KNOWING
Justin

Knowing Justin

Copyright © Lisa Rogers, 2024

First Edition

ISBN (paperback) 978-1-914447-82-2

ISBN (ebook) 978-1-914447-83-9

KNOWING
Justin

LISA ROGERS

I am dedicating this book to everyone I love and have passed, and to all my family, friends and acquaintances that I have grieved with. You have taught me so much and changed my understanding of life.

A special dedication goes to my beautiful friend, Sharon Whitfield, who helped me to hold on to my spiritual beliefs and encouraged me to walk my talk through some of the darkest days of my life.

Your love and support helped me more than you know

xxx

CONTENTS

1. Justin - The End   1
2. Sally - The Big Sister   10
3. Natalie - The Realisation of Death   18
4. Peter & Justin - The Accident   23
5. Natalie - And So It Begins   36
6. The Funeral - Reality Kicks In   46
7. Scott - Where Am I?   52
8. The Principal - Shock   64
9. Scott - The Breath   68
10. John Lucas - Unpredictable   81
11. Sally - Denying Reality   87
12. Peter - There Is No Going Back   92
13. Scott - When You Expect Nothing, You
    Receive Everything   98
14. Scott - Getting A Hold Of Himself   119
15. Tina & Jane - Absence   123
16. Tina - Life Goes On But Time Is Broken   127
17. Peter - Guilt   139
18. Michael - Making A Connection   146
19. Natalie - Helpless   151
20. Kate - Gratitude   155
21. Jane & Scott - Helpless   162
22. Jane - Will Ego Take Over? The Truth Will
    Set You Free...   178
23. Tina - So Much Pain   192
24. Scott - He Found His Heart   205
25. Peter & Michael - That Is What Love Is...   212
26. Emma - How Is She Coping?   221
27. Jake - Grief Is The Price You Pay For Love?   226
28. Tina - Waking Up From Nowhere   233
29. Tina & Natalie - Moving Forward   240

30. Tina & Jane - Unspoken Forgiveness 244

31. Jane - She Thought She Was Doing Okay 248

32. Peter - He Missed Him Everyday 257

33. Peter & Michael - Plans Are Underway 270

34. Peter & Michael - Being Honest And Truthful 277

35. Joe & Jane - Finding Peace, What Does Your Soul Want? 280

36. Tina - One Foot In Front Of The Other 289

37. Sally - Pushing, Pushing, Pushing 294

38. Sally & Kate - Determined Not To Let Anyone In 299

39. Sally & Grace - Time To Reconnect 303

40. Jake - Anger Beginning To Bubble To The Surface 308

41. TINA
Work Work Work 318

42. Jake - Downward Spiral, Ready To Stop 327

43. Peter & Michael - Justin's Adventure 330

44. Jake & Joe - Finding Some Peace 337

45. Jake & Tina - Do You Want To Live Like This Forever? 349

46. Tina & Joe - Forgiveness 354

47. Joe & Jake - The Homeless Man 362

48. Sally - Never Healing 370

49. Sally - The Birth 380

50. Kate & Sally - Forgiveness 385

51. Lucas Johns - You Never Know 391

52. Tina - The Pain Continues 397

How to Nurture Your Spirit Through Grief 405

A Note From The Author 411

Acknowledgments 419

*"Pain is inevitable.
Suffering is optional."*
- Buddha

JUSTIN - THE END

SHE SAT WITH HER HEAD RESTING ON THE BED WHILE HER hand rested on his chest. She wanted to know exactly when the last breath was. She wanted to know when her sweet boy was leaving this world. She needed to know with all her heart. She willed him to stay alive but she knew there was no hope; his brain was too damaged. She didn't dare to close her eyes in case she missed it, the end, when life was removed from his body. Slowly she raised her head and his hand and rested it against her face. She squeezed his hand and said, "It's ok baby."

She was choking back her tears, "You don't have to stay here for me."

She was all alone with him; nobody else could watch her son's decline any longer.

"I don't want you to suffer anymore."

Her eyes filled with tears and, eventually, began to roll down her face. She hadn't cried for a long time about her son's impending death. She felt she had to be strong, she had to show no fear, no sadness. Although inside, she was disheartened and discouraged with life. The reality was she didn't know how she was going to put one foot in front of the other.

"I remember so vividly the day you were born. You were so

laid back, you never cried, you had so much hair and the fattest little cheeks. I loved you from the moment I knew you were in my belly."

She took a loud breath to gather her courage, "You have grown into such a beautiful soul and I don't know what I will do without you. Who is going to make me laugh like you do? How will I fill the gap you are leaving behind?"

She began to cry loudly now, she stood and kissed him on the cheek that was opposite to the side she was standing. His face was pale and disfigured and around his eyes showed remnants of bruises from his injuries but all she could see was her beautiful baby, lifeless and so helpless.

"It is ok to go my sweet boy, don't stay here for me," she repeated, as if willing him to go.

She bent down to whisper in his ear. "I love you so much and I will never forget anything about you."

Her tears fell from her eyes onto his face and as she lifted her head, he took a big breath in and she realised in that instant that this was his last. She sat and watched with the tiniest bit of hope that he would open his eyes and say, "Ha Ha Mum! Fooled ya."

He was such a joker, jumping out from behind corners in the house to scare her, making jokes that only made him laugh which in turn made her laugh. She thought just maybe it was all a joke. In reality it was her worst nightmare, her son had just taken his last breath on earth. She was there for his first and his last. It wasn't fair. No Mother should have to see or experience that. She was paralysed with grief in that moment. How would she go on? How would she see another day? He lay before her with no sign of life. He was dead...

Tears flooded her face as she sat and laid her face on his hand, "Oh my baby boy, this wasn't supposed to happen. You were supposed to be with me when I die in my old age".

She raised her head and looked at him, his face, the way his hair fell on his forehead, his eye lashes and how they were so long, his nose and how he had his father's nose. She noticed his shoulders and how he had gotten so broad; he really was the same size as an adult even though he was only 16.

She rubbed his chest, "I am going to miss you so much."

Minutes passed and, before she realised it, her two daughters, Sally and Emma, were standing on the opposite side of the bed holding hands. The girls had hardly seen their mother shed a tear during this whole process. Now she stood before them sobbing, her face covered with tears. Sally realised what had happened; her brother was grey and lifeless, every last earthly piece of energy had left his body. Sally was eighteen years old she was no fool, she knew exactly what was happening in their house; her brother had come home to die. Conversely, Emma was only eight and so she was not sure what death looked like or what they were actually waiting for with her brother laying in a hospital bed in their living room.

"Mum?"

Sally's voice was high pitched and sounded desperate for some support. Tina was in no state to offer any support to her girls, she was lost in her grief.

"Mum, why is Justin so weird? He's a funny colour... what is wrong with him? I think he needs to go back to the hospital."

Emma had panic in her voice. She hadn't realised that Justin had come home to die, she thought that leaving the hospital was a great sign that he was getting better and would wake up soon.

"Mum, quickly ring someone."

Emma had not seen Justin at his worst at the hospital, ventilated and unconscious from the accident. She had come to terms with the situation by thinking that he was asleep and would wake up some time soon.

3

"Sally, you do it. Call the ambulance."

Emma jerked on her hand. Sally didn't know what to say to her little sister, tears welled in her eyes and Emma begin to panic even more.

Tina finally looked over at the girls as a wave of reality rolled over her and she spoke, "Sally please go and get your Father."

Her voice was as calm as Sally had ever heard it before. Sally dropped Emma's hand and headed up the stairs with urgency in her step. Tina picked herself up off the chair and walked around the bed and looked directly into Emma's eyes

"Justin is gone, sweetheart."

"What do you mean, Mum? This doesn't make sense," she began to cry in terror.

As Tina sat down on the chair beside Emma, Emma threw her arms around her mother's neck. She didn't understand what was happening but she just wanted the safety of her mother's embrace. Tina could barely lift her arms so she struggled to embrace her youngest child, she wasn't even thinking about comforting her. She was just so exhausted, saddened and lost in her own mind.

Footsteps came from behind them and a moment later Jake and Sally stood there, together, staring at the lifeless body before them.

"He's gone, Jake."

Tina didn't even turn her head to make eye contact with her husband. She had distanced herself emotionally from everyone around her, including Jake. She couldn't bear the thought of having to console him. Jake walked to the opposite side of the bed, sat in the chair and picked up his son's hand. He wrapped his own hands around Justin's and leant forward on his elbow resting their intertwined hands on his forehead. As he rocked, his sobs became louder and louder. He didn't acknowledge anyone else in the room; he too was wrapped up in his own loss.

Tina had Emma on her lap and Emma was holding her mother so tightly that it was clear she was not going to let her go any time soon. Sally just stood behind her mother, staring at her brother, mesmorized by what she saw before her. Both her parents distraught with grief and her little sister terrified. She had no idea what was to happen next.

"Hello?" A voice shouted out from the front door. "Hello?"

Then the sound of footsteps on the timber floor followed. Sally didn't recognise the voice, it was like she had risen up out of her body and was hiding in the abyss, away from what was before her.

The footsteps slowed and then stopped right beside her. She didn't even turn her head to acknowledge this person.

"Oh dear," the voice whispered.

Sally felt an arm wrap around her shoulders in an attempt to comfort her, but there was no acknowledgement as she was somewhere faraway in her mind, body and spirit. Then she felt a kiss on her face and recognised the smell of her grandmother. Her grandmother was someone she hadn't spent much time with because she lived far away from them which had created a limited relationship. However, over the past few weeks, they had spent a lot of time together as Tina and Jake had been at the hospital a lot and so Grace, Sally's grandmother, had taken on the household and childcare duties. Jake's sobs didn't waver in the presence of his mother, he didn't even know she was there. His tears had begun to dampen Justin's favourite t-shirt that Tina had put him in after she last helped the palliative care nurse wash him the evening before.

It was 5:45am and the sun was just beginning to shine through the windows in the living room. Tina had not touched the curtains for a few days, leaving them open so she knew if it was day or night. She was not orientated to regular life; she had spent the days since Justin returned home by his side, talking to him and caring for him as best she could.

Grace had silent tears run down her face and she squeezed Sally as strongly as her strength would allow. Soon, before anyone knew what was happening, Tom, Grace's husband, Jake's father and Justin's grandfather was standing behind Jake with his hands on his back. Tom had been side-tracked putting a few dishes of food in the kitchen. He had been a distant father and grandfather and he was stern, abrupt and unloving, but he stood there fighting back tears like he had been punched in the heart, crippled by the pain of what had been triggered within him. Tom had no idea what to do, so he just stood there with his hand on Jake's back to ensure his son knew he was there. After a few minutes had passed, and with no reason, Jake stood up and embraced his father. It was as though he had only just realised he was there and all of a sudden needed him. Their embrace broke Grace's silent tears and her crying became unrestrained, her breaths loud and grief stricken. Jake sobbed loudly and rocked in his father's arms.

To the outside world, Jake and Tom had a pretty good relationship, but it certainly wasn't close. When Jake was growing up, his father was busy working and earning a living and didn't have much time to spend with his children. They had love for each other but probably didn't know each other that well. However, in that moment in the living room, their embrace lasted and lasted. Tom was not going to let go of his son until he let go first. Tom knew he had not been there for his son over the years and wanted to be closer to him, but he didn't know how and the physical distance between them did not help. He had made a promise to himself on the interstate flight when Justin was injured, that he would be there for his son now - he would make the effort, even though he was not sure how. He thought that just being together might help, so that is how he planned to start.

"Why? Why... Why... Why... My son..." Jake wailed. "Why? Why... Why... Why..."

Tom was lost for words. What do you say to your son who has just lost his child? Tom was so intensely sad, but finally responded, "I don't know, Jake."

"Mummy, what is happening?"

Emma began to cry because she was scared and confused and feeling so vulnerable. She took her mother by the face, with one hand on each cheek.

"Mum, what is happening? I don't understand... Mum, please tell me."

Tina couldn't speak. She looked through Emma like she wasn't there. She couldn't find any words, so she just shut her eyes and cried.

Grace could see that Tina had lost herself and gently let Sally go, walking around to pick Emma up. As she did, she wiped the tears from her face and gathered herself. She put her own emotions aside and found some strength deep deep within. Emma was a slight child, only weighing 22kg. Grace scooped her up and walked from the room, looking for a quiet place to talk Emma through what had just happened. They ended up in the kitchen and Grace placed Emma on the kitchen bench so they had direct eye contact.

They could still hear Jakes sobs of grief.

"Emma," Grace said.

"Yes Granny?" Her eyes thick with fear and bewilderment.

"Emma..."

She paused. *What do I say now? How do I tell her that her big brother is dead?*

"Emma," she said again, "Justin has gone to heaven."

"What do you mean, he has gone to heaven? He is right there in the bed. I still don't understand."

Emma was pissed off, Grace could see it in her eyes. Maybe they had not prepared Emma enough for what was going to happen or maybe she was just young and couldn't comprehend.

"Emma, darling, heaven is not somewhere your body goes to, it is somewhere your spirit goes. It looks like he is there but he is not breathing, there is no life left in him."

Emma stared blankly at her grandmother and Grace couldn't tell if she had understood what had just been said. A few seconds passed and Grace asked, "Do you understand now Emma?"

Emma's posture slumped and her line of vision fell to her lap and she nodded a small and insignificant nod that, if you weren't looking for it, you wouldn't notice.

"He is with God now, Emma."

"Just like Poppa?" Emma responded.

"Just like Poppa, darling."

Emma reached up and wrapped her arms around her grandmother's neck, "I don't want him to be in heaven. I want him to be with us, here in my house."

"I know sweetheart. We all want him here, we all do."

Grace cried in silence as Emma sobbed her little eight year old's tears while they embraced. Emma lifted her legs and wrapped them around her grandmother's waist. Grace stroked her hair and her thoughts raced. *This is so unfair. Why is this happening to us? That boy in there does not deserve this, this family does not deserve this. Why? Why? Why?*

Her thoughts resonated with her son's wailing.

"I'M NOT SURE WHICH PAIN IS WORSE, THE SHOCK OF WHAT HAPPENED OR THE ACHE FOR WHAT NEVER WILL BE."

- UNKNOWN

2
SALLY - THE BIG SISTER

Sally stood there, frozen to the spot, unable to see the tragic portrayal before her. Her brother didn't look like her brother; his face was swollen and distorted and his eyes dark and bruised. He was normally so full of life, full of jokes and chit chat, hyperactive and always doing something... never still. She just couldn't comprehend that he was laying there in a hospital bed, lifeless and grey. It didn't make any sense to her. She could see her parents reactions to what they saw but she didn't want to believe it. She didn't want to believe that Justin had left her here, on her own; they were brother and sister but they were also best friends. Her mother was sitting holding his lifeless hand as silent tears passed over her cheeks and her father was distraught, wailing and rocking in her grandfather's arms.

Sally turned on her heels, walked out of the room and promptly out the front door. She could no longer cope with the situation before her. When she crossed the front door frame, she felt relief. She continued to walk down the front path and she felt even better. As she walked out the front gate, she felt free, so she just kept walking. She had no idea where she was going but the further from the house she got, the further away from her family she got, the better she felt and so, she began to run. She ran down the block, around the corner, and before she knew it, she found herself in the park where her run slowed to a walk. She slowed down and stood still. She had no idea what she was going to do in the park but she felt better being there, away from her life. She walked towards the playground and found herself sitting on the swing. There was no one around because it was so early, so there was nothing to distract her.

She watched her toes in the sand and felt the texture of the grains, cold and soft. As she moved her feet around, the swing began to move in a back and forth motion and, suddenly, Sally remembered how much she loved to swing. She began to swing, higher and higher. The breeze was cold and crisp but she didn't care. A smile came to her face. Justin and Sally loved to come to the park and, even as they grew older, they still went there with Emma. They would all laugh and swing and chase each other. Memories of many days messing around in the park flashed through Sally's mind. She laughed out loud at some of the fond memories, so real in her thoughts.

Just then, a gust of wind sweep through the park. Sally's hair twirled around her face and her mind shifted from her beautiful happy memories to the reality that was in her living room. The swing slowed down and eventually stopped, her hands fell to her lap, her head slumped down and she began to cry... her brother was dead, he had left her.

What am I going to do without him? Her thoughts raced.

She cried and cried. The wind was cool and her hair was blown over her face and stuck in her tears. She lost connection with reality and, in her grief, many minutes past by as Sally sat in the swing; alone, cold and grief stricken. Sally's heart ached like someone had blown a hole in her chest. The reality had knocked her, hard. She was sure that this is what it would feel like if someone took a gun, shot her through her heart and blown it to pieces.

Her mind was scrambled, she didn't understand why this would happen. Who would do this to a sister? Who would do this to the love she had for her brother? Her heart was broken and her tears had glued her wind swept hair all over her face. She felt as if she would now be alone, forever.

"Sally, is that you?" A voice came from nowhere. "Sally?"

The outline of a figure was moving closer and closer but Sally didn't want to acknowledge who it was and her head remained slumped. The figure crouched down in front of her and placed their hands on her knees.

"Sally, are you ok?" they asked.

It was Natalie, one of the neighbours. She had seen someone on the swing from the other side of the park and she wouldn't usually have paid any attention, but as she got closer, she realised they were in their pyjamas and had no shoes on so she was concerned. Natalie knew Sally very well because she had spent many days at her house with her daughter and son, playing from a very young age.

"Sally, what are you doing here, love?"

Sally raised her eyes to meet Natalie's and shrugged her shoulders. Natalie knew what was going on in her neighbour's house. She didn't like to think of it but she knew all the same. Natalie reached up to Sally's face and wiped the hair that was wet with tears away from her eyes.

"Are you cold, love?"

Natalie took off her coat and wrapped it around Sally's shoulders, and then she rubbed the girl's arms as if to warm her up.

"Why don't I take you home?"

"No," Sally immediately snapped back.

"No. I'm not going back there, it's too awful."

"Tell me what's wrong, love. Is it Justin? Where are Mum and Dad?"

"They are at home with Justin but Justin has gone. He's not here anymore, he's left me."

Sally's face crumpled and tears flowed from her eyes.

Oh my God! Natalie thought, *Justin has died. Oh my Goodness! What do I do? What do I say? The poor sweet child.*

"He's gone... it's only this distorted body there in the living room." Sally's voice was angry and loud. "Justin is not there anymore, he's not."

She slammed her hands on Natalie's that were resting on her knees.

"Do you understand he is dead, Natalie? Dead."

Her tears did not stop running down her face, her hair was a mess and she began to shiver with grief.

"I understand, love, I understand."

Natalie could see that Sally was grief stricken and unaware of her surroundings; the cold, the wind, the fact she was in her pyjamas in the park at 6.05am. All Natalie could think about was getting Sally warm and cleaned up. What else could she do? She couldn't make it better, she couldn't change her reality.

"Why don't we go to my house and get out of the wind and cold?" Natalie asked, rubbing Sally's arms again in an attempt to warm her up.

Sally didn't answer, she just sat and sobbed. Natalie stood up and looked around the park but no one else was there. She put her hands around Sally's shoulders and gave her a little pull to get her to her feet. Natalie adjusted the jacket to ensure it covered Sally as much as it could, she brushed the hair out of her eyes, again, and walked with her arms around the girl's shoulders. Sally, slowly, walked alongside her.

"You know he is gone, right? He's not here anymore. He's

left me and you. He doesn't care about us, he doesn't care!" Sally sobbed.

Natalie squeezed Sally a little tighter knowing that whatever she said at this point would make no difference. They walked slowly towards their houses but, as they caught a glimpse of their street, Sally stopped still on the path and said, "I am not going in there. I am not going home."

"I know, love. We are going to my house. It's just there, see?" and Natalie motioned towards her house, just metres away.

As they walked through the door, Natalie directed Sally onto the couch and covered her with a blanket that was sitting on the arm of the chair, ensuring her feet were covered. They sat side by side and Natalie wrapped her arms around Sally.

"It will be ok, Sally," she said to try and comfort her.

"It's not ok. It will never be ok. He's dead. Do you know what that means? He is gone, never to return... never to return. Dead, Natalie. Dead."

Natalie immediately felt terrible about what she had just said. She was only trying to comfort this child she had known all of her life.

"I realise, Sally. I'm sorry, I didn't mean to upset you," she tried to placate her.

"Oh Natalie, this is not what is supposed to happen."

Sally's head fell to Natalie's shoulder as she continued to sob. Natalie raised her eyes to the ceiling and thought, *You are damn right, this is not supposed to happen. That poor boy. How are they going to move on with life? Oh my God, help me to stay strong.*

After about 15 minutes, Natalie stood up from the lounge, went to the bathroom and found a clean wash cloth. She wet it with warm water and took it to Sally. She sat beside her and gently wiped the tears from her face with the washcloth and brushed her hair back. Their eyes connected and, in that moment, Natalie felt Sally's pain. Natalie couldn't find any words so they just sat there and cried together while both their hearts ached.

Natalie's 16 year old son appeared before them, wiping sleep from his eyes, "Hey, what is happening here?"

He took a closer look at them both and realised what was happening; everyone had been waiting the last couple of days for this moment. Actually, for the last couple of weeks.

Natalie didn't want to answer but she also didn't want Sally to have to answer, so she quickly interjected, "Just what we have been expecting Peter."

Sally sat as if not a word had been spoken. Peter was shocked, even though he was expecting it. He sat next to Sally, deflated, and rested his hand on Sally's knee. Tears came to his eyes. He and Justin were very good friends; they grew up together and were born only two months apart, Peter being the oldest of the two. He never let Justin forget it either.

Sally leaned on Peter's shoulder and cried. He wrapped his arm around her and they cried together. They were warned about this tragedy, but you can never be prepared. Peter was shocked and shaken with the news. The three of them sat there, together, and Natalie did not know what to do or say. She could feel her son's pain, but what could she do to help?

How must Tina and Jake have felt, seeing and experiencing Justin's pain but being unable to help or fix it? It must be so torturous, heartbreaking and cruel. As Natalie thought about this, she suddenly realised that they must be concerned about Sally's whereabouts, not knowing that she was at her house. *What if they are in a panic looking for her? I better do something.*

With that, she stood up to go and let someone know.

"Peter, I will be back shortly."

Both their faces looked up at her, but their stares went straight through her.

"BEING LEFT BEHIND IS HARD."

3

NATALIE – THE REALISATION OF DEATH

Natalie raced next door, to Number 42. She ran through the gate, up the step and through the front door, which had been left wide open. Her head started to swirl, she felt dizzy and light headed. *What am I doing, what am I going to say? Oh my god.*

Her stomach turned to knots and her mind went blank. She had known these people for 18 years; they had spent holidays together, BBQs together, had games nights, been camping and fishing together, but never had they experienced such tough times.

What do you say? Natalie's mind was going wild.

She stopped, rested against the doorway and caught her breath. A voice whispered in her ear, "You need to be strong."

She looked around for someone as the words were so clear and not her own.

"You need to be strong," again, the words very clear.

Natalie had no idea what was happening or who was repeating these words, but they calmed her down as she took some slow, deep breaths. She found her weight back on her feet instead of the door frame, inhaled deeply, and headed into the house to see if she could help. However, most importantly, she entered to let them know that Sally was safe.

It was like a whisper but Natalie voiced the words, "Tina... Jake... Hello?"

Nobody in the house could possibly hear her and she didn't really want anyone to hear her; she didn't know what to say or what she was going to find. Also, it was very unusual for their front door to be wide open and that, in its own right, put Natalie on edge.

Natalie slowly crept into the house, giving her time to prepare herself for what may lie ahead. She walked towards the lounge and her worst fears were realised, she could see the back of Tina's head and Jake clenching Justin's hand against his face. She couldn't see Justin's face but she knew that he was dead from Sally's recount. Her pace slowed so she was hardly moving and as she got closer to the bed, she realised she had no idea what to say or do. She aimed for the foot of hospital bed. As she reached her destination, Jake made eye contact with her. She could tell that he had been crying; his eyes were completely blood shot. It was a meaningful glance but not a word was spoken. As she placed her hands on the foot of the bed, Tina turned around, red faced, hair dishevelled and posture slumped. It appeared to Natalie that Tina held no hope for life. Their eyes met and Natalie could physically feel Tina pulling her in, so she walked over and sat beside her.

Tina was exhausted. She had been awake for approximately 38 hours, ever since Justin returned home, and the lack of sleep was taking its toll. She rested her head on Natalie's chest and sobbed. Natalie could feel Tina's tears soaking through her shirt. She closed her eyes and embraced Tina like she had never done with anyone before; she felt like she was putting a protective shield around the poor woman. What else could she do? She couldn't change anything, although she wanted to; she couldn't take the pain away, although she wanted to; she couldn't bring him back, although she wanted to. All she felt she could do, at this point, was to hold Tina and give her some protection.

Jake quietly moaned. "Why... Why... Why?"

Natalie closed her eyes and tears ran from the corners. What a tragedy she was seeing and experiencing. She wanted to do something but could think of nothing. She just sat there and held her friend.

Natalie's eyes opened and shifted to Justin; his poor battered body, grey and lifeless.

How could this happen? She thought, *How did we get to this point? Why is this happening to us, to my friends, to my family? How are the kids going to cope with this? How is Peter going to cope? How can I fix this? How can I help?*

Her mind raced uncontrollably, an anxious flurry of thoughts and worries. The aftermath of this crescendo ended with Natalie's mind going blank. She closed her eyes and saw a beautiful white light that made her feel safe and calm. She watched as the light flowed outside of her and surrounded the whole room and everyone who was in it. There was nothing else she could do. The pain was too much, the shock was too much.

In that moment, Natalie realised that she couldn't change anything about the situation. She couldn't change the sadness, the distress or the fear of loss. The prayer she practiced as a child at school, flowed freely in her mind...

"God, grant me the serenity to accept the things I cannot change,
the courage to change the things I can
and the wisdom to know the difference."

She squeezed her eyes shut, consciously felt Tina in her arms and drank in every word of the prayer.

Natalie took a deep breath and prayed, "Please God, give me the wisdom."

Natalie and Tina were good friends, both nurses and both familiar with death. They had spoken about their own beliefs and faith in the past but neither of them knew their faith would be tested like this. At this moment, Natalie could not fathom how life was going to go on while Tina was only just capable of breathing.

"GRIEF HAS MANY LAYERS, MANY FACES AND MANY CHALLENGES!"

4
PETER & JUSTIN - THE ACCIDENT

On the day of the accident, Peter and Justin were at the skate park doing their usual thing, zipping and skating all over the place. They both got their first skateboards at 7 years old for Christmas, the same year. Of course, it was orchestrated by their parents that Santa bought them both a skateboard but they never realised this, they thought it was an awesome coincidence and never looked back. This day Peter knew he couldn't stay long as he had to work so he had to get home to prepare. They both worked at the local supermarket stacking shelves, collecting trolleys and working the registers, but Justin wasn't on the roster that day.

As they said goodbye, it was like any other day that one of the boys had to leave without the other. They performed their detailed hand shake, bumped chests and Peter rode off towards home. However, this day, Peter got to the edge of the skate park, stopped, looked back and took one last mental picture of Justin pushing off from the top of the bowl.

"So cool," he said, "Wish I could stay."

He spoke very quietly so no one would hear him and then rode off down the road.

―――――

Tina was a midwife which meant she worked shifts, but this particular day she was off work. It was a usual Saturday when Peter turned up at the front door looking for Justin to go skate boarding at 8.15am. Tina stopped Justin at the front door as he reached for his skateboard which routinely sat leant up against the wall in the door way.

"Hey now, you boys be good and more importantly be careful, don't do anything silly."

Tina often warned the boys to be good; they played hard and fast and didn't stop for much, especially Justin, he was always doing something adventurous.

"Yep Mum, we will be fine," he reached over and hugged his Mother, something he didn't normally do, but that day he embraced her with a warm and loving hug and then charged out the door.

"See ya, Mrs P!" Peter yelled from the front gate.

Tina watched the boys ride down the street in the direction of the skate park, laughing and pushing each other all the way. *Oh, those boys!* Tina thought and she shut the door.

―――――

Natalie was anxious and unsettled that day, she didn't know why. It wasn't an unusual day in her house, she was just doing the normal weekend stuff, but she was uneasy. Peter raced through the door up the stairs and she could hear him in the shower.

"Hey, Mum," he yelled "Where are my work clothes?"

"In the laundry," she yelled back.

With that, Natalie heard Peter scream down the stairs to the laundry and then run back to his room. She knew he was cutting it fine to get to work on time but she was sick of rushing and reminding him so she just left it up to him to get it together.

"Ok, ready Mum."

Natalie grabbed her keys and raced out the door with him. As they drove along Natalie asked, "Is Justin working today?"

"Nah left him at the skate park, lucky bugger."

"Remember that you are funding your skating habit, aren't you saving for a new board?"

Natalie tried to divert Peter's attention. He never wanted a job but Natalie had pushed him to help learn responsibility.

"Yeah, but I would still prefer to be hanging with the J man at the bowl."

———

AT AROUND 2.30PM, Tina rang Natalie, "Hey there, just wondering if you have seen the boys?"

"Oh, well I dropped Peter off at work at 11.30 and from our conversation in the car, Justin was still at the skate park."

"That's weird... it means that he's been at the skate bowl since 8.15. He's missed lunch, I thought they both must have been at yours, eating you out of house and home."

"No, I haven't seen him."

"I might go for a walk down to the skate park and see what he is up to. Bloody boys, they have no idea of time," Tina was obviously annoyed.

"Want me to walk down with you?" Natalie asked.

"No I will be right, I'm a big girl."

"Ok no worries, I'll talk to you a bit later."

Tina was getting herself all worked up. Her thoughts were racing about how she was going to lecture Justin. He was irresponsible and had gotten so wrapped up in what he was doing that he forgot about the rest of the world.

She put the phone down and headed straight for the door. She didn't say anything to Jake, she just marched out of the house and headed for the skate park. She was boiling with anger as she stomped along the pathway. The lecture she planned to give Justin was bubbling through her brain.

Tina had no conscious idea of her surroundings until she turned the corner to walk through the gate of the skate park and was confronted by a sea of police cars. Her paced slowed and her heart began to race. There was police tape with 'Crime Scene' plastered all over the place. It was like a movie scene in a dramatic movie about criminal investigation. Tina stood there, staring at what laid before her. Her son was missing and the police were investigating at the skate park where her son was supposed to be. *Oh my God, Oh my God, Oh my God,* her thoughts raced. She glanced over at the skate park but there was no one to be seen. As she looked back at the investigation area, her hand came up to her face and covered her mouth. She closed her eyes.

"Oh my god, Justin."

"Are you ok, madam? Do you need some help?" A helpful young man in a police uniform approached her. "Madam?"

She turned her head and made eye contact, "Oh my god Justin," she said a little louder.

"Sorry Madam, I didn't quite catch that," he responded.

"My son, Justin, is missing. Last I knew he was at the skate park but he hasn't come home. What the hell is happening here?" Her voice getting louder.

As she turned her head to the grassed curb, she saw Justin's skateboard sitting there, all alone. Tina knew Justin loved that board and would never leave it behind. As the realisation sank in, that Justin had abandoned his prize possession, Tina fell to the ground in a heap and began to sob, and her body began to rock back and forth.

"Justin, Justin, Justin," she cried.

The policeman crouched down beside her, "Madam, are you ok? What's wrong?"

Tina made no coherent response. He stood and motioned for a colleague to come over. He crouched again and, this time, he put his hand on her shoulder, "Madam, what is it?"

"It's my boy," their eyes met through Tina's tears. "My boy," she cried.

A female policewomen came over to assist, "James, do we need an ambulance?" she asked as she approached.

"No, I don't think so. I think we might have found the family of the boy..."

James' face showed his pain and distress. He was a rookie, only out of the academy for a few months, and he was still struggling with all the heartache he had already witnessed. The female police officers eyes widened as she crouched down to speak to Tina.

"Madam, how can we help? What's wrong?" She didn't want to put words into Tina's mouth.

"My son is missing and that is his skateboard, just there," Tina gestured towards the board.

"Right, I see. Do you live around here?"

"Just down there," Tina pointed to the direction she had just come from.

"You better get Serg, James."

James was more than happy to remove himself from the situation. He was one of the first police officers who had arrived at the scene and so he understood the gravity of the news that was about to be delivered.

"Are you sure that is your son's skateboard?"

Tina stared at the board but it was a distance away. *Maybe it wasn't?* The policewomen must have realised it wasn't close enough to identify and so she went over and picked it up to give Tina a better look. As she approached with the board, Tina knew for certain that the board was Justin's and, as the policewomen handed it to her, Tina leant back on the grass as if she was being handed the plague. Tina had no idea why she recoiled, but she knew she didn't want to touch the board.

"Yes, yes, yes." Tina wailed.

The police women withdrew the skateboard.

"Oh Justin, Justin," her rocking returned and the sobbing rolled on.

The Sergeant appeared out of nowhere.

"What is happening, Sarah?" he asked with authority.

"We have found the owner of the skateboard," she paused, "This lady's son... and I think his name is Justin."

Sarah placed her hand on Tina's back, it was all she could think of to do. *Oh damn, this isn't good. What do we do now? Poor woman.*

Then, without warning, Tina jumped to her feet, angry and wild, "Where is my son? What have you done with him?"

"I am not sure who your son is, Madam, but we may be able to find out for you."

"Where is my son?" Tina screamed in the Sergeant's face and then again, "Where is my son? Where have you taken him? Where is he?"

By this stage, Tina was hysterical, lost in anger and fear.

"Madam, you have to calm down."

Tina bashed the Sergeant on the chest.

"Where is he?"

Tina glared at him with all the hatred she could muster. She hated the man in front of her who she had never seen before, in that instant, she hated him with every inch of her body, her mind and her soul. She wasn't thinking clearly. All that she knew was that Justin's skateboard was beside the road where there was police tape, police cars and a hell of a lot of people.

In her hysteria, she didn't realise that the police wouldn't know who the boy was. The boy who was just whisked away in an ambulance with tubes and lines hanging out of him everywhere.

The sergeant grabbed at Tina's hands and nodded at Sarah to let her be.

"Madam, let me help you find out some information," he held her around her wrists and pushed her back a little so he could make eye contact with her. He was forceful but gentle, "If you can calm down a little and give us some information, we will be able to locate your son."

Tina looked through the sergeant.

"Madam..? Madam..?"

Tina shook her head, looked him in the eyes and nodded in agreement - it was all she could manage, her voice was not working in that second.

"Now, what is your name?" the sergeant asked as he walked Tina over to a park bench beside the road.

As they sat down, Tina responded, "Tina Point."

"Right, can you give me some information about your son's whereabouts today?"

Tina sniffed and wiped her face with the back of her hand. There was silence for a few seconds before she responded, "He and his friend, Peter, came here to the skate park around 8.15 this morning."

A switch seemed to have been flicked in Tina's head; her posture straightened and her chin lifted to keep eye contact with the sergeant. She wiped her face again and pushed the hair off her face.

"Right, do you know where your son's friend is?"

Again, a pause. It seemed as though Tina was taking a long

time to digest the questions that were being asked. Finally, she said, "Yes, he is at work."

"So your son hasn't been home since 8.15 today?"

"No. I thought he was at Peter's house until a little while ago, which is when I came to look for him."

Tina turned her head and looked at the scene before her. She caught sight of a pool of blood that lay on the road and had been cordoned off by police tape. Panic overcame her and she raced over to look at the scene.

"Oh my God, what happened? Oh my God, Justin!"

Tears began to flow down her face, again. The situation was only getting worse; the blood, the police tape, Justin's abandoned skateboard.

The sergeant looked directly at Tina, "There has been an accident, but I don't know if your son was involved because the victim had no ID on them."

Tina nodded, "That's my son's board. Was he hit by a car? Run over? Fell off his board? Bashed up? What has happened?" Tina pleaded with the sergeant.

"A boy seems to have fallen down this gutter here and was found unconscious. He has been taken to hospital, but like I said, I don't know if it is your son."

Tina put her head in her hands and sobbed.

As the sergeant gently rubbed her shoulder, a voice came from behind them, "Tina? Tina are you alright? What's happening?"

It was Natalie. She had been overcome with worry and, after some time, couldn't help herself but to come looking for Justin herself. Tina turned and fell into Natalie's arms.

The sergeant looked at Natalie and brought her up to speed, "There has been a serious accident and a boy has been injured but we have been unable to identify him as he had no identification on him."

Natalie nodded and her attention was drawn to the road where Tina had just noticed the pool of blood.

"Oh my goodness."

Tina continued to sob in Natalie's arms, so grateful for a safe place to hide her face from the world.

"It seems to be that the boy fell down here," the Sergeant motioned to the gutter where the path was much higher than the road and large tree roots infiltrated the area. "We don't know how long the boy was lying on the road before that gentlemen over there found him. The boy was not in a good way and it seems that it had been some time since he was injured."

Natalie squeezed Tina in her arms and rested her cheek on the side of her head and, as she did, she noticed Justin's skateboard on the ground. She recognised it instantly; he had been so proud of it when he brought it about 18 months ago, he had shown everyone. Natalie had probably seen it every day since then, in amongst the boys antics.

"That's Justin's skateboard, right there," Natalie pointed out.

"James!" The sergeant shouted for the rookie to return.

James ran over, "Yes, Serg?"

"Ah mate, you were first on the scene here?"

"Yeah."

"What was the boy wearing?"

"Um, well, um, he had some cool green and blue converse shoes..."

James only realised the enthusiasm in his voice about the shoes after he had said it.

Tina cried out, "Oh my god, Justin!"

James was flustered by Tina's outburst, "Um... Um... He had light blue shorts and a black t-shirt on."

As Tina's crying got louder, the sergeant realised that this must have been what her son had been wearing that day and he had to get Tina to Justin as soon as he could.

"Just give me a minute, I need to make some calls," he rushed away.

Natalie continued to rub Tina's back while she fought back the absolute terror that was bubbling up inside of her. The pool of blood on the road screamed at her that the worst possible thing imaginable had occurred.

James, the rookie, stood before them, lost in the pain and anguish he saw. He was certain that the boy belonged to this lady who was so distraught in front of him, but he didn't know what to do in this situation. Sarah had discretely removed herself to pursue her duties at the crime scene. James felt like an idiot just standing there, not doing or saying anything. Neither Tina or Natalie were aware that he was still there, they were lost in their own thoughts.

The Sergeant was on the phone, checking in with the hospital to see if the boy they just scraped off the road was still alive. He didn't hold much hope considering the condition he had been in.

The officer had gotten so used to, and indifferent about, what he saw on the job these days. He had been working the streets as a police officer for 24 years and he was maxed out with the devastation that existed in society; the beatings, the drugs, the abuse, the killings and the deaths, but what upset him the most was the cruelty of human nature. The hatred and conflict between family and friends that caused harm and jail time. He couldn't fathom why people would hurt and abuse their loved ones, why they couldn't grow past their own hurt and abuse and be what they wanted for themselves. He had lost all faith in human nature and was emotionally paralysed. His wife had been on at him for the last few years to do something about his emotionlessness, but he felt too scared to change.

However, with this situation, he found himself anxious and uneasy. He, too, had a 16 year old son that loved his skateboard, and so the sergeant was finding resonance with the situation before him. He was struggling to hold onto his indifferent attitude because he could see his own family in the situation before him.

As he spoke to the nurse on the other end of the phone line, the anxiety began to swirl deep in this belly. His thoughts crossed from the family before him to his own family. The panic rose inside of him and all he could think of was his own son, hoping he was safe.

"Are you there sergeant?" A loud voice beamed into his ear and broke him out of his agony.

"Sorry, yes," he paused for a second, realising that he didn't hear a word she had said about the boy's condition, "Could you please repeat that?"

"The kid is hanging on by a thread. They have taken him for emergency surgery. He has had a massive brain bleed and has a broken neck."

"Right, right, I think we have found his family so I will bring them down. Where should I take them?"

"Bring them to Emergency. We will find out where he is and find a doctor that can speak to them."

"Thank you," the Sergeant acknowledged and ended the call.

He stared at the phone screen and, lost in his own thoughts, he dialled his wife's number. He could think of nothing else but his own son.

"Hi love," his wife answered.

"Where is Josh?"

"In the front room... Why? What's the matter?" She knew something was wrong because her husband, usually, had a much better phone manner than he had just demonstrated.

"Oh, thank Goodness! Tell him not to go anywhere until I get home from work."

"Oh, why? He was just about to go and meet his mates at the skate bowl?"

"I said, tell him not to go anywhere. That's the same for Amanda. I don't have time to argue, just tell them they are to stay home until I get there," he was fired up by his sudden anxiety to keep his family safe, triggered by the situation before him. "Right, do you understand? I have to go."

There was no goodbye or apology for his snappiness, he just hung up. His wife was left standing in the kitchen, absolutely gobsmacked by the conversation. For a few seconds she thought about what could possibly be wrong. Why was her husband going on like this? She was already worried about his emotional state but this was well out of character.

The Sergeant walked over to Tina and Natalie. Natalie was still embracing Tina and she could feel the quiver of Tina's body against her chest. James was still with the ladies, standing there not knowing what to do. The Sergeant liked James but he knew he was struggling with the emotional side of police work.

As he got closer to the small huddle, his eyes connected with Natalie and he could feel her distress. Tina's face was still buried.

"From your description, I think your son has been in an accident. He is now at Lady Mary's Hospital undergoing emergency surgery. Let me take you to him,"

"Ok," Natalie responded. There was no response from Tina.

"EVERYONE HAS A STORY WHICH INFORMS THEIR LIFE AND BEHAVIOUR."

5

NATALIE - AND SO IT BEGINS

NATALIE FOUND HERSELF RACING THROUGH THE emergency room at Lady Mary's Hospital, being ushered into a small meeting room.

"The doctors will be with you in a minute," a young lady quickly advised, before racing off.

The police had driven Natalie and Tina to the hospital and helped them to find the team of staff looking after Justin. Natalie looked around the sterile room, wondering how they ended up there. Tina sat at the table with her head down, fiddling with a tissue she had used to dry her eyes.

"Why do we have to wait?" Tina sneered through her teeth at Natalie, anger had started to bubble to the surface. "Justin is my son and I deserve to know everything. I deserve to know, right now."

Her breath was heaving through her chest, her teeth were clenched and she was ready for a fight.

"Hey now, Tina, these people here, the ones that are trying to help Justin, they are not our enemy. They are our heroes," she paused, "Look at me, look into my eyes." Natalie took Tina's hands and gave them a little shake to try and snap her out of her rage, "Let's be angry later. Let us just try to think about Justin and what they can do to help him, not rip them apart."

Tina's eyes meet Natalie's, "Come on, Tina, we need to help not hinder... take a deep breath and let's focus on Justin."

Tina finally nodded at Natalie, looked down and began to sob. Natalie knew the anger was only a defence; Tina was trying to protect her heart as it was breaking. Natalie held Tina's hand and concentrated on breathing deeply. She was also on the edge of falling apart but knew she needed to be the brains and listen to what was about to unfold.

Before they knew it, three doctors raced into the small meeting room, which suddenly felt cramped and uncomfortable.

The tallest one sat down and began speaking first, "I am the neurological surgical registrar, I am here to talk to you about your son."

He looked directly at Natalie as Tina was still looking into her lap, not wanting to connect with the newcomers in the room. Natalie pointed to Tina and gave the registrar a small nod.

"Your son has had numerous tests and we can confirm that he has had a severe head injury causing extensive bleeding in his brain. He also has multiple fractures in his neck and a punctured lung from a rib," he paused,"Things are not looking good... The consultant has just taken him to theatre to alleviate some of the pressure in his head from the bleeding and I would say he will be in there for quite some time."

Silence fell over the room Tina lifted her head, "What do you mean, things are not looking good?"

"Sorry, I should have explained things better. The tests have shown a lot of serious injuries and we have resuscitated your son twice since his arrival. His brain has been extremely damaged and I didn't want to come in here and give you false hope. Things are dire and the chance of Justin's survival is low."

The pained look on the doctor's face said it all to Natalie - she had seen it before many times in her 20 year's nursing experience and seen the outcome of the words that the doctor had just spoken multiple times.

"I see," Tina managed to squeeze out. "You are telling me that my son is dying."

"It is not looking good, I'm sorry," the doctor stood from the table, ready to leave the room.

Tina raised her voice, "You know what?" The doctor looked her directly in the eyes, "I am still going to pray for a miracle."

"I think you should."

Within a few seconds the room was empty again, leaving Tina and Natalie alone.

Neither Natalie or Tina had their phones with them and no one else knew of the tragedy they were dealing with. A nurse came into the room and showed them to a waiting area outside of the operating theatre. When Natalie explained to her that they needed to make a few phone calls but had no way of contacting anyone, the nurse quickly returned with a cordless phone for them to use. Natalie held the handset and felt the anxiety well up inside of her. She had to ring someone to tell them, to share the burden of the tragedy, but fear was driving her. She froze and her palms became sweaty, her thoughts raced as a vision of Justin's face flashed in her mind's eye. His eyes were swollen shut and purple bruising was running down his face, the image frightened her and she began to hyperventilate. As she tried to catch her breath, a glimpse of Tina distracted her, *Pull yourself together, Natalie, now. Stop and breath.* She closed her eyes and took some slow, deep breaths to centre and focus. The feeling of the phone in her hand became apparent to her again. She dialled her home number hoping for James her husband to answer.

"Howdy!" Her husband's voice beamed from the other end of the phone.

As Natalie responded, she got up and walked out of Tina's hearing range, "James it is me, you need to listen carefully."

"Are you alright, love?" James interjected, feeling things were going to get serious.

"Listen, I am at the hospital. I am ok but Justin has been in an accident and they are not holding much hope for his survival."

"What? What? Justin has been in an accident? What the hell happened?!"

"Look, we haven't been given any details except that they found him on the road and think he fell from the path. Justin has been taken for emergency surgery, so we need to find Jake and get him here ASAP."

"Where are you?"

"Lady Mary's Hospital."

"How did you get there?"

"I'll fill you in later. Find Jake and bring him here. Get Peter and Kate to go and be with Sally and Emma until I can sort something else out. Actually, Peter is at work so can you go and get him?" Natalie didn't even know the time.

"Ok, ok, I will work it out. I will find you when I arrive with Jake."

"See you soon... hurry."

James was stunned at the other end of the phone.

Natalie spoke quietly as she didn't want to startle Tina, "James has gone to get Jake and bring him here."

Tina looked up with swollen red eyes, "Ok."

Natalie sat down beside her friend but words alluded her. She was restless with worst case scenarios flashing through her mind. Tina began to cry and rock in her seat; the scenario before her was obviously way too much. Natalie wrapped her arm around her and pulled her in tight. They had been good friends for many years, they had seen each other through all sorts of dramas and celebrations, but nothing like this. Natalie closed her eyes to stop the flow of her own tears but her efforts were in vain. She was a nurse, so she knew that the injuries Justin had sustained where either going to end in death or severe brain damage. Severe brain damage was a terrible option that Natalie didn't want to think about.

They sat together shedding tears of pain and anguish.

Before long, Tina and Natalie realised Jake and James were standing in front of them, but Tina had no strength to stand and embrace her husband. Jake sat beside her and took the place of Natalie, wrapping his arms around Tina.

"Have you heard anything, Natalie?" He said as he made eye contact with her.

"Not a thing," she replied.

Jake was remarkably calm considering the circumstances, "Tell me what they have told you already, how did you get here and what accident was Justin involved in?"

Jake had many questions that Natalie answered as best she could. When the questioning was over they all sat in silence, lost in their own living hell.

———

NATALIE WAS RUNNING checklists in her head when she realised that she hadn't checked to see if Tina's sister, Jane, had been told about the accident. Natalie knew Tina and Jane had a very close relationship and she began to panic that she was there at the hospital when Jane was not. She turned to Jake and asked the question and he confirmed that he had called Jane and she was on her way. The waiting became too much for Natalie, so she got up and began to wander around the large waiting area. She trawled her thoughts for some peace but it was very difficult.

Natalie thought of herself as spiritual - she practiced mindfulness, meditated and did yoga - and she thought she had a handle on life, but this event had truly thrown her off her game. Terrible thoughts of Justin's condition rolled through her mind and her heart ached with the fear of losing him. Her heart not only ached for her own loss, but also for her family's loss. Justin was like her son and she knew the love that Peter, Justin and her daughter, Kate, shared.

Her thoughts were wildly out of control as she paced around the room.

Finally, Jane and Scott arrived and Natalie felt such relief when she saw their faces. She felt the burden she was carrying to support the inconsolable was finally lifted, it was now shared. Jane and Scott were also friends of Natalie and her own family; they had spent a lot of time together over the years and Natalie knew that the closeness of their relationship would help now in their time of need.

James and Natalie moved away from Tina and Jake and allowed Jane and Scott to comfort them for a while. Jake and Scott discussed what they knew about Justin's condition and the accident while Jane listened and embraced Tina. Natalie watched in despair from the other side of the room. Her nursing experience gave her the realisation that things were pretty hopeless and her mind kept going to places that were torturing her soul.

She was knocked from her nightmare when James touched her back and asked, "Why don't we take a walk?"

Natalie nodded quickly. She wanted to get as far away from this place as possible, her heart was aching and she wanted it all to stop. As they walked out of the room, James wrapped his arm around Natalie and she rested her head on his shoulder. They were no more than 20 metres from the room when Natalie lost it and began to sob. They stopped in the hallway and Natalie buried her head into her husband's chest as the stress of the afternoon took its toll. Natalie and James had been married for 21 years but had been together for 26, so they knew each other very well and their relationship was close. Of course, they had had their ups and downs, but their relationship had grown because they had fought for it and worked hard.

James knew Natalie was the strong one, the one with the advice, and she always was the guiding light. She was like this for everyone in her life. She didn't realise it but she was an amazing person who helped anyone she knew, by just being there. However, at that moment, James knew by the way she was behaving that Natalie was shaken by the situation. He had noticed in the waiting room that her eyes were darting and the pacing was very unusual. He wanted to protect her and help her, as she had always done for everyone else, but he didn't know what to do, so he just held her tight for a few minutes. He felt his heart race, his throat tighten, he felt the pressure of the situation. He knew he was being selfish, but each time he thought of Justin, he found comfort that his own children were at home safe.

James could feel the grief shaking every part of Natalie's body. The sobs subsided and Natalie turned her head so her voice could be heard, "What do we do James? I don't know what to do to help."

There was a pause before James could answer, "I know you always have an answer or a way but, Natalie, this is not for you to fix. We just have to be there for them and see what happens."

James was a man of few words. To the outside world he seemed strong and resilient but he knew that he depended on his wife for her support.

Natalie could not control the thoughts in her mind: visions of Justin in a vegetative state, constricted within his body and with no quality of life, or his poor body, dead in a coffin. She could also see her own son, Peter, draped over Justin's dead body, distraught with sadness - it was this image that hurt her the most in this moment. She knew the boys were close and Peter's life would mean nothing to him without Justin. Her thoughts were tormenting her with the possibility of such a loss. Thoughts of her future always included the Point family, and Justin was a big part of that. She had thought about the boys being friends as middle-aged men, and of their own children becoming friends, how they would be each other's best man at their weddings. How they would go skateboarding all over the world. She couldn't shake off the racing thoughts.

Over the years, Natalie had experienced a spiritual awakening. At first, she was very reluctant to share this with anyone, but recently, she felt she had to live her life truthfully and not hold her spirituality back by hiding it. She had learnt and integrated the understanding that your mind is only a computer and controlling it is key to living peacefully. However, at that moment, all her work with her soul was swept away as the grief took its toll. All these thoughts of the future, of the consequences of Justin's injuries and possibility of death, plagued her and there was this nagging voice right at the back of her mind telling her to stop with all future prospects.

Natalie realised that James had guided her as they had walked, she had no recollection of how she had arrived in the lobby of the hospital. The busy nature of people rushing from here to there distracted her and, as Natalie became aware of her surroundings, her thoughts slowed down. James ushered her to a chair and they sat down together.

"Breathe, Natalie. Take some deep breaths."

Their eyes met and James could see pain in her eyes, but he shook it off. Natalie closed her eyes she breathed through her thoughts to try and find some peace.

As they sat in the lobby of the hospital, James began to wonder how he could be so numb. This was a tragedy, life was hanging in the balance, and he felt indifferent. *What sort of unemotional robot am I?* James looked as his wife, he could see she was not coping. *Why am I so numb? Why am I like this?* He continued to question himself. His brain began to scan memories and life events, searching for answers, when a loud crash rang from the other side of the lobby and distracted him from his thoughts. He decided to push the uncomfortable feelings aside and concentrate on comforting his wife.

Life was about to change forever.

"THE PAST SHAPES YOU.
YOU BUILD A WORLD AROUND
YOURSELF THAT MAKES YOU FEEL
SAFE ACCORDING TO YOUR LIFE
EXPERIENCES."

6
THE FUNERAL - REALITY KICKS IN

THE COFFIN WAS LOWERED INTO THE GROUND, THE SLOW creaking sound of the winch echoing through the cemetery. The crowd that attended the burial service was silent, you could only hear the sniffles and snobs of the attendees. There must have been at least 900 people gathered in the small cemetery. It was a grey, cold, windy day, and almost every person there didn't want to remember. They all had one thing in common that day and that was to forget; forget the trauma of such a senseless accident and of an innocent life of a boy being taken. A boy who had the world at his feet, a boy who had been becoming a man. The gathering stood solemnly and quietly, forcing themselves to forget.

As the coffin lowered, Justin's mother, Tina, fell to her knees. Her hands were holding her heart as though she was holding it in her chest, in case the broken pieces were going to fall out onto the grass. Her sobbing started a ripple of heartbreak amongst the crowd, as if Tina's pain was contractable like a contagious disease.

The creaking of the winch stopped as Justin's coffin reached the bottom of the grave. In that moment, the reality of Justin's death hit Tina and the actuality of his lifeless body being buried under the earth fell hard on her heart. The nightmare she thought she was going to wake up from, was, in that moment, realised as a harsh reality. The complete unfairness of her son being taken from the world, and from her, caused indescribable pain.

Jake bent down to comfort Tina and he rested his hand on her shoulder. He was like a zombie: no words, no emotions. He was not affected by his wife's sobs and cries of pain, he just stared blankly towards his son's grave. Tina was inconsolable and Jake appeared to be unaware of her extreme grief.

Tina's sister, Jane, was standing behind the couple. She could see what was unfolding and decided to intervene. She nudged her husband, Scott, and motioned for him to support Jake as she proposed to gather her sister.

Jane had never seen her sister grief stricken before; when both of their parents had passed away, Tina had been her rock. Jane didn't know how to deal with this role reversal, but she knew she must do something. She pulled her sister up from the ground to a standing position and, as she stood up, Tina's sobs started to quieten. She wiped the tears from her face as she came back to the reality of the situation she was in.

Jane wrapped her arm tightly around Tina's shoulders and drew her close, ensuring she was able to hold her up.

All Jane could think was, "Keep quiet, keep quiet. Keep standing, keep standing."

As Jane held her sister, she could feel Tina's physical and emotional pain. *How do we move on?* Her head shook in disbelief.

Jane lost awareness of her surroundings for a while until she heard the minister's final words, "Ashes to ashes, dust to dust... We return Justin to your love and care. Until we meet again..."

The crowd of people began to move and Jane could hear

the rustle and whispers amongst them. As Jane looked around to fathom what was next, she saw Scott still firmly grasping Jake. It was customary for the family to greet the attendees but Jane knew, with absolute certainty, that neither Tina or Jake were up to this. Jake's father, Tom, walked to his son and stood beside him, ready to field anyone who came close.

Tom turned his head and made eye contact with Jane, "It is time Tina went home."

Jane nodded and Grace, Jake's mother, began to guide them to the carpark so that they could escape the hordes of people.

Tom handled the situation with poise and dignity, shaking people's hands and accepting their condolences. His son stood beside him like a battered soldier, shell-shocked from the horrific happenings. Jake held his hand out to acknowledge the people in front of him; he allowed people to kiss him, but he did not utter a word.

As Jane, Tina and Grace reached the car park, Jane noticed Sally and Emma trailing behind them. Emma's reddened face said it all; grief was amongst them in all forms and it was affecting each and every one of them in a different way. Jane stared at the girls as they came across the carpark and realised she must get everybody home as soon as possible. She shuffled Tina into the car and motioned for the girls to join her.

Suddenly the thought came to her: *Where is Justin? We have to get out of here!*

Grief flooded through her and tears dripped from her eyes as she wrapped her arms around the girls and kissed them both on the top of their heads. She wiped her eyes and motioned for the girls to get in the car. Grace got into the driver's seat and the group began their drive home, leaving the cemetery behind them.

————

Tom pulled into the driveway about an hour after the girls arrived home. Jake was in the front seat, beside him, while Scott sat in the back. The entire ride home had been in silence. The car came to a halt and, after Tom turned off the ignition, the three men all sat still and remained silent for a moment. All that could be heard was Jake's breathing, fast and laboured. Scott didn't know what to do next, so he didn't dare make a move. He didn't know Tom very well, but he did know he was a strong and foreboding man that demanded respect with his mere presence. He would wait unit Tom made a move.

Jake showed no signs of movement. Unbeknown to Scott and Tom, he was panicking inside, his mind unable to comprehend the loss, the trauma, the things he had seen and experienced. It all seemed unreal; a reality that he was suffering through but could not partake in.

Seeing his son's coffin being lowered into the ground had made him panic. How could he just leave him there, in the ground, alone, cold and lifeless? Surely there was something that he could do to bring Justin home?

Jake's breathing sped up, his posture slumped and, for the first time in days, tears fell from his eyes.

Tom reached over to support his son, "Things will get easier, Jake. I don't know when, but they will... We will be ok."

"Justin won't be though, will he?" Jake voiced. "He's dead, Dad. We left him back at that cemetery. He's deep in the ground, all on his own, without any of us. It's just not fair, why couldn't I have died and Justin lived? I am no one special but he was a special kid - just looking at him made me feel alive and extraordinary. He had a way to make me feel love, like I had never felt before. A love that connected us in a way no one else could feel or understand. What am I going to do without him? Who am I without him? I want to die so he can live... I want to die!"

Jake sobbed into his hands.

Scott sat in the back of the car, silent and stunned. He felt like he was invading Jake and Tom's privacy. Hearing their sadness was breaking his heart. His heart and chest began to ache. He didn't want to feel like this; he was always in control of his feelings and never, ever, cried. Grief was getting the better of him. A glimpse of his own father flashed before his eyes, lying in a hospital bed, grey, skeletal and unconscious. He never cried when his father got sick and passed away, but this was just too much for him to bear.

Tom was lost. *A grandfather should not have to bury his own grandson. Why couldn't I have died and Justin lived? I am old and have lived my life. I want to take Justin's place, in that grave, in that coffin, in the ground.*

Yet, nothing could change, there was no negotiating with God. God's plan had played out and Justin was dead while Tom and Jake were alive. How was life going to go on? How were they going to move on?

"I know the desperation you feel because I feel it too. He was a special kid," Tom's voice broke.

Scott could hear the quiver in Tom's voice as tears began to roll down his own face, "I don't know. I don't have any answers for you, mate." Tom had no idea of what to do or say to his son.

Scott wanted to open the door of the car and get the hell out of there. His eyes remained firmly shut in an attempt to shut out the world. He was choked up with grief, he didn't want to feel what his was feeling.

"EVERYONE HAS THEIR OWN
WAY OF COPING"

7

SCOTT - WHERE AM I?

Both Tom and Jake were sobbing in the front of the car and Scott couldn't stand the pain. Before he knew what he was doing, he was out of the car and walking down the footpath. Scott was a Real Estate broker and spent his days trying to pressure people and convince them to buy. It was a high-pressure job so Scott was always on the move with something to do. He liked it that way; he liked to always be busy so that he didn't have to think or feel.

Scott was not good with difficult situations, he was a man of avoidance and distraction. His life often involved running from his inner truth. By the time he reached the end of the path, Scott was walking so fast that he felt as though he was floating. The further away he got from the car and the house, the better he felt. The distance began to rescue him from his discomfort.

After a while, Scott realised that he was some distance from the house and didn't recognise where he was. In his scurry to get away, he hadn't noticed his surroundings passing him by. He found himself on a busy main road and amongst a few shops.

"Where the hell am I?" Scott whispered under his breath.

He stopped still and, as he did, his mobile phone rang,

startling him and releasing him from his disorientation. Scott grabbed the phone out of his pocket and answered on autopilot, "Hello, Scott speaking."

As he spoke, he realised that he didn't actually want to speak to anyone.

"Hello, is that Scott Watts?" The accented voiced beamed from the other end of the phone.

"Umm, what?"

Scott was noticeably annoyed, knowing all too well that the call was from a telemarketer, but then realised it was a blessing in disguise because he didn't have to continue the conversation.

"Not today, thanks," and Scott ended the call without waiting for a response.

Scott and his wife didn't have any children. From a young age, he had always known that he didn't want children. He didn't see himself as a father and Jane, his wife, didn't mind either way. So, very early in their relationship, they made a decision not to start their own family. Because of this, Scott found it hard to relate to kids, hold a conversation with them, play or spend time with them. Except for with Justin; Scott found a lot of enjoyment and had a connection with Justin. They related to one another well. Justin had a great sense of humour and Scott really loved his company.

The day of the accident, Scott was closing a deal on the biggest sale he had ever undertaken, a fourteen million dollar sale - the biggest sale in his office and the biggest sale of his career. He was sitting in his office, signing the last pieces of paperwork, shaking hands and congratulating everyone on a job well done, while Jane was repeatedly ringing him. Scott had ignored the calls for over half an hour and he knew he should pick up but, inwardly, he had this enormous aversion to answering it. It was like his hand just could not reach across the table and pick up the phone. He didn't know why; he only knew that he just didn't want to listen or hear it.

Jane didn't ring him much during the day, so Scott knew that she wasn't ringing over something trivial. They were not a clingy couple, they were both driven and independent. Jane worked as a legal secretary and was dedicated to her job. She was passionate about being the best she could be and she didn't rely on her relationship with Scott to feel worthwhile.

Scott's phone lit up; twelve missed calls in half an hour. Everyone else had since left his office and he was sitting looking at the signed paperwork before him. The biggest deal of his life and he could not find one ounce of joy in it. The phone began to vibrate, again, and Jane popped up on his screen, a photo of her on the beach from a holiday they took last Christmas. Scott forced himself to pick up this time and answer the call.

"Hey," Jane squeezed out, "I take it you have been in a meeting?"

"Yep, just closing the deal with the Hubners," Scott could not muster any excitement in voice.

"Ok, sure. I remember now."

"What are you chasing me for?" Scott questioned awkwardly. He really felt in the pit of his stomach that he did not want to know.

"I was ringing to see... I need to tell you... I am not sure where to start..."

Jane hesitated and started to sob on the other end of the phone. She was sitting in her car in the hospital car park with the ignition turned off, not knowing what to do next.

"Jane, what is the matter? Are you ok? Is it you?" Scott's mind began to run wild.

"No, no, it's not me... it is Justin."

"What's happened to Justin?"

Justin's face popped up in the forefront of Scott's mind.

"He's been in an accident. I'm not sure what happened but he is in a bad way. Jake rang me a while ago and asked me to come to the hospital to be with Tina, but I just can't move out of car. I am so scared... Jake said things are really bad and that Tina needs me. I don't know if I am strong enough for all of this Scott," she sobbed.

Scott's mind was racing. The phone line was quiet as neither Jane or Scott muttered a word, Jane was distraught and Scott was in shock. A long minute passed with Jane's quiet distress being heard through the phone.

"I will come to you and then we can decide what to do. Where are you?"

Scott didn't want to go but knew he was mandated to support his wife. He wanted to run a million miles away but, instead, he gathered every bit of strength he could find.

"Where are you?" He repeated.

"Lady Mary's Hospital in the undercover carpark," Jane looked up and saw the concrete pillar in front of her, "I am on level two, purple."

"I will get there as soon as I can."

———

Scott pulled into Lady Mary's car park and began scanning for Jane's car. It was only a few seconds before he found it. He could see Jane sitting in the front seat with her head hung low. As Scott approached the car, his gut tightened and the anguish within him rose. He tapped gently on the car window and, as Jane turned around, he opened the door.

Jane seemed to crawl out of the car in slow motion.

"What the hell has happened?" Scott was bewildered.

"Justin was in an accident," Jane sobbed as she tried to explain the few details she was aware of.

Before they knew it, Scott and Jane were standing in front of Tina and Jake in the surgery waiting room. As Scott stood there looking at Jake, his brother-in-law but also his mate, he consciously pushed all his own feelings deep, deep, down. He could see that Jake needed him to be there and Scott assumed that Jake wouldn't deal well with him losing it. Jake was stressed; he was sweating and was rocking back and forth in his seat. Natalie and James moved to the side and explained that Justin had been in a senseless accident and he was in a critical condition. Justin suffered from a massive brain haemorrhage which had resulted in pressure in his skull where it shouldn't be, so the doctors had taken him for surgery to relieve it. The situation made logical sense to Scott; Justin had experienced a bleed and they were going to drain the blood so that his brain wasn't damaged.

James and Natalie then disappeared.

A female approached them with surgical scrubs on, "Mr and Mrs Point?"

Tina and Jake jumped to their feet.

"I've come to talk to you about Justin's condition," she paused, "Let's sit down."

"Don't tell me to sit down," Jake raised his voice, "Just tell me what is happening with my son."

Tears of frustration began to well up in Jake's eyes.

Scott wrapped his arms around Jake shoulders, "Mate, let's sit down so we can work this out."

Jake and Scott's eyes met, and Scott didn't have to say another word. Jake sat down next to Tina, ready to listen. Scott was pushing his emotions down into depths of his soul - this was his solution to everything in life when he felt uncomfortable; shove, shove, shove.

Scott's childhood had not been one filled with love and sweetness. His mother left when he was eight years old, after years of verbal and emotional abuse of him and his father. Scott was the product of a teenage pregnancy which his mother had always regretted and never hidden from her only child. Angry and pissed off with the world, his mother drank a lot, from morning until night, while his father worked long hours to support the family. On the other hand, his father was a loving, kind and gentle person but the bitterness of Scott's mother took its toll on his father's spirit. By the time she left them, his father was downtrodden and depressed from the constant ear bashings he would receive about the poor choice they had made by going through with the pregnancy, how having a baby so young had deprived them of their own childhood.

In contrast, his father would tell Scott that having him in his life made him so incredibly happy.

Scott was scarred from his childhood and didn't like a reality that challenged his emotional state and challenged how he managed himself. The way he coped was pretty simple, he shut down and would pretend something wasn't happening. It was a habit from when he was young, a coping mechanism that ensured his survival!

Back in the hospital, Scott was sitting there trying to calm his emotions, when the lady walked into the room.

"Hello, I am Doctor Timms. I need to tell you that Justin is in a very serious critical condition and, at the moment, we don't think he will survive his surgery," she looked very uncomfortable. She took a deep breath and continued, "I am sorry to have to tell you this but the bleed in Justin's brain is more extensive than we thought, he has suffered much more damaged than expected. The neurosurgeon has asked me to come and explain the gravity of his injuries to you so that you are prepared."

There was a pause and Scott saw Tina look at the floor in dismay. Scott quickly looked away as he didn't want to see the aftermath of this information on Tina's soul. Similarly, Jake's eyes didn't leave their connection to the floor, it was like he was frozen. Scott still had his hand on Jake's back and he could feel Jake's shock radiate through their physical connection. Scott took a deep breath and held it. *What the hell?* His thoughts raced. *What do I say? What do we all do?*

As quick as she came, the doctor stood up and left, "We will keep you updated."

As she walked off, Scott thought about what a crappy job she had dealing with this sort of thing.

"My poor baby," sobbed Tina, her voice muffled by her embrace with Jane. Jake was leaning forwards and Scott could see tears running through his fingers. Panic began to consume Scott and he realised that the anguish of the situation was getting to him. He took a deep breath and tried to remember how he got there, to the point where he was comforting this man and woman who he was only related to by marriage.

This is not my responsibility, his thoughts raced. He had to get out. He couldn't take the strain and he was willing to use any excuse to be free of it all. His wall of iron went up, protecting him from the pain of loss, he was becoming emotionally free of this situation. He closed his eyes and took a deep breath.

Scott was brought back to the present by Jane trying to convince Tina things would be ok, but it didn't feel alright to him, he felt as though Justin was gone already. It all felt horribly wrong. He didn't want to deal with it. Unwanted feelings were bubbling up to the surface again and panic began to rise. His heart began to beat so fast that he thought it was going to crawl up his throat and out of his mouth. He wanted to jump off that chair and run as fast as he could but, as he turned, the image of Jake kicked in. Scott realised that he couldn't leave, he couldn't run away, he needed to be there.

What the hell can I do? I can't change this or even make things slightly better. I'm not a miracle worker! His thoughts were so loud in his head, he felt as though he was being yelled at by himself. *I am not God.* He shook his head. *Screw this, this is not my thing.*

Scott stood up and turned to face Jake. Jake lifted his head, his face wet from his tears. "Where are you going, man?" Jake's voiced trembled under the pressure.

In that moment, Scott was caught between how uncomfortable the situation was making him feel and to be there to support Jake.

Scott paused for what seemed like eternity, but finally responded, "Nowhere, man. Just standing up."

"Please don't go."

Scott nodded in agreement. In his heart, he knew he wanted to stay and be with his family, but he had to really force himself. He sat back down in the chair and placed his arm around Jake, again. He thought about how these people were his family; he had to let his own demons go and put them first.

Scott looked down at his watch and he saw the minutes tick over to 6.18pm. It had been a good hour since the lady in the scrubs had been in to talk with them. As he looked up, a small army of people dressed in scrubs marched towards them. By this stage, it felt like the family had been waiting forever. The army all had the same look about them, scared and tired.

"We are here to talk about Justin."

Tina, Jake, Scott and Jane all looked up. The man who looked like he was in charge grabbed a chair from the main seating area and dragged it over to sit in front of the two couples.

"Who are Justin's Mum and Dad?"

No one wanted to own up to the role, it was a terrifying thought. However, the doctor persevered and, when everyone was identified, he continued. They were told that Justin's condition was hanging in the balance; the neurosurgeon thought there was little hope but, if Justin was still technically alive within 24 hours, they would need to conduct tests to assess brain death. They were told that the surgery hadn't gone well - the bleeding was severe, the worst the surgeon had ever seen, and there was nothing they could do.

From that point on, Scott checked out of life. For the next eight days, he simply zoned out. Except for the eight minutes he was left alone in the hospital room with Justin, just before they transported him home to die.

———

THE DOOR SHUT with a swish and Scott was left alone with the body that had once housed Justin's cheeky and bright personality. Scott looked at his nephew's face, he forced himself to, but it was so bruised and swollen it was difficult to recognise him. A wave of sadness flowed over Scott's body and tears welled in his eyes. Reality was setting in. Scott had to face it Justin was gone.

"Justin, mate..." He paused, "I don't know what to say to you. I'm struggling to understand, or believe, what is happening. Life is just so messed up." His voice got louder and anger tinged his tone. "This is so damn cruel. Why do you have to go? Why do you have to leave?"

There was no response. It was clear that life was no longer residing in Justin's beaten and bruised body.

Scott had to face reality; he could hide no longer. Someone he loved was leaving him once again. First, his Mother when he was a child, then his father as a late teenager, and now Justin. His chest and throat ached.

"I'm sorry this happened to you, mate. I wish I could take

your injuries away and you would sit up and tell me some cheeky joke," he paused, "God, you made me laugh."

Scott realised he had spoken in the past tense and, in that comment, he realised Justin was gone. His eyes fell to his lap and the tears ran down his face.

"Thanks for us," Scott whispered.

The machines were beeping and buzzing around Justin's lifeless body. Scott was stunned when a cool breeze flooded over him. He instantly looked around to see where it was coming from, but nothing he could see allowed for the breeze. Then, again, he felt it. He gazed over at Justin; no change or movement, just the buzz and beeps of the machines. Scott's head dropped, his posture slumped and his sadness returned.

In that moment, a warm embrace wrapped around Scott. It was comforting and he could feel his chest begin to glow. He began to straighten up to look over at Justin and, as the warmth wrapped around him, a gentle white light fell over his nephew. Scott was mesmerised by the happenings. He didn't try and explain what he saw, he was just there, in the moment, in awe of the splendour before him. Scott wiped his eyes, as if to wipe away the light he saw being cast over Justin, but he realised that it was real. The light began to fill the room and spread to cover Scott. As the light spread, he experienced an intense feeling of love. Tingles ran up and down his body, and he felt light and peaceful. He had never felt anything like this before. It was intensely beautiful and was a welcome relief from how he had felt since learning of the accident.

Scott stood and held Justin's lifeless hand and allowed the feeling to take its course. A feeling of gratitude filled him, a great gratitude of knowing Justin. He had never felt such intense feelings of love before and the experience was amazing. Something had shifted within him.

As quickly as the light, love and gratitude arrived, it was

then gone. The door to the room swung open as Jake, Tina and Jane returned to the hospital room. No one spoke for a few minutes and Scott continued to stand by the bed, holding Justin's hand. In his mind, he said his goodbyes. *See ya, mate. Thanks for the memories.* He closed his eyes and took a deep breath.

He let Justin's hand go and turned to face Jane. As he looked at her, he felt an intense love and a need to embrace her. Scott hoped that Jane could feel the love that was emanating from him, and he hoped he was passing on some of the peace he felt in that moment. They embraced and melted into each others arm.

Their eyes met as they pulled away, "I needed that, Scotty."

"THERE IS NO GREATER POWER IN HEAVEN OR ON EARTH THAN PURE, UNCONDITIONAL LOVE."

- DR. WAYNE DYER

8

THE PRINCIPAL - SHOCK

LAWRIE GEORGE, JUSTIN'S SCHOOL PRINCIPAL, WAS REALLY hit hard by losing Justin. He had been a school principal for twelve years and loved his job, but he had never lost a member of the school community in all his years. He saw Justin as a kind, funny kid, who was full of enthusiasm and also just the right amount of cheeky.

Lawrie knew Justin quite well because he helped coach the football teams and Justin had been playing since he started at the school. Lawrie was always glad to see Justin because, a lot of the time, the kids were hard to motivate, but if Justin was around he seemed to be able to razzle the team just by being himself. His energy enveloped the field and all its residents, he was such a pleasure to be around. It was kids like Justin that made Lawrie's job worthwhile.

It was Monday morning at 8.12am, when Lawrie heard of Justin's accident. He knew the time because he had looked at the clock to check if it was time to address assembly when his phone began to ring. As he answered, he was greeted by Natalie Wood, the Point family's friend and neighbour.

"Hi Lawrie, this is Natalie Wood."

"Oh, hi Natalie. What can I do for you today?"

Lawrie was upbeat for the Monday morning he was generally a happy and friendly chap.

"Look, I have some devastating news, Justin Point has been in a horrific accident and is not expected to live. His sister, Sally, won't be at school and neither will my son, Peter." Natalie took an enormous breath; she didn't want to discuss the details. "I will be back in touch with any changes."

Natalie hung the phone up without waiting for a response. Lawrie sat, staring at the clock on his desk, completely shook up by the news. Many thoughts raced through his mind, but those few words repeated and repeated, "Justin has been in a horrific accident and is not expected to live."

Lawrie felt as if someone had punched him in the stomach and knocked the wind out of him. He was frozen, the phone handset sitting on his desk with the beeping sound audible in the background. Eventually, the clock clicked over to 8.18am and the branch of a tree suddenly brushed against the window which was situated behind Lawrie's desk. It snapped him out of his trance as he shook his head from side to side. *Justin, really? Justin... What on earth could have happened that meant Justin would be so injured that he may not survive? He is such a good lad.*

Lawrie flopped back in his chair and his breaths became short and laboured. He didn't cry but sweat began to build on his forehead.

It was 8.21am when the door of his office flung open and Susan stepped in, "Lawrie do you know what the time is? Parade is waiting for you!"

Susan was a bit annoyed that she had to chase him, it wasn't usual, but as she got closer to Lawrie she saw that he was pale and sweaty, "Are you alright Lawrie?"

She rushed over by his side, "What is the matter you are as white as a ghost, do you feel ill?"

"No, no, I'm not ill, just shocked," cold sweat dripped down the side of his face.

"About what? What's happened?"

Lawrie took a deep breath, "Justin Point has been in a horrific accident and is not expected to live."

"DISBELIEF IS PART OF THE PROCESS."

9

SCOTT – THE BREATH

Scott put his phone in his pocket and began to take notice of his surroundings, trying to work out where he was. He was in a tizz trying hard to push his emotions aside, but he was struggling. When he had left the car, he hadn't taken note of the direction he headed.

After some time, he finally recognised the takeaway store that he and Justin had visited to collect fish and chips for everyone on their Friday night get-togethers. It was always Scott and Justin's job to collect the food.

He was beginning to get lost in his thoughts again, when he noticed a coffee shop open. It was only 12.21pm, which made sense as the funeral was at 10am. *Good,* he thought, *I will go and get a coffee to see if I can use up some time here, instead of heading back to Jake and Tina's.* Having some time alone was a bit of a relief from the intensity of the situation they were all in.

Scott entered the coffee shop and wandered over to a table in the corner where he picked up the menu. A lovely bubbly waitress appeared to take his order.

"Hi there, what can I get you today?"

Scott looked up, "I'll have a flat white in a mug and the quiche and salad, please."

"What salad would you like with that, Greek or garden?"

"Whatever is going."

Scott was not interested, he just wanted to order something so he could sit at the table. "Coming right up," the waitress rushed off.

Scott's thoughts started to tick away, *What is happening here? What am I doing?* He began to list things that he needed to do, things that he could get done for work since he'd lost some time over the last few weeks. He was desperately trying to distract himself from the happenings of the day. It had been so hard, working all day to squash his feelings and not let anyone else penetrate his shield of exclusion. He grabbed his phone out of his pocket and messed around clicking in and out of apps, until he finally settled on thumbing through endless social media posts.

After a short while, the bubbly waitress flew by his table with his coffee. He placed his phone down beside the cup, added two sugars to the drink, stirred his coffee and took a sip. He looked out across the street, scanning for a distraction. His gaze settled on a homeless man who was pushing a trolley up the street, filled with zipped up bags. There were random items shoved down the sides of the trolley; he could make out an umbrella and a hat. Scott was enthralled with what he saw. The man looked about the same age as he did. *Why is he homeless? Surely he can find a job and somewhere to live? Why would someone choose to live rough with no food and no money?* As Scott was thinking of the man pushing all of his worldly possessions up the street in a shopping trolley, the waitress returned with his food.

"Here you go," she placed the plate down on the table and noticed that Scott was distracted, "I see you're interested in Joe."

"Oh, I was just watching him pushing all his stuff around in that trolley."

"He's ok, you know. He has money for food and what not. He's a good fella, he just doesn't want to be a part of the rat race. He pops in here most days for a coffee, reads and wanders off. He is good for a chat."

"Oh, he is ok then?"

"I think so, as ok as he can be," the bright and chipper waitress replied and then left him to it.

I wonder why he lives rough and is homeless? He doesn't want to be part of the rat race, what does that mean? I wonder what happened to him, why doesn't his family help him, why doesn't he ask his family for help?

Scott's thoughts completely distracted him from his own life troubles. He tucked into his lunch, he didn't really want to but he felt compelled to eat it. As he sat and ate, the time passed and he began to feel more at peace.

Scott was startled by the rumble of wheels behind him. He spun around to see Joe squeezing his trolley through a tight space so he could sit at the next table.

Their eyes locked and Joe extended a bright, "Hey, mate! Nice day we are having, isn't it?"

Scott was taken aback by the salutation. He looked up at the sky to notice, for the first time that day, that the sky was now a beautiful shade of blue, different from the gloomy day he experienced at the cemetery.

A few seconds passed when Scott responded, "Yeah, I suppose it is."

"Haven't you noticed it before just now, mate?"

"Actually, I haven't."

"That's a shame, the day is half over and you've missed it."

"I'm sort of glad that I did, it's been pretty crappy." Scott didn't realise that he shared so much in one short statement. He didn't mean to, it wasn't like him to share, at all.

"Bad day, hey? I don't seem to have them anymore. When you expect nothing, you receive everything," Joe replied.

"Well, you're lucky mate," Scott paused.

With that, the waitress reappeared to take Joe's order. Scott noticed they greeted each other like old friends. He was surprised that the staff didn't kick him out, instead, they didn't seem to judge him. The waitress took the order and disappeared, while Scott sat and stewed on the goings on.

He was mulling over Joe's last remark, "When you expect nothing, you receive everything."

Scott had worked extremely hard for all his adult life; he didn't have anyone to count on financially and no one pushing him to do better or be better. *If I didn't expect anything, I would have nothing. I would be like him, feeling sorry for myself, and have given up on life.*

"Hey, mate, what's made your day so crappy? It can't be that bad," Joe prodded for conversation.

"Oh, but I think it is," Scott paused, he didn't know if he should spill his guts or shut his mouth but then figured that Joe asked so he must want to listen.

"I buried my nephew, Justin, today. He was 16 and I have literally run away after the service. I'm hiding here from my family because I don't do emotions."

Their eyes never lost connection.

"Man, that is a tough day. How did he die?" Joe continued to probe, even though he knew that Scott was finding it tough.

"A senseless accident... severe head injuries... his parents had to turn off the ventilator as he was deemed brain dead." Scott's voice was monotonous, he was doing his very best to hold it together.

"Man, that is tough. How do you feel about it all?"

Silence fell between them as Scott didn't know how to answer that question.

"Who are you? What are you asking me that for? Shit, man, I don't know if I want to answer that. I don't know you?"

Scott was scared to talk about how he felt, so he attempted to distance himself from Joe.

"That's cool, man. You don't have to talk about it, I just thought that you might need an ear."

Scott turned away from Joe to hide himself and the men fell into silence.

After a few minutes, Joe pressed on with their conversation, "Sorry, mate. I will introduce myself; I'm Joe, currently roaming the streets, happy, enlightened and presently very hungry."

Joe was trying to lighten the mood. He could see Scott was shrouded by a cloud of despair that was weighing his soul down, he didn't want to push him.

Scott couldn't stop seeing flashes of Justin's bruised and battered face and a few uncomfortable minutes passed while he tried to clear his head.

The waitress interrupted and placed Joe's coffee on the table.

"Thanks Tammy, you're a gem."

Joe was truly grateful for his coffee; he knew that most people say thanks purely out of politeness, they didn't really think about what they were saying, but he meant it.

Joe relaxed and began to enjoy his coffee. Scott noticed that he looked well fed and nourished, he was clean and his clothes appeared washed. He didn't look like the "typical" homeless person you would expect, he wasn't begging or sitting on a street corner. He could obviously pay for his food, or the waitress would not have taken his order. Scott was now looking in Joe's direction, judging Joe's life decisions.

"Good food here, hey?" Joe made eye contact again.

"Yeah," Scott responded by looking down at his plate of half-eaten food. He picked up his fork and continued to eat his quiche, "It is really good."

Scott only just realised what his lunch tasted like.

"Hey, sorry. My name is Scott, nice to meet you. Do you want to sit with me, Joe? We can talk better if we sit closer."

Scott was feeling guilty about how he had spoken to Joe because he realised Joe was only trying to be kind.

"Sure, mate," and with that, Joe got up with his coffee and sat opposite Scott at the table.

Tammy arrived with Joe's lunch, "Oh, you changed tables! You always find someone to talk to, Joe."

"What can I say?" Joe lifted his arms in the air with a shrug.

"Enjoy!" Tammy walked off.

The men sat in silence and ate, but when Scott was finished he asked, "Do you need somewhere to stay?"

After he finished the question, he realised he didn't have anywhere to offer Joe but it was out in the open now, too late.

Joe giggled in response, "No, I'm fine, but thank you for your kind offer."

"Really?" Scott hated the thought of having nowhere to call home.

"I'm ok Scott, don't worry about me."

"Aren't you worried about getting attacked and robbed?"

"I actually did get attacked once. Well, sort of. A guy held a knife to my throat and told me to give him my money, so I did. I told him to chill and all he had to do is ask and I would give him anything. Think this caught him off guard because he backed right down and we ended up chatting for about an hour. He was a busted man - no food, no clothes, no bedding and no plan, and it was cold. He had lost his job and his flat mate kicked him out for spending his money on pot and not rent, so I gave him all that I could. I still see him from time to time. He's back on track; found a job and somewhere to live. Given up the pot."

Joe spoke with such a matter-of-fact attitude that Scott thought he might have been making it up, "Is that all true, Joe?"

"Sure is," Joe looked Scott directly in the eye, "Look, mate, fears aren't real, they are only worries about the future or of the past. If you live fearing the future or battling your past, you cannot live in the present."

"What do you mean?" Scott was completely puzzled by this statement.

"Well, for me, right now, in this very moment, I am ok - no danger, no worries and I am having lunch with you, having a nice conversation."

"Sure, because it's the middle of day and you're eating. You are not thinking about where you are going to sleep or the safety of the place you are going to sleep in, you're busy, but things can happen."

"As I told you, Scott, I'm doing ok. I don't need to think about those things 'cause everything will work out and I am happy, right now."

Joe wriggled back in his chair, sat bolt upright, took an long breath in and an even longer breath out.

"I don't get you... Don't you think about what you are going to do next? And, what you have done in the past? Or, what got you here? I can only imagine that someone has hurt you or you are here hurting yourself."

"Well, you hit it right on the head, Scott... you IMAGINE. Let me ask you something, what problems do you have right now?"

Scott was caught a little off guard but responded with a bit of drama, "Well, my nephew just died, everyone is distraught, my wife doesn't know where I am, I should probably be a work... What am I going to say to my mate that has lost his 16 year old son? So many problems and issues."

Scott lent back in chair and ran his fingers through his hair, Joe could see he was really triggered.

"What if we can just think of this moment, right now? What if we could just breathe and see what is right in front of us?" He paused, "Do something with me... Take a deep breath in for the count of six, and out for the count of eight."

Scott didn't respond so Joe waited for him.

After a few seconds, Joe continued, "Let's do it together; breathe in 1...2...3...4...5...6... Ok, now out, 1...2...3...4...5...6... 7...8... Ok, again, 1...2...3...4...5...6.... Ok, out, 1...2...3...4...5... 6...7...8..."

They did this for about two and half minutes before Joe intervened, "Now just look at your surroundings and see what is right there before you. Notice the beauty in the sky, notice the breeze on your face. What colour is the table?"

Joe allowed a minute or so to pass as he noticed that Scott was listening and examining the world around him.

"Yeah, wow. That makes me feel at bit better..." Scott paused and shook his head a little, "...but isn't that just ignoring what my reality is?"

"The worries and stress you perceive you have, is about the past and the future. Think in this moment only. Do you have anything pressing, anything real, you need to deal with?"

Scott took a breath and really thought about this question. He thought to himself, *Well, Justin has passed away but there is no point in worrying about the effect of that because it won't change anything; my wife is not looking for me because I don't have a missed call; work told me not to return for a few weeks; Jake isn't here with me, so I don't have the pressure of dealing with him.*

After some time, he responded to Joe, "Well no, I suppose not."

"A lot of what you are feeling is worry for a different future, or worry for how you can fix things and what you could, or couldn't, do."

Joe felt Scott was understanding a little. He looked at Scott the whole time; he wanted to stay connected to him for Scott to really grasp the concept he was explaining.

"Joe... How do you do that when there is a pressing issue in the moment? What about the day we had to make the decision to turn Justin's ventilator off? The day we had to listen to the news that Justin would not survive surgery? These are really stressful moments that force us to think about the future and the past; what we will miss, what we won't have, who we will or won't be, without him. How? How do you do that? It's ok here, removed from the situation, but not when you are in it."

Scott was obviously frustrated with Joe's simple suggestion for deescalating stress.

"I know it seems easier here, removed from your family, but believe me, it will make each moment easier. This way of thinking is not trying to devalue the gravity of your loss or how hard your life may seem currently, it is just trying to show you how your brain expands the pain. Work at staying in the moment during these stressful times and dealing with what comes in that moment. Stop your brain from stirring up unnecessary scenarios and emotions, stick to the actual moment."

Joe studied Scott to see how he was coping with the information.

"Yes, we all have tough things to work through, but thinking and controlling your brain this way will assist in making life much less painful."

Scott began to see Joe's point, but he was not totally convinced.

"Ok, I understand. Here is another example; if you are lying in bed tonight and you are thinking about how your life will be affected by your loss, you are creating stress and pressure for yourself that is not necessary. You are using the future and the past to power your thoughts. You should try the breathing exercise we just did and appreciate the present moment; you are safe in bed in your house with your wife and your family. What is so terrible about that reality? You will find that you drift off to sleep in a relaxed state until the sun rises. Is that so bad? I know that things are raw and hard to hear right now but, believe me, this helps."

Joe wanted to reach out and comfort Scott because he could feel his pain and anxiety, the air was palpable with raw emotion. He knew the pain, he had been there himself, but he wasn't ready to share that with Scott.

"I can see you are sceptical about what I am saying, so let me try and explain one final way. By not worrying or thinking about the past or future, you are allowing yourself to live in the moment. I know this sounds strange, but most people don't really experience life properly, moment to moment; their brain is too busy thinking about how a specific experience will affect their future or comparing it to the past. Let's take you, here today, you have attended your nephew's funeral," Joe looked to Scott for agreement.

Scott wasn't giving much away and simply raised his eyebrows in response.

"What would that experience have been like if your brain wasn't focusing on the consequences of not having Justin with you and your family? I bet, today, you were reminded of other funerals you have attended and your heart ached with anguish over missing not only Justin, but also others in your life?"

Scott jumped in quickly, "It's natural that I would feel and think of these things."

"Actually, I agree, it is, but does it have to be so painful?" Joe paused, this was a tough subject to approach and an even tougher concept to integrate into life, "Funerals are about a celebration of life and goodbyes, and it doesn't mean that goodbyes are not painful."

Scott was lost.

"What if you didn't think about the future impact of not having Justin in your life; the loss, the pain, the things that you will miss out on? What if you didn't compare this to past experiences? I can guarantee that a lot of the sadness and despair you experienced today arose from reflecting on your past. Memories compound the current pain tenfold. Can you see that we use a lot of the past and future to digest or, shall we say, deal with the issue at hand?"

"I can see that, but I think it's obvious. Of course, we use past experiences to deal with a situation. We live and learn, that's life," Scott argued.

"But, what if we just dealt with the situation as it was, or is, and left the future and past alone? A lot of the torture and unhappiness on our planet would disappear..."

Scott understood the concept Joe was trying to explain, he just wasn't convinced of its validity. The two men sat in silence, Joe finishing off his food while Scott worked at digesting the information.

"Scott, I am going now to leave you with your thoughts and allow you to find your way home to your family."

"Yep, righto mate," Scott was distracted and distant.

Joe disappeared while Scott was lost in thought. He attempted the breathing exercise again, while he sat there, alone, trying to work through the information he had just been given. Then, out of what seemed like nowhere, Tammy popped over to the table, "Can I get you anything else?"

Scott looked up with a blank stare, "Ah, no thanks, but I do need to pay and get on my way."

He reached into his pocket for his wallet.

"It's all paid for," Tammy tried to lighten the mood but silence persisted, "Joe paid the bill so you are good to go. See you next time."

Scott sat there for a moment and contemplated, *What the hell is happening? I buried my nephew then run away, gotten lost and had lunch with a cashed-up, wise homeless man. Life is definitely not what I was expecting today.*

He sat and grinned to himself and realised that he had not felt any degree of relief about his situation until his conversation with Joe. He counted his blessings, turned on his phone, opened up his social media account and was pleasantly surprised to see a particular quote jump out at him:

"No one is sent by
accident to anyone."
– A Course in Miracles

"You can say that again," Scott didn't care who heard him talking to himself.

"NO ONE IS SENT BY
ACCIDENT TO ANYONE."

- A COURSE IN MIRACLES

10

JOHN LUCAS - UNPREDICTABLE

"WHAT DID HE SAY?" LUCAS WHISPERED TO A FRIEND sitting beside him.

"Mr George said that Justin Point has died."

"What?" Lucas paused, he was shocked. The blood drained from his face.

His mate, John, noticed his face change, "Are you alright? You don't look too good."

Silence fell over Lucas, he couldn't speak, he just stared through John, lost for words. His face was pale, white as a sheet.

"Dude, what's wrong with you?"

Still, Lucas couldn't answer.

"Hey, Sir!" His mate whispered, trying to get the nearest teacher's attention.

Mr George was still talking about Justin, "He was a great guy and a great friend."

Lucas heard nothing but the dismay in his head, *What the hell? Dead? Justin, dead?*

"Hey, Sir!" John's whisper grew a little louder.

Mr Belan made eye contact with him but furrowed his eyebrows, angry that someone was being disrespectful. John pointed at Lucas but Mr Belan couldn't see his face. John began to point furiously; Lucas was looking paler and paler by the second. John was worried Lucas was going to pass out, so he put his arm around his shoulders to ensure he remained upright. Mr Belan noticed something was wrong and began to look concerned. He shuffled down the row and crouched down to see what the problem was, his eyes widening when he finally saw Lucas' face.

"What happened John?"

"I'm not sure, Sir. He just asked me what Mr George said about Justin and then just went all weird."

"Ok, ok, thank you," Mr Belan paused, puzzled by the situation. "Lucas? Lucas?" Mr Belan tried to get the boy's attention.

Still, silence, no response.

Lucas had slipped into another world, far away from the reality before him, lost in the shock of what he had heard. In the background, Mr George was finishing up the assembly.

Mr Belan reached around to Lucas's back and gave it a rub, "Lucas? Lucas..?"

The other students began to move off to their classes; normal assembly had been cancelled and everyone had been sent to their home room to process their shock of the news of Justin.

Lucas rested his face in his hands and whispered, "Justin is dead."

"Lucas, mate, how are you feeling?"

He looked Mr Belan in the eye, "I'm ok, I'll be fine." He stood and walked off, saying nothing further.

"John, do you think he will be ok?"

John shrugged in response.

"Keep an eye on him if you can."

"I'll try, Sir."

Lucas walked aimlessly around the school campus, trying to work through his emotions: shock, anger, sadness. He walked so fast that he lost John and, before he knew where he was, he was standing on the football oval. It was his safe place, the place where he felt strong and alive. It was actually the place he got to know Justin. The universe had brought him there to find some sense of calm. Justin had been his football team's assistant coach. He had helped Mr George coach the under-fourteen's team and Lucas had felt a true, and real, connection with him.

Flashes of their last conversation came to Lucas, like beams of white light in his mind. It was half-time in the match against their rival school and Justin was giving Lucas a tough talk. Justin had grabbed Lucas by the back of the neck and pulled his head until they were face to face, eyeball to eyeball. Justin was always telling Lucas that he was incredibly talented and encouraged him to trust himself enough to use it. Justin was right. Lucas was scared of being the best, scared of the limelight, but he loved the game, he loved the ball and he loved the fight that was involved. He just had trouble investing his whole being into it.

Lucas recalled Justin gritting his teeth and growling at him, "Come on, mate. It's up to you, you can make or break this game. Release the bear within you, it's dying to come out. Anything other than your best will not do. Time to be your best, nothing else will do."

He slammed Lucas on the back and yelled, "Get out there, only your best will do!"

Lucas remembered nodding in agreement. He had been so nervous about being the best version of himself. When he was in the moment, and playing in the present, it was clear that he was incredibly talented and Justin had been encouraging him all season, at every practice and at every game.

After that pep talk, it was the game Lucas let it all out; he played his best, with all his heart. He didn't hear the massive cheer of the crowd, he didn't hear his teammates chanting his name, all he saw was the ball. He allowed the skill he had to sparkle, he lost his ego and played from his soul. When the game ended, Lucas looked up at Justin and their eyes met. Justin nodded at him and grinned. Nothing needed to be said.

Lucas recalled the feeling of being on the field that day and how good it had felt. He hung his head and his posture stooped.

"Be my best," Lucas whispered to himself.

He was overwhelmed, short of breath and dismayed. He sat on the ground and shook his head, thinking about what life would look like without Justin high fiving him on the path at school, yelling game plays across the field and forcing him to be the best.

It wasn't just him, it was everyone on the team. Everyone thrived on Justin's energy.

"Lucas!"

A voiced called from behind him. Lucas didn't recognise it but, as he turned his head, he realised that it was Mr George. Lucas acknowledged him with a head nod.

"What are you doing down here? Shouldn't you be in class?"

Lucas nodded again, unable to find the words.

Mr George had walked to the oval to get some space, just like Lucas had. He knew Lucas well from coaching him, he also knew he was a quiet kid with a lot of potential but needed encouragement to be his best. He had noticed how his relationship with Justin had boosted his confidence on the field and allowed his ability to excel.

He stood beside Lucas, knowing why they were both there. The grass was green and lush, the sun was bright and warm. Mr George had no words, so he just stood there, thinking about how life had changed in the last sixty minutes. His stomach ached and a tight knot had formed in his throat.

"Is this real Mr G, is Justin really dead?" Lucas' words surprised Mr George.

"I'm afraid it is, mate. I spoke with Justin's grandmother."

"I just can't believe it. I knew he had had an accident, but I thought he would be back soon."

Lucas had no previous experience with death, so he was finding his emotions overwhelming.

"GRIEF IS UNPREDICTABLE."

11

SALLY – DENYING REALITY

As soon as Sally walked in the door after the funeral, she wanted to leave straight away. Her mother was a mess, with her aunt desperately trying to comfort her, while her grandmother was intently trying to distract her little sister from the distress around her. They all seemed lost in their own worlds and Sally just wanted to get away. There was no one there for her. Justin was her go-to person and he was gone.

She wandered through the house, searching for some comfort, to sit or lay somewhere that would take away her feeling of panic. Nothing was working, so she ended racing for the back door; she thought if she could just get outside, she might feel better. Sally burst through the door with great anticipation. In the back yard she paced around but could not find any comfort.

With that, Sally headed for the side gate with only one thought in mind, I'm going to the Woods' house.

Sally and Justin rarely knocked as they entered the Woods'; they were so comfortable together they were like family. Sally burst into the house wild-eyed, looking for someone, anyone, to talk to. Kate was walking down the stairs as Sally walked through the house. "Kate!" Sally called out.

"Hey Sal."

Kate could see that Sally was clearly upset. They had known each other their whole lives, Kate was only a year older than Sally, and they had been best friends forever. As Kate got to the bottom of the stairs, they embraced.

"I hate it over there! As soon as I walk in, I just want to get straight back out. It feels like I'm suffocating there, like I'm drowning and I just can't catch my breath."

Kate didn't know what to say so she just held her friend in her arms, hoping that it was enough.

Sally found herself in Kate's room, curled up on her bed and staring out the window with thoughts of Justin overwhelming her. She felt abandoned by him which pissed her off. Ever since the accident she had been angry, really pissed off, that Justin had been injured. The anger consumed her days and nights, stopping her from sleeping, eating and feeling the sadness of her loss (although she wasn't aware of this herself!). Kate had left her to go and find something for them to eat and drink but Sally didn't care about her stomach.

Kate returned with a tray of food her Mum had prepared for them, "Here we go, something to eat, Sally."

She placed the tray on her desk which was covered in papers from the university assessment she was completing on the day of Justin's accident. She hadn't touched it since. "Why don't we have something?" Kate suggested as she sat on the edge of the bed where Sally was lying in a ball.

As Kate finished her sentence, Sally sat straight upright, "Why would Justin do this to me? I am just so pissed off. He is punishing me." Sally's face was red with anger.

Kate had no idea how to handle Sally, she was battling her own sorrow and sadness.

"What a stupid bastard falling down that gutter and dying!" Sally's voice was getting loud.

Kate didn't know how to react, she knew that Sally was angry but didn't know how much it was consuming her.

"Don't you see, Kate? He has abandoned me and left me all alone. What am I going to do without him?"

Peter was sitting on the other side of the wall from Kate's room and he could hear every word. He leant against the wall beside his bed, closed his eyes and felt the pain of his loss deep in his chest. He had closed the door and locked himself away from his family. He was sick of everyone asking if he was ok - how would he know if he was ok? His best friend, his brother from another mother, was dead and he felt that it was his fault. With Sally yelling from the room next door, the burden of his guilt beared down hard.

Peter's thoughts raced, *If I was with him, this never would have happened, he never would have fallen. If I was there, I could have stopped it, I could have helped him.* These feelings of guilt had been washing over Peter since the accident, it made him feel terrible to think that he could have saved his friend. He just couldn't get past his guilt.

"Don't you see? I'm alone now, Kate," Sally yelled in Kate's face.

Kate knew the abuse Sally was hurtling her way was not specifically for her, but she felt fragile and unwilling to take it on the chin.

"Sally," she interjected, "I don't think that Justin died to punish you, it was just an accident. He loved you." Kate paused, "You were... are... great friends."

Sally glared at Kate in retaliation. In essence, she didn't actually hate Kate, she just hated the realisation of the past tense of her relationship with her brother.

"Oh Kate, I'm sorry, I am just so pissed with him."

"I know, I can feel your pain."

Kate moved closer to Sally and wrapped her arm around

her shoulder, their foreheads rested together, "We still have each other, Sal, we will get through this, somehow."

Sally broke down at this point and the grief came pouring out; her breathing was short, the tears flowed and her sadness came in a huge wave as the anger began to disappear.

"I just feel so let down by him," she said frustratedly, "Why would he leave me on my own? We are supposed to be brother and sister, forever."

Sally's face was red and flustered. Kate grabbed Sally and hugged her as tight as she could because she didn't know what else to do; she had no idea how to comfort her, she had no idea how to comfort herself. Sally held on tight, closed her eyes and cried.

Sally had spent most of the time since the accident at the Woods' house, the thought of her own house triggered anger and pain, so she had unconsciously positioned herself with her friends and neighbours. Sally, so far, had avoided her own life. She had successfully denied the reality of living without Justin and she was desperate to keep it that way. In the moment of that embrace with Kate, she confirmed that she would not return home.

"GRIEF IS AN UGLY REALITY THAT CAN WARP AND TORTURE YOU. YOU CAN BEGIN TO STRUCTURE YOURSELF JUST TO HARNESS A FEELING OF SAFETY, RATHER THAN REALITY."

12
PETER – THERE IS NO GOING BACK

PETER COULD HEAR THE CRYING FROM THE OTHER SIDE OF the bedroom wall go on and on and he was also sobbing, sobbing with guilt and disbelief that this had all happened. He couldn't let the guilt go as his thoughts swirled around his head, around and around. They caused his heart to race and the tears to flow. Peter was distraught that his best friend in the whole world was gone. They had planned so many things together that could no longer be fulfilled. The biggest plan the boys had made was to go to America on a skateboarding and adventure holiday at the end of Grade 12, in 18 months' time. Their trip felt all so real when Justin was alive; they had researched the cost, the dates, the flights, everything you could think of. Now, Peter felt lost and alone. He cried, despairing at the future.

In reality, his mother and father were worried about him. They knew that the boys' relationship had been close; they were more than best friends, they were brothers that were inseparable. When they finished primary school, they had convinced their parents to send them to the same high school although they were originally booked into different ones. They convinced their parents to holiday together, eat together, spend Friday nights together, and the list goes on. The boys thought that they had arranged their families' friendships but, little did they know, they were all kindred spirits.

James, Peter's father, was especially worried about his son. He could see he was shut down emotionally from everybody and, at every opportunity, he was running away to be alone.

Peter had cried himself dry and found himself laying on his bed, staring at the wall, thoughts of Justin circulating in his mind. He was worn out. He hadn't talked to anyone about how he felt and didn't plan to. James knocked on Peter's bedroom door but Peter did not respond. James knocked a little louder and Peter still did not answer, so James just opened the door.

"Hey mate," James walked towards Peter but Peter didn't flinch, he lay lifeless on the bed. "Just wanted to check in and see what's happening?"

James sat on the bed and Peter still lay lifeless. James rested his hand on Peter's hip in an effort to connect with his son, but nothing shifted Peter's gaze.

"Mate, it has been a big day... well, actually a draining few weeks really," he paused, "This whole situation is really crappy but we can't stop talking, dude. When we stop talking, we lose connection with one another and that is when we stop being family."

James longed for his son to open up to him, he had been so quiet since the accident and he was worried about how Peter was feeling. A few minutes passed and the silence was killing James.

"I just want you to know that I'm here and I want to help you through this, but if you don't talk about it I can't help you process this," Peter remained silent and completely still, so James had no idea if he heard him or not. "Alright mate, I am going down to sit with Mum for a while."

He rubbed his sons' hip, stood up and headed to the door. Looking back at his son, a lump formed in his throat, the pain of watching his son suffer was a lot. As the door shut, Peter rolled on his back and stared at the ceiling. He was tired and worn out and, within minutes, he fell asleep.

A few hours later, he was woken by his mother, "Hey, mate. Matthew popped in to see you. He is downstairs, so do you want to come down?"

"No, thanks, Mum."

"Come on darling, you can't stay in here forever."

"Mum!" Peter yelled "I am not coming down."

Peter sat up, yelled at his Mother and then threw himself back down on the bed and resumed staring at the wall. It seemed to be his favourite past time these days, just staring all day long. Natalie was offended by his outburst but let it slide.

"Ok buddy, no need to yell."

She shut the door and went to explain to Matthew that Peter wasn't up to company. As she walked down the stairs, she knew that it was going to be a long road ahead for any healing to take place and she began to ache in the pit of her stomach.

As Peter laid there, his thoughts returned to how he hadn't been there for his mate, his best friend. He had left him at the skate park and if he had stayed, it all never would have happened. The pain in his gut made him draw his legs up into the foetal position. Flashes of Justin lying on the bitumen, lifeless, kept sweeping through his head and, with every flash, Peter's gut wrung with pain. He closed his eyes and allowed the pain to take over him, he thought he deserved it, and he began to rock in pain.

Without any notice, Peter's father entered the room and sat himself down on the side of the bed. It didn't give Peter a fright, it actually didn't even disturb him. He was so overcome with grief that he didn't care.

"Pete, mate, someday this all won't be so painful."

Peter stopped the rocking and made eye contact with his

father. His father had no idea how to deal with loss, he always just pushed his emotions away. He had no idea how Peter could tackle the world without his mate but he had to try and get through to him. Peter had spent almost all the time in his room since the accident and he knew things couldn't go on like this.

Hatred pulsed through Peter's veins; he hated his father for saying his pain would go away. He wanted to suffer so he never wanted the pain to go away. He never wanted to forget Justin and the pain was keeping him alive in Peters mind.

"Sorry, mate, I didn't mean it like that," James saw that he had upset his son.

Peter turned his head swiftly towards the wall as if to reject his father. James didn't know what to say or do, so he just sat in silence and let time pass, hoping that Peter would forget what he said.

After a while, James' mind drifted off to memories of the boys when they were little; playing in their back yard dressed as superheros, the Christmas they both got skateboards, first time in their school uniforms. The happy memories of them together flowed.

James felt the gravity of their loss and felt the need to pull his son close and hold him as tight as he could. James had successfully squashed his emotions until now, but his son's reaction was crushing him. He reached down and pulled Peter to his chest. Surprisingly, Peter allowed his father to embrace him, he didn't fight it. Peter began to feel the warmth of his father which distracted him from his thoughts. James began to rock with Peter in his arms and tears welled up in his eyes.

"Pete, we can't change things, we can only look forward. I know this hurts."

Peter actually heard what his father was saying, mulling the words over in his head, *That's right, I can't change things, I can't go back and make it right. It is my fault, there is no going back...*

James knew in his heart that the loss of Justin would change Peter, forever. James was right - Peter's heart had closed tight shut.

"LOSS AND GRIEF CAN CHANGE YOU FOREVER, IT CAN CLOSE YOUR HEART AND YOUR MIND TO LOVE AND CONNECTION."

13

SCOTT - WHEN YOU EXPECT NOTHING, YOU RECEIVE EVERYTHING

JANE AND SCOTT DROVE IN THE DRIVE AND, AS THE headlights beamed across their garden, the time became apparent to Scott. It was 10.25pm, they had been at this thing, the funeral, since 7.30 this morning. Scott was completely worn out, completely spent. He was overcome with exhaustion and he was on the edge.

In his exhaustion, he let his impenetrable outer shield come crashing down. He had spent the afternoon listening and taking on board what people were feeling in his family. He saw the very best in some of them and the very worst in others. He was shattered, all he could think of was bed.

He turned the ignition of the car off and, as the engine came to a stop, Jane interrupted their silence, "I'm not sure where to go to from here, everyone is broken."

Quietness filled the car. Scott finally responded as best he could, "You know what, sweetie? I don't think we are supposed to know right now. I think we need to get some sleep and see how the world wakes up in the morning."

Jane looked down at her hands, fidgeting, "I'm sure you are right Scott."

In that moment, Jane remembered how she missed her husband today, "Where did you disappear to today, anyway? I thought you were with the Jake and Tom?"

Scott hesitated, he wasn't sure what to say, "I gave them some space, seemed they needed some time alone. Jake was distraught and I didn't know how to help, so I went for a walk and had a coffee."

Their eyes met in silence; both their souls were exhausted.

"Yeah, tough day."

Jane grabbed Scott's hand and squeezed it. Scott was pleased Jane didn't probe him anymore about his whereabouts. It was not that he didn't want to tell her, it was that he didn't have the strength to put it into words.

That night, Scott found himself in bed, staring into the darkness while Jane was asleep. He was going over the events of the day in his mind; the lowering of the coffin, Tina's reaction at the funeral, Jake's vacant expression... Justin's bruised and swollen face haunted him.

How did our lives turn into such a tragedy? The last few weeks have been a nightmare.

Scott's thoughts escalated over the next 45 minutes. He was restless and sweaty and the centre of his chest ached. He was so tired but just couldn't close down. His mind was a mess and, for the first time in his life, he couldn't pull himself together.

Then, Joe's face appeared in his mind, remembering how he predicted this situation at lunch. A restless and out of control mind, thinking about all the could-be's for the future and all the happy memories of the past. It was making his heart hurt. Scott began to change the topic of his thoughts to Joe and he had a little giggle about how a homeless man had brought him lunch and provided emotional advice, all because of a chance encounter. Suddenly, he remembered the breathing advice.

Right, let me test Joe's theory. It can't hurt, I'm so exhausted and I need some sleep. Anything is worth a try, my thoughts are killing me.

Scott found a comfortable position on his back, arms laid either side of him. He closed his eyes and began to breathe in for a count of six and out for a count of eight. He began to notice the rise and fall of this chest with each breath. Random thoughts of Justin's face, Jake, Tina and the girls did pop in and out of his head, but he let them leave his mind with his breath outwards and began his cycle of breathing again. Scott's exhausted body was giving into sleep as his mind began to slow right down. Eventually, his mind stopped inventing the future and revisiting the past and Scott fell into a deep and well-deserved sleep. He didn't get a chance to agree with Joe that the breathing technique worked because he was asleep before he knew it.

When Scott woke up, he noticed sunlight peeking through the gap between the windowsill and the blinds. He rolled over and lifted his head, looking for Jane, but she wasn't there. Scott and Jane had hardly connected since the accident, after all, Jane was Tina's sister and her main support. Jane had spent every waking hour with Tina that she possibly could. Scott flopped his head back down on the pillow and sighed. It was at this moment that he realised the breathing technique had worked and he had fallen asleep peacefully. A little grin grew on his face. As he lay there, he realised that meeting with Joe may have been of great consequence and benefit to his life right now. He flicked the sheets back and literally crawled out of bed; he certainly didn't want to face the day but thought he should go and find Jane.

Scott found Jane pounding away on the treadmill he had gotten her for her birthday – a gift because he hated her running around the streets in the dark, alone. She was covered in sweat, her face was bright red and around her lips were pale to bluish.

"Hey, what's happening?"

Scott spoke as he walked into the room. He had set the treadmill up in the spare room at the back of the house.

"Woke up super early and felt the need to run."

Jane was extremely fit and she ran everyday, if not twice a day, if she could.

"How long have you been running for?"

Scott was curious because she looked physically wrecked.

"I'm not sure," Jane responded as she looked down at the timer on the treadmill, huffing and puffing. "Wow, two hours and three minutes."

Scott hit the emergency stop button and Jane came to a screaming holt.

"I didn't know what to do and you know that when I run, I feel calmer."

Out of nowhere, the tears began to roll down her cheeks. Scott leant towards her and wrapped his arms around her.

"I don't know what to do," Jane sobbed, "Of course, no one knows what to do. We are living a nightmare!"

Scott didn't want Jane to beat herself up, "You need to take care of yourself, your sister needs you to be her strength. You can't break yourself running like a maniac!"

Scott was overcome with concern for his wife and anxiety began to swirl in his gut, the feeling of loss overcame him. Jane was still crying and he felt tears spill down his own face. In that moment, he wasn't sad about Justin, he was sad and anxious that he could lose his wife, lose the person he fell in love with. He knew that grief changes a person. Fear froze his body; he would have nothing without her, his whole world would fall apart. His chest started to ache.

Jane pulled away from Scott and looked directly into his eyes, "I just don't know where to pick up from."

A few seconds passed and it seemed that Jane didn't realise that Scott was crying.

"I've got to go, I've got to get to Tina's house."

She pushed Scott away and rushed out of the room. Scott was left standing alone in the room with the treadmill. He reached up and wiped the tears off his face. He took a few deep breaths, in for six and out for eight. He noticed the sun beginning to beam through the window onto the carpet.

He needed the light on in the kitchen as the sun wasn't completely up yet. He turned the coffee machine on and began the task of making scrambled eggs and toast. The fear of losing Jane came back into mind, something that he had never thought about before, and it was now plaguing his thoughts and evoking terrible scenarios in his mind. As he put the toast on his plate, the pain of his thoughts were more than he could bear. He stopped, put his hands on the bench and leant forward. He closed his eyes to block out the world and took a deep breath, then another, and another. The counting of six in and eight out as he breathed happened without too much mental effort.

Eventually, he became calm. *Everything is ok now. Jane is safe and well, we are safe and well. I am ok, things are all ok.*

Homeless Joe's wisdom seemed to be having a real impact on Scott.

Before Scott knew it, he was walking down the same street he visited the day before, when he was lost. He headed for the coffee shop again, hoping for another chat with Joe. He felt like he had been ungrateful, rude and distant. He really wanted to say thank you for the advice and thank Joe for lunch. Scott felt that he should have paid for lunch, not the homeless guy. Also, he had had enough with the sadness and the devastation at Justin's house, he felt he had not recovered from the previous day and he wanted to get away. He thought he could thank Joe with a cuppa and another chat.

As he approached the coffee shop, he could see Tammy rushing at her normal pace, serving and smiling at the customers. Scott scanned the café for Joe but no luck, he wasn't there. Scott was ok with it, it had been a long shot, he was just happy to be away from everyone. He resigned himself to the fact that he was to have coffee alone. Tammy rushed over to Scott not long after he found a seat.

"Hey, back again? You must have liked it yesterday! What can I get for you?"

"Hey, yeah, I did like it here yesterday," Scott smiled.

"What can I get you?"

"A flat white and a mud cake please."

"No problem, coming right up."

Scott was disappointed that Joe was nowhere to be seen, he scanned the street on both sides but nothing, no trolley with an umbrella. Scott sat and reviewed their conversation from yesterday, *Joe was saying something along the lines of 'why think about the possibilities of the future or dwell in the past?' I think that's what the breathing technique prevents. I proved it last night, concentrating on my breathing stopped my thoughts. If my thoughts stop, then the feelings stop. Then, I suppose you feel better.*

He kept thinking about the night before and how he was able to go to sleep, and then the panic and stress of this morning when he thought of losing Jane. Tammy interrupted Scott's thoughts with the delivery of his coffee and cake.

"Thanks, Tammy."

She smiled and left him with his thoughts. Scott sat and

contemplated the advice from Joe, over and over again. What was bugging him the most was his reaction to the thought of losing Jane, it seemed out of proportion this morning. Why would he have such a reaction to these thoughts? Considering this again now, his heart started to beat very fast, anxiety began to swirl in his gut and sweat started to bead on his forehead. His coffee and cake were left untouched in front of him as he was lost in his thoughts.

Scott began to evoke memories of his life from when his mother abandoned both him and his father. The fear of being left behind and blamed for a life lived in sadness and frustration beared down on him. He had buried these memories for at least two decades, why the hell were they being dug up now? Flashes of his mother yelling at him for being born and ruining her life were taking their toll, right here, in the present moment while he was sitting in the cafe. He felt it in his chest and his gut. He remembered crying himself to sleep as a young boy, no one knowing how sad and alone he felt. He never told his dad how bad the abuse was when he was not in the house, because his father had his own ordeal of abuse to deal with. Even as a young boy, Scott felt he couldn't burden his father in this way.

His father's smiling face flashed into his mind. He had loved his father, but now he was gone as well. Scott had looked after him through his terminal illness and nursed him at home for as long as he could manage to. His father was a good man and did his best for Scott and the sadness of not having him around now burdened his current emotional space.

Life is really screwed up. My life has been filled with devastation and Justin passing away has just topped it off. I don't know if any of this is worth it.

He wallowed in his memories and emotions for quite some time, forgetting the coffee and cake in front of him.

Scott was so deep in thought that he did not realise Joe had pushed his trolley up beside him and sat at the table opposite him. Scott was squarely focused on the table in front of him and his misery and nothing was going to distract him.

"Hey, mate. You're back again?"

Joe offered a greeting to Scott, but he didn't even hear the salutation. A few minutes passed as Joe studied Scott sitting there, consumed by his thoughts. Tammy came and took Joe's order for a cappuccino and a hamburger and yet, still, Scott had no consciousness of his surroundings.

Joe raised his voice a little, "Mate, are you alright?"

Scott was plucked from his mind and looked up, his eyes meet with Joe's.

"Ah, yeah. Hey, hi, Joe. You're here!" Scott was surprised by the sight of Joe.

"You seem distracted, are you ok?"

"To tell you the truth, I am a little plagued by misery today."

"That is understandable, mate, you have been through a lot."

Scott stared at Joe and Joe could see the pain engulfing him.

"Do you want to chat or do you want to keep to yourself?"

"Please join me, Joe. I wanted to talk to you about what you told me yesterday. Please come and sit down?"

Scott stood up, pulled a chair out and pushed the table decorations out of Joe's way, as if he was a very important person. The truth was, Scott felt relieved that Joe had found him. He felt he needed some counsel in his time of turmoil.

Joe immediately got up and moved across to join Scott. They sat together and silence fell over the table. Joe wasn't going to push Scott, but he knew he was troubled by something and could clearly see it was weighing him down.

"Firstly..." Scott spoke slowly and with purpose, "I truly want to thank you for lunch yesterday, it was very kind of you and I surely didn't deserve it."

Joe's eyes furrowed, "Surely you did deserve some kindness Scott, everybody does."

Scott was still not convinced that he did deserve it, but he let the moment pass without any objection and, with that, Tammy arrived with Joe's coffee and food.

"You must have been sitting there for a while before I noticed you, Joe. I'm sorry because, truth be told, I came looking for you and when I couldn't see you, I got lost in my own thoughts."

"Maybe eight or ten minutes," Joe responded. He wanted to make it clear to Scott that he had been lost in his own thoughts when he arrived.

"I am glad you still want to talk to me after yesterday, Scott. You seemed upset with my advice."

"You know what, Joe? I think I was upset, not with you, but with the reality of what you said to me," Scott paused, "I really wanted to tell you that I used your advice last night when I was in bed. My head was running wild with thoughts of the past, it was torture really. I don't even want to repeat what I was thinking about because it causes too much pain. I was able to catch myself, it took a while though. I lay on my back in a comfortable position and I breathed in deeply to the count of six and out to the count of eight. In and out I went. When a thought popped into my head, I just let it go and concentrated on my breathing again. Before I knew it, I was waking as the sun was coming up."

"Wow! Great job, Scott."

Joe was so happy that Scott had listened to his advice. Unbeknown to Scott, Joe had experienced horrific times in his past that he needed to escape from and he used this breathing technique to find peace, day and night.

Joe was eating his lunch by this point. Scott picked up his own coffee and took a sip. It was stone cold and Scott shook his head with disbelief.

"My coffee is cold! I must have been so lost in my mind that I didn't notice how much time had passed."

"Pity you didn't catch those thoughts, Scott, you might have drunk your coffee while it was hot," Joe grinned.

Scott laughed and paused for a few seconds, "You are so right."

Tammy whisked past and Scott hailed her over, "Can I get you something?"

"Another coffee, please. Do you want something, Joe?"

"No thanks, mate."

"Is there something wrong with your current coffee? I can replace it."

"No, not at all, I just forgot to drink it," Scott smiled at Tammy and, with that, she left.

"You are right, Joe. Just now, I was thinking about so many events from the past, mad stuff... What the hell is going on?" Scott paused for an answer but Joe had his mouth full of food.

"I admit, this has not just started now, after Justin. I have battled with my thoughts all my life. I think about my dad a lot but not my mum. Battles in the past have been mainly work related, trying to do my best and prove myself. I have always been insecure and I've always doubted myself."

Joe responded, "Amazing what you become aware of when you realise how much thinking you do about the past and what-ifs for the future, hey!"

"I feel like since you said that stuff yesterday, I have seen things differently, I have really got lost in my own mind and thoughts."

"That's the thing, Scott, when you become aware it blows your mind how much time you spend in the past and in the future which, of course, makes you miss the present moment in your life," he paused while Scott was processing.

"Holly crap! It seems that I may have missed most of my life, just thinking about stuff and not living."

"I know it all seems harsh when you realise your habits and how your mind drives you, but every experience has got you to this point in your life. Every experience has made you into you and got you to this moment, it is all how it should be."

Scott looked at Joe and nodded, what Joe had said had made him feel a bit better.

Scott's coffee arrived, hot and ready to drink.

Tammy smiled, "Now, remember to drink this one."

"Interesting exercise, Scott, you have a coffee there... I figure you drink coffee a lot. When was the last time you sat and truly enjoyed it? Lived in the current or present moment and did things like smell the coffee, feel the cup on your lips, feel the temperature and texture of the milky goodness? Every single sip, notice it slipping down your throat and enjoy the taste."

Scott was gobsmacked. He paused and thought about Joe's question, "I am not sure that I ever have."

"I'm not surprised, most people have not, they are thinking about all sorts of other things; the next sip, when it will run out, what's on the television or radio, having a conversation, working, walking, all manner of things. Why don't you do it consciously and see how you feel?"

Scott had never thought about drinking a coffee consciously before and the realisation of how he had lived his life up until this point was taking a toll. Scott stared across the table, contemplating his life. He began to get lost in his mind and thoughts yet again, *I have missed my life, the experiences and enjoyment.*

Joe interrupted, "Stop thinking. Have an experience with your coffee and I will with mine."

Joe smiled and glanced at his coffee, like a visual nudge for Scott.

"Right, I will then," Scott returned a smile.

After their coffee 'experience' was over, Scott was blown away by how he felt and how much he enjoyed his coffee.

"Good coffee, hey, Scott?" Joe smiled and pushed his cup away from him as he was finished. "Now, what if you could stay with whatever else you are doing during your daily activities?" Joe paused and allowed Scott to think this through, "Things would be a lot more enjoyable, hey?"

Scott was quiet and contemplative, running through many life events and wondering if he had actually lived them or if his brain had been living in the future or the past.

The men sat and chatted about this and that but, in his mind, Scott was troubled as to why his childhood issues with his mother were coming to the front of his thoughts. He was supposed to be grieving for Justin, yet his mother was hounding his thoughts. Finally, he brought it up with Joe whose response was, yet again, profound.

"When you are faced with tragedy or a life threatening event, every fibre of your being is challenged and your mind looks for coping strategies to deal with things. In your case, your mother leaving was another time in your life where you suffered an enormous loss. Your mind resonates with the pain and anguish, so memories can hound your thoughts as you are looking for ways to cope. From what you just told me, it seems that you emotionally shutdown and try to run away. You try and close yourself off from everyone, either close or distant relationships, and hide away in your own thoughts."

Joe's words were confronting for Scott; he had never identified with his behaviour before and he was having an ah-ha moment when Joe interrupted, "Do you see? Does this fit with you, can you see it in your life?"

Silence fell over the table and Joe was confident that Scott was going to respond - the look on his face said a thousand words.

"I can see it over and over, again, in my life."

"Be careful that you don't get lost in your own mind there, Scott. You don't want your identification with the past to wreck your presence in this moment."

Scott looked at Joe and nodded.

"You see, the events of your life, and how you cope, manage and deal with them, shape you. The most shaping that goes on in your life happens as a small child. You learn from your family how to manage emotions, how to feel, how you use those emotions and what to do with them. I'll give you an example from my own life that I have become aware of. When I was a small child, my parents always behaved in a very proper manner. They always told me not to cry, it was a sign of weakness, and in fact, looking back, they never really showed any emotion at all. Not sadness, happiness, excitement, peace, love, their reaction was always nothing. If we fell over and cried, it was always 'no need to cry, be tough' or if I was fighting with my siblings and I was frustrated or hurt by their actions or words, I was told to behave and ignore how I felt. So, when my grandmother died suddenly from a heart attack, I was told to be tough and not to show how I was really feeling, that I was being weak. I was eight years old and to be truthful now, my grandmother was the only one throughout my young childhood that showed me any love and affection. She let me cry and comforted me when my feelings were hurt, or if I fell. When she died, it felt as though my heart was being stabbed and the only one that could possibly comfort me was her, but she was dead."

Scott was listening intently, trying to take in every little piece of information.

"So, you see, growing into a young man I began to hide myself away; hiding my feelings, my wishes and desires because, in my family, you were not to show any human side of yourself. My siblings dealt with it differently - one rebelled and, in the end, got locked up in juvenile prison and the other suffers with extreme anxiety, it seems she is just so insecure with her feelings she is always thinking she is feeling wrong. So, Scott, you see how your young life shapes you in ways you cannot even imagine. But why I am telling you this? It's because this insight holds the key to grow within yourself. Awareness heals, so if you can get some connection between your behaviour patterns and your life experiences, you can grow and evolve. If you don't, you can get stuck in the same cycles over and over."

It took a while for the information to settle in Scott's brain before he spoke, "So, are you saying that how I was raised has created how I cope with issues, today?"

"Yes, that is exactly what I am saying."

Scott's eyes wandered around the coffee shop, not seeing anything in particular, simply scanning his life for repeated patterns and coping strategies. Scott had suffered in silence as a child. He had hidden all his fear and sadness away, keeping it from his father and the outside world because he was made to think that his mother's lack of acceptance for her own life decisions were his fault. He was made to believe that he didn't deserve love and he learnt to hide away behind a big emotional barrier to protect himself. When his mother finally left them, life became lighter and happier. His relationship with his father was filled with love and acceptance and Scott felt his mother leaving was a blessing, although his father was gutted.

Scott never told his father about the abuse heaped on him as a child because he didn't want to tarnish his father's opinion of the women he loved. When she left, Scott felt like his father just got on with life. The two of them moved to a small house close to Scott's school so he could walk home. His father stopped all the overtime and his obsession with money fell away. During this time in Scott's life, he did feel loved and supported. His father was a good man but never went near women again. He died when Scott was 19 from a rare type of cardiac cancer, they didn't find until it was too late to treat. Scott looked after him until the day he died. The love between them was real and Scott knew that, without his father's love, he would be nothing, Scott did all he could do until he died. Although, now, in adulthood, he never spoke of his father or his mother for different reasons.

Finally, Scott spoke to Joe, "Can I just run something by you?"

"Sure."

"So, you are saying that the emotional barrier I used as a child to protect myself from my mother's abuse, is one I still use today to deal with rejection and loss?"

"Yep, unless you have learnt a better way to protect yourself."

"Since Justin has passed away, I can see that I have been hiding and running away from how I feel, I have been so uncomfortable in my own skin. I haven't wanted to admit to myself he's gone. I shut down when I see how someone else is feeling, also. I seem to run away from all feelings."

"Scott, you have to understand that it sounds like you have survived some tough times growing up. Now that you are faced with a difficult situation again, you can either close down or you can just feel and try to support the people around you."

Scott nodded in agreement. Scott was overwhelmed by the realisation of what Joe had explained to him, but he was more overwhelmed by the thought of feeling the loss of Justin. His mind flicked to seeing his father take his last breath, his breath caught in his own chest and a lump grew in his throat. The pain of it all was becoming real.

Joe allowed Scott to sit with his pain for a little while. Scott's pain was jumping between the agony of losing Justin, his dad's grey emaciated face and his mother's abuse. The pain was the same and he was lost in it.

Eventually, Joe interrupted his thoughts, "Hey, Scott?" Their eyes connected, "I didn't give you this insight to torture yourself, man. Remember to always bring yourself back to this moment in time and allow the pain to pass."

Scott was lost for words, the pain was too great for him to bare. He managed a smile in Joe's direction and then picked himself up and extended his hand, "Thanks, mate. Your time means a lot to me." Scott placed a $50 note on the table and said, "My shout this time."

"This too shall pass, Scott, nothing stays the same."

Scott nodded, "Thanks, again," and he walked away from Joe and his emotions.

———

As Scott got further away from the hustle and bustle of the street, his emotions got the better of him. He was overwhelmed with his realisation and felt so sad about losing Justin from his life. All the traumatic pictures of his demise that Scott experienced in his last days flashed before his eyes. There was never any sign of life after the accident; every time Scott saw Justin in the hospital or, in the end, in Tina and Jakes lounge room, he felt he was gone. Justin was gone and Scott was finally feeling the loss. Grief took over him.

By the time he got back to Tina and Jake's house, Scott was pretty upset. He didn't want to go inside the house and add fuel to the already blazing fire, so he sat in the gutter to give himself some more time. He kept reliving the past events of Justin's death, it was horrific, the physical implications of the family's decisions and then the emotional burden of it all. He was the main decision maker regarding turning Justin's life support off and now, with all his emotions on board, he was second-guessing his decision. A quote from Stephen Hawking entered his mind, 'Where there is life, there is hope.' Justin's body did have life, so had Scott helped in making the right decision to turn off the life support? The question overwhelmed his thoughts.

Twenty minutes passed without him realising. He had already been away from the house for a good two hours; everyone would be wondering where he was. He just couldn't stop his pain and anguish rolling around within him and, as he looked around, he realised that no one had any idea of the agonising pain he felt. He felt cheated and alone.

Scott didn't notice that Tom came up behind him until he spoke, "Oh, you are out here. Are you getting some fresh air?"

Tom lowered himself to sit beside Scott. Scott wouldn't turn his head because he didn't want Tom to see his face, but Tom could feel the pain radiating from Scott, regardless.

"Ah, yes... I suppose I am."

"I need some air too. To tell you the truth, I have no idea what to do in there. The pain in that house is incredibly hard to bear." Tom paused, "You knew Justin a lot better than I did. I feel like I have been an absent grandfather, but it seems you have been a pretty good uncle from what the girls have told me."

Tom had spent the majority of his time with his granddaughters during this ordeal. His oldest granddaughter, Sally, had taken it hard and had clammed up, but Emma had spent the whole time nattering about all sorts of family matters. Scott had been a part of that natter. Tom had come to understand that Jane and Scott were an important part of his son's family.

"Maybe," Scott replied after a long pause. He was in no mood to chat.

Tom finally got a look at Scott's face and he was surprised to see it. During the past days he had spent in the house, Tom had not seen Scott expend any sort of emotion other than stability - someone they all could depend on. Yet, now, Tom was taken aback and silence fell on them. Scott was still trying to get a hold of himself when Tom extended his arm and draped it around Scott's shoulders. He was extending the hand of love.

"These are hard times, the hardest of times..." Tom corrected himself, "and you have been an absolute rock for these guys. I wanted to thank you for all your love and support."

"You want to thank me, Tom? Thank me for helping in the decision to turn off Justin's life support, thank me for ending your grandson's life! What have I done? What have we done? Where there is life there is hope... Have you heard this before, Tom? Justin's body had life and we just let it slip away." Scott was now distraught. His voice was raised and his fist was slamming the palm of the other hand, "I deserve to die, not Justin. What have we done? What the hell have we done?"

Scott had not even questioned their decision to turn Justin's life support off since the decision had been made. It was only now, when his understanding of life was being challenged with new ways and new beliefs, that the doubt and anguish started to pour out of him.

"Scott, that is so not the truth. There was no hope of any sort of recovery for Justin. If there was, he would have been able to breathe on his own. His brain was so messed up... Don't blame yourself, you did nothing but help bring some peace to the situation."

Scott was crying and anger was pouring out of him, "That's such a load of crap, Tom, such bull crap! We should have tried, we should have waited!"

"I am going to put a stop to this right now. You helped make the right decision, without a doubt. Justin had left his body many days before his body gave up. There was nothing left to save or help. Justin is gone by no fault of ours, it was an accident that no member of our family could have done anything about. Now, stop this blaming yourself, I won't have it."

Tom was breathless when he finished. What Scott said had hit a nerve. He was exhausted physically, but also emotionally, and he felt Scott had been a hero for the family. Scott stopped, placed both hands on the side of his face and cried. Tom felt relieved that Scott had given up on voicing his guilt but worried that he was falling apart.

"Look, mate, I am no expert but things will get easier. Justin was a great lad, we have to remember him for that. We should place no emphasis on the last part of his life because it will only torture us."

Scott had calmed down a bit.

"Look, take some deep breaths and let it go."

When Tom said take some deep breaths Scott was snapped out of turmoil and a picture of Joe sitting at the table opposite him popped into his mind. In that moment, he knew that he could listen to Tom or he could stay in his misery.

Scott began to take some breaths, in for the count of six and out for the count of eight. As he did, memories of the peace and love he felt when he was left alone with Justin in the hospital room flooded over him. Peace that now settled within once again. He continued to breath consciously.

"TO AWAKEN SIT CALMLY,
LETTING EACH BREATH
CLEAR YOUR MIND AND
OPEN YOUR HEART."

- BUDDHA

14

SCOTT – GETTING A HOLD OF HIMSELF

After another long day with the family, Scott found himself in the shower with racing thoughts, the same racing thoughts he had had all afternoon since his conversation with Joe at the coffee shop. He stopped the automatic nature of his actions and found a second of insight. A voice in his head kept pounding away at him, stop, just stop.

He decided to listen and stop. When his thoughts and actions stopped, he realised that his thoughts were driving him. It was like his mind was a computer and he was just feeding it the same horrific thoughts and emotions, over and over. He thought about the conversation he had with Joe, about concentrating on his breath, and he decided that it was time to stop the torture even if it was just for a few short minutes. He began the breathing exercise, breathing in for the count of six and out for the count of eight. Scott managed this for a good two minutes and he could feel his body physically relaxing. As a stray thought arose in his head, he returned to the counting and the feeling of his either inward or outward breath. He had come home to sleep for the night but his wife, Jane, had decided to stay with Tina. Tina and Jane had a very strong bond and Scott didn't want to stand in the middle of it, so he had decided to come home for some respite for the night.

Scott continued to stay in the present moment and take note of his surroundings, he was very mindful of exactly what he was doing with his body. He got back to washing himself, feeling the soap on his hands and smelling the fragrance as he rubbed it over his body. He noticed that the water was pretty cool, so he adjusted the temperature and felt the smooth flow of it all over his body. He looked at the shampoo bottle like he had never seen it before, he read the label and he started to wonder what Jane was doing and how the hell was she coping over there, but something twigged him back to his breathing. His hand remained on the shampoo bottle, he hung his head and closed his eyes. I am breathing in 1 2 3 4 5 6, I am breathing out 1 2 3 4 5 6 7 8, over and over he went until he found peace again.

As thoughts came into his head, altering his emotional state, he returned to his breath. Minutes passed and he felt his arm had pins and needles as he still had a hold of the shampoo bottle on the ledge in the shower. He stopped with the conscious breathing and began to think about how easy it was to block out what his arm was doing and just think about his breathing. With the next thought he made a connection between the power of his thoughts and happiness. How much you allow your mind to control your present moment determines your emotions and, most importantly, your happiness. He stood in the shower, shaking his head over his newfound understanding of life.

As his thoughts returned to Justin and his family's loss, Scott recalled the day in the hospital room when he felt extraordinary love come into the room. He remembered how beautiful it felt and how he felt this love for Justin when he was alive and now in his death. He pondered the thought that recalling his love for Justin was just as powerful as recalling the trauma and pain. Your thoughts control your feelings, which control your ability to live life in the moment. That your positive feelings such as love and peace can also influence you in a powerful way. He could use his feelings for good. This realisation for Scott was a game changer! Scott's chance encounter with a homeless man had, forever more, changed his understanding of life.

"DON'T LET YOUR MIND CONTROL YOU."

15

TINA & JANE - ABSENCE

Jane and Tina sat in the lounge where the hospital bed once was that had carried their beloved Justin. Jane had made some herbal tea and they were sitting where they had most evenings since Justin passed, in silence, consumed by their thoughts and not tasting the tea. Jane realised that Tina was just going through the motions of her life, not really experiencing anything but her loss. Her eyes were glazed over and puffy from the tears, she was pale and appeared to be just the shell of who she was before this all happened. The two women were close and had been all their lives, they didn't fight like typical children did when they were growing up and they were always great friends, kindred spirits. As children, they had a good life, growing up in a loving home with two attentive parents. Both their parents had passed away a few years earlier, first their mother from a heart attack and, 18 months later, their father from a stroke. With each passing, they were both devastated, but they kept it all together with the realisation that their parents had had good lives. However, they missed their parents terribly and Jane did feel a little empty inside not having them around to go to for support. Tina seemed to cope better as she had her own children and family to support.

This situation, Justin's death, hit them both very hard. Tina had not been present in her own body for many days. Jane was struggling herself, but she had tried and succeeded in keeping things together, stepping up to make the big decisions about the funeral and treatment options etc. She was screaming inside, worried to her core, about her sister. Tina wasn't connected with any sort of reality and Jane wasn't sure that she even knew where she was.

"Are you going to drink your tea, Tina?" She paused, "While it is still hot... I know you only like your tea hot."

She grinned as they made eye contact, not to signal happiness but to acknowledge the words spoken. Jane felt as though Tina looked straight through her, no meaningful response. She was there with Jane in body, but certainly not intellectually or emotionally. Jane tried not to worry about her as it was only early days, but she had never seen her sister like this before. She wasn't even acknowledging the girls or Jake, she just seemed lost in her own grief.

Tina's thoughts were skipping over memories of her son until a streak of reality infiltrated, her heart began to ache and her throat throbbed from holding back her grief. Just as a good memory or the feeling of complete love overcame her whole body, just as she was appreciating the good, grief came flooding back. Her despair that Justin was gone plagued her every moment.

The tea had gone cold in her cup. She felt a shiver up her spine and as she moved with the shiver, the tea spilt in her lap. Jane watched in despair as she witnessed no response to the spill from Tina. She watched as the tea dripped down Tina's lap and dripped onto the floor. Tina was pretty particular about her belongings, including the level of cleanliness in her house. Jane couldn't believe what she was watching, Tina was so distant. Jane got up and walked to the kitchen, grabbing a dishcloth and a tea towel to clean up the mess. As she wiped and dried Tina's lap, she watched her eyes - they were glazed over, puffy and appeared bruised. She stared outside into the black of night and did not acknowledge Jane at all.

That night when she was tucked up in her own bed, Jane hoped and prayed that this stage of Tina's grief would pass quickly. It was horrific to watch!

"GRIEF HAS MANY LAYERS."

16

TINA - LIFE GOES ON BUT TIME IS BROKEN

T INA FOUND HERSELF ALONE IN THE HOUSE, IT WAS A COLD and dim day and that was just as she felt; cold and dim on life. She gazed out the window and watched the street go about their business. A little girl, no older than five years, rode past on her scooter while her mum power walked behind her trying to keep up. A small smile came over Tina's lips, but then her gaze dropped to the footpath and she remembered Justin was gone. In every moment of everyday Tina was reminded that Justin was gone and her heart ached. When she thought of something other than Justin and her loss, she found herself guilt ridden. How could she possibly think of anything else when Justin was gone? Her gaze raised to watch the cars going up and down the street. *How can life just go on when we are suffering and Justin is gone? It seems so cruel that everyone doesn't think of him every minute, like I do. Don't they care? Don't they realise my boy is dead and cold in the ground, lifeless? How can everybody not be sad like me?*

It had been four weeks since Justin's death. Tina looked through her tears and saw that everything in the room had returned as it was before. Secretly, Tina hoped when Justin had been brought home to die that he would wake up and be ok. It was a fantasy she kept close to her chest. She hated that every little piece of Justin's death was gone from their house. Jane worked hard to ensure that the house was like this, she didn't want any trigger to remind her sister of Justin's demise. Jane thought that this would help with the healing and grief, so her sister didn't have to think about those terrible days while Justin faded away. Tina hated it. She hated that everybody seemed to be moving on, that everyone was forgetting, that life went on without him. She cried hard and started to rock, and really began to hate the world for time passing.

The house was quiet and lonely which is how Tina had begun to like it. She had grown to hate when the girls came home from school, when visitors came or when a conversation grew out of anything but Justin. She was obsessed with keeping him alive by holding on to him in her every thought. The misery within her was growing by the second. She stopped rocking and began to stare out the window, willing the world to stop so she could keep Justin alive in her mind. As her sobs grew quieter, Tina felt the gravity of her exhaustion. She rested her head back on the lounge and her eyes slowly shut as she drifted off into a troubled sleep.

Jane had been spending every day with Tina, doing all the things for her sister that she couldn't bring herself to do: shopping, washing, cooking, homework with Emma, cleaning. Tina could not care any less about life than she did, she wasn't interested in anything or anyone. She saw straight through the kindness Jane was providing, she didn't acknowledge it, was indifferent to it, she just wanted to swim around in a pool of memories of Justin. She had this overwhelming need to keep him alive in her mind. Thinking of him and ignoring the world made her feel safe. She had gotten herself into such a state that reliving memories was the only way she felt any relief from herself. She was getting lost in a world that no longer existed.

Tina was woken up by the front door slamming shut and Emma running through the house.

"Mum...? Mum...?" Emma yelled.

Tina didn't want to respond to Emma, so she ignored her daughter.

Emma called again, "Mum...? Mum...?" but when she got no answer, she gave up and went to the kitchen in search of food. A few minutes passed and Sally came through the front door, but she didn't mutter a word. She walked directly up the stairs and into her room and slammed the door shut. Emma was disturbed by the noise, realised that Sally was home and raced up the stairs into Sally's bedroom carrying an arm full of snacks.

Tina sighed with relief. She didn't want to interact with the girls, it was too painful. Especially with Emma because she was capable of getting on with life and Tina swore she would never move on. Tina's body felt heavy and incapable of anything, she couldn't move or talk. Her gaze fell over the street again and the repetitive thoughts of contempt that the world was forgetting Justin flooded her mind. The afternoon passed with the girls upstairs and Tina downstairs, trying to ignore her life.

Unlike Tina, Jake had returned to work. He couldn't sit around the house anymore listening to how sorry everyone was for their lost, feeling the uncomfortable silences and awkward chatter, not knowing what to say and everyone being lost for appropriate conservation. Jake began to think that there was no appropriate conversation anymore. He didn't want to talk about the past, he didn't want to talk in present tense because Justin wasn't in the present, and the future was not even conceivable. He found himself in a daze of simply getting through each moment. Jake hated going home; every corner and crevasse of the house reminded him of his boy, the only thing keeping him standing was his girls.

He was getting through each day by knowing they needed him.

Jake came in the back door from the garage and noticed the house was dark, as if no one was home. He put his keys down on the kitchen bench and turned the light on. Looking around the kitchen, he found everything in its place. On any given afternoon before Justin died, the kitchen would seem as if a cyclone had passed through. He would usually come home to afternoon snacking scraps strewn across the benches, the TV blaring and stray kids visiting. Coming home to nothing, darkness, made Jake's heart sink. Tina knew Jake was home but, again, she didn't want any interaction with him.

Jake called out, "Anyone home? I'm home!"

He tried to sound cheery but he came out sounding flat and exhausted. Within a few seconds Emma came racing down the stairs and around the corner of the kitchen.

"Hey, baby," Jake conjured up a smile for her.

Emma knew her father wasn't the same man she had grown up with, his eyes were dark with accompanying bags and his posture was slumped. She loved him all the same and threw her arms around his waist. Jake rubbed her back as he closed his eyes to gather his strength, he wanted to cry out of complete exhaustion but controlled himself. He felt uncomfortable with the love, like he was cheating or unworthy of feeling it anymore.

Life before Justin's tragic demise had been relatively happy and optimistic. Emma felt the deep change in the energy of the house and it made her squirm inside.

"Dad, you're home," Emma said with a sigh of relief.

She was only young and often couldn't articulate her feelings but found solace in the arms of her father.

"Do you know where Mum is, Bub?"

Jake had always called Emma Bub and the rest of the family had followed suit.

"No, I haven't seen her."

Jake knew she was around somewhere because her car was in the garage. He also knew she wasn't ready to leave the house. Jake picked Emma up and sat her on the kitchen bench. "Where is that sister of yours, young lady?"

"She's upstairs on her bed."

Emma's response upset Jake, What kid sleeps from when she gets home from school until morning? This was starting to become an unhealthy habit of Sally's and Jake didn't like it.

————

WHERE DO you start with life when a major part of it has disappeared? When everyone you hold dear is changing and sadness fills every breath of your life? Jake had no idea where to start with life, no idea what to do with the girls, including Tina. Sally was really starting to worry Jake, she was isolating herself and trying to escape life. Sally usually was a girl with a full social calendar, plans for everything and a camaraderie with her brother that made Jake proud and full of love for his children. But where do you start when everything hurts? When everything you do without them hurts? When everywhere you look you see them and it hurts? When everyone you look at has a broken heart? Life was just shit all over. Jake was dragging himself around, praying that no one would notice him and mention Justin's name. Life was painful in every way. Jake realised that he was broken and would never be the same, how was he going to feel any love or joy again was beyond him. Life was beyond him, only holding it together from moment to moment.

Emma nattered on about her day, describing every second

of it. Jake was trying his best to listen but grief was bubbling up in his chest and, in the middle of Emma describing how she dropped her chocolate biscuit on the ground at lunchtime, Jake lost his emotional control. He looked deeply into Emma's eyes and could see Justin looking back. He was remembering the day he first looked into Justin's eyes when he had been born and fortunately, or unfortunately, Emma's eyes resonated. Tears ran down his face as he gasped for air. He drew Emma close to his chest and rested his chin on her head. He cast his mind back to when Justin was Emma's size, when he used to talk through his day with his Dad. The pain was tearing him apart.

Emma felt her little heart ache in the middle of her chest. Before Justin died, she had never seen her Dad cry. He was the rock and the funny man of the family and she found herself feeling unsafe and unprotected when her father showed his vulnerability. Silent tears fell from her eyes as she became engulfed in Jake's emotions, swallowing up the grief that surrounded her in her father's arms.

Tina continued to sit in the darkness of the lounge room on her own, hiding from the world. In the quietness, she could hear her husband and her youngest child sob. The air began to fill with the horrific pain pouring from Jake and pushing through Emma. Tina remained still and silent and, for a while, she was happy that Jake and Emma had not forgotten Justin, they were feeling the pain she felt. She was elated that someone else on the planet wasn't forgetting him. Every sob, every grief-stricken breath, she revelled in. It was a sad fact but so true. Tina wasn't sure why it felt so good to her that others were hurting, but her pain was temporarily lifted. She felt the burden of the continual sadness melt away. Someone else could carry the sadness of Justin's loss, it wasn't her responsibility for just a little while.

As Tina sat there, feeling her relief, Sally began to walk down the stairs and turned the lights on so she could see her way. The sun had gone and the blackness of night was kicking it. As Sally glanced down the stairs and across the lounge, her eyes connected with her mother's. Both their hearts sunk and the grief and sadness within them both smashed together and bubbled to the surface. Tina gasped as Sally turned on her heals and raced straight back up the stairs. The house rocked with the slamming of Sally's bedroom door. Tina didn't know why, but over the last few weeks she disliked the sight of her girls. It made her skin crawl and she became so uncomfortable that she wanted to get as far away as possible. Justin wasn't her favourite child, in fact she didn't have a favourite, but all she could think was how to avoid the girls.

Jake was intrigued by the slamming of the door; his tears had subsided and he lifted Emma back down from the bench.

"Let's go see what all that noise is about, hey."

Jake led Emma out the kitchen door and, as their eyes adjusted to the dull light in the lounge room, they could see Tina sitting in the dark. As soon as Emma set eyes on her mum, she released her grip on her father's hand and leapt across the room to embrace her. Tina didn't reject Emma but there was no exchange of love from her. Emma was trying with all her might to drag some love from her mum, but nothing was happening.

"Mum?" Emma tried to engage her mother.

Tina turned her head to Emma but offered no eye contact.

"Mum, I have student of the week presentations tomorrow and I feel like it's my turn to get it, finally. Will you come along to parade in case I do?"

"No, Emma, I have too much on tomorrow."

Emma let go of her mother and slumped in the chair beside her. She turned herself around and looked at her dad's face.

"I should be able to make it, Bub," Jake tried to console her.

Jake could see what was happening, Tina had no interest in anyone. The worst part was that Jake could clearly see how much Emma needed her mum and how much it was breaking her little innocent heart. He could not get her to engage in life, but he kept telling himself it hadn't been long and he needed to give his wife time.

"How about I come and pick you up, Tina, and we can go to parade together?"

Jake wanted Tina to connect with Emma, he could see the pain that the lack of connection was having, but there was no response from Tina, she continued to stare into the empty space in front of her.

Emma piped up, "Yeah, come on, Mum, that would be great."

Tina shook her head, indicating she would not come.

"Oh, come on Tina, you can see how much Emma wants you to come."

"No," Tina responded in a quiet voice.

Within a few seconds, Tina was yelling, "No, no, no!"

She pushed Emma aside and took herself up the stairs. Emma looked at her father and burst into tears, "Mummy doesn't love me anymore, Justin took all her love with him to heaven," she sobbed as Jake reached down to pick her up. She wrapped her legs around her father's waist, clinging to him as if she would never let go.

"It's ok, Bub. Mum is just a little bit broken, she can't see her way anymore," Jake paused not knowing what to say. He took a deep breath and asked for some help, he didn't know from whom he was asking but wanted someone or something to help. He continued, "She does love you very much, but with Justin going to heaven she can't find her love."

"She doesn't love me Dad, she can't. I dreamt that Mummy would never love me again, I saw her without her heart sitting in a broken chair with darkness all around her," Emma's little sobs continued to flow. "The dream made me so scared and sad, now I know it is real."

Jake thought for a minute, "You know what, Bub? I think your dream is right, Mum's heart has stopped loving but only for now. I am sure if we give her some time to be sad, her heart will come good."

Emma's head was buried into Jake's chest, so he carried Emma into the kitchen to scratch something up for dinner. Tina had disappeared into Justin's bedroom to hide away.

After some discussion, dinner was boiled eggs and toast soldiers, as negotiated by Emma. Jake and Emma held hands as they ventured up the stairs to get Sally to come down to help. Jake never cooked before the Justin thing, he always cleaned up. His cooking skills left a lot to be desired. In the past, Tina would monitor all meals, ensuring that everyone was eating a balanced diet. Now, she was barely eating herself, let alone worrying about what anyone else was having. Jake was relieved the choice was boiled eggs.

As they walked up the stairs, Emma checked that Jake was going to make her eggs just the same way Tina usually did, convincing her dad that he needed to cut the crust off her toast. All Jake could think about was how easily Emma moved on, how easily she allowed life to distract her from the damaging situation around her. He was pleased about that, but also began to think how Emma would be the first to forget Justin and that made his heart ache, he never wanted Emma to forget.

Justin and Emma had a lovely relationship. Yes, Justin did get frustrated with Emma; she was little and often annoyed him, but Justin always tried to include her if he could. Jake often found Justin playing with Emma on her bedroom floor or watching a Barbie movie while he rolled his eyes. Jake loved it when he witnessed these moments, he could feel the love they shared. He also remembered how the screaming echoed down the stairs when Justin wanted some space and was trying to get Emma out of his room. Jake felt deeply sad and so lethargic he could barely walk the stairs, but as they reached Sally's door, Emma let go of his hand and pushed through to announce dinner.

Jake found it very hard to comfort Sally. She always had questions and misery that Jake found very hard to address because he had no answers for himself that he could share. Every day was a struggle, every meal and every conversation, life was at an all-time low.

Jake stopped outside Sally's door as anxiety welled up inside him. He didn't realise that the feeling he was experiencing was anxiety, he just knew that it made him uncomfortable. As he took a step forward, he was saved by the doorbell chiming.

"Oh my, thank god," Jake whispered to himself, "Sally, time to come down and help with dinner."

Jake was able to get his message out without any extensive interaction. He turned and began to make his way to the door. As he got closer, he began to think who could it be and what he thought had saved him he also began to dread. He would have to interact with a world that may or may not know of his painful life. Before he knew it, he was opening the door.

"Hi, Jake," a familiar voiced shot into the darkness.

Jake quickly realised it was Natalie, his long time neighbour. She was holding out a baking dish filled with lasagne. Jake nodded in response to Natalie's greeting, he couldn't find the words but was relieved to see Natalie. Over the years, Natalie's friendship had been a great blessing; she was wise, loving and so helpful.

"I made you guys some dinner," she nudged the baking dish forward, "I won't come in, Jake, just wanted to drop it off."

Jake smiled and took the baking dish from Natalie's hands.

"No, no, please do come in and see Emma and Sally."

Jake had a motive, he wanted someone Sally loved to talk to her because whatever he said was not working.

"You sure you want me to? I don't want to intrude..."

"You could never intrude, you're family Natalie. Your input or conversation would be really helpful, I'm struggling with Sally."

Jake turned and hoped that Natalie would follow him and she did.

As they walked through the house, Emma had convinced Sally to get up and eat and they all met in the kitchen.

"The lasagne is still hot, so all you have to do is cut and serve it."

As Natalie spoke, Sally realised Natalie was in their kitchen and she raced over wrapped her arms around her with great enthusiasm.

"Hello, sweetheart."

Sally didn't respond, she just melted into the embrace. She closed her eyes and felt safe. Natalie rubbed Sally's back and gave her a squeeze. Jake looked on with a harsh pain in his throat, fighting so hard to stop a gut-wrenching howl from his lips. He knew that Sally was struggling and he felt so helpless. To see her with Natalie in this embrace made him truly realise how he couldn't help her. She had shown no interest in interacting with him, but with Natalie there appeared to be an instant connection. Jake's emotions were mixed, he was relieved that Sally was connecting with someone but also deeply sad that he couldn't help her himself.

"PEOPLE'S REACTIONS TO
GRIEF IS UNPREDICTABLE,
WITH NO TIMETABLE,
AND THE URGE TO CHANGE
OR SOLVE THEIR EMOTIONAL
PAIN IS REAL."

17
PETER - GUILT

Peter's life felt empty and he was surely lost. His mum, Natalie, found him distant and his sister, Kate, knew how lost her little brother felt. Peter and Justin were like brothers; they could fight and argue but, in their next breath, all was forgiven and they were back to being mates. They had lived next door to each other all their lives and the love they shared was deep. Both Peter's mum and dad were working hard to engage him but it was futile, Peter's grief ran deep.

Peter knew his mum had gone next door, as she did most days, his dad was still working and his sister was not home. The swirling sadness in his gut drove him out of the house, down the stairs and to the front door. As he put his hand on the door handle, his reflex reached down to pick up his skateboard. He hesitated and anger welled inside him but he picked it up, opened the door and began to run as fast as he could towards the skate park.

Justin and he spent many hours at the park, firstly learning how to skate then mastering many skateboard tricks. Peter had not ridden his board since Justin's death, and in his fury, he had vowed never to ride again. When he got to the park, he was breathless and so wild with anger his jaw was clenched and his face a deep red. He stood at the top of the bowl and threw his board into it with all the anger he could muster. It came crashing down and a wheel flew to the other side of the bowl as the board came to a stop. Peter was breathing rapidly and he was shaking his head. With all his gumption, he launched himself into the bowl to get a hold of his board and, as he slid down the side of the bowl, one of his shoes clipped the other and he began to tumble, uncontrollably, down the concrete side. As he came to a holt, he felt excruciating pain in his left forearm and warm blood drip down the side of his face. He glanced down and saw the blood colouring his white shirt with a deep red. He got to his feet, picked up the board and smashed it against the side of the bowl. He picked it up again and smashed it again and then again. He face was red, now covered in blood, and his board was in pieces shattered all over the floor of the bowl. He looked around in fury for a big enough piece of his board to pick up and smash but there was nothing of significance. He knew nothing of his surroundings; who was there at the park, who was skating, who was watching him lose it. Peter's chest was all puffed up, blood was trickling down his face continuing to fill his shirt.

"Man, are you alright, Pete?" A voiced called from the opposite side of the bowl.

Peter didn't respond as he was still all in his own head, his rage was throbbing through every part of his body and his breathing was in a furious state. His gaze couldn't move from the fragments of his board shattered in front of him.

A second later, "Pete?" Then a pause, "Pete, mate, are you ok?"

The body attached to the voice was Peter's friend, Michael. They had known each other for many years and he was a fellow skater with Justin and Peter. They had met skating at the bowl and this was where there friendship stayed. When they met at the park it was never planned, simply a happy coincidence. They talked of boards, wheels, tricks and tracked the progress of their abilities with a friendly banter, always trying to outdo each other.

"Pete, mate?"

Michael could see that Peter was emotionally unstable and he didn't want to startle him, so he slowly reached out to put his hand on his friend's shoulder. Michael was experienced with this sort of thing; his mother was an alcoholic that frequently experienced manic and psychotic episodes. Michael felt like he was just treading water at home until he was of an age so he could legally remove himself from the horror of where he lived.

Michael's hand was just about to touch Peter's shoulder when he spun around with wild eyes and a boot full of anger.

"What?" He screamed into Michael's face.

"Mate..." Michael whispered.

"What? What do you want from me?" The screaming went on, "I can't do this shit anymore, this is just too much for me, I can't do it!"

"I know, I know," Michael raised his hands as if to soothe the air around Peter.

"I just can't do it."

Peter's head fell like he didn't have the strength to hold it up anymore. Michael was a kind and gentle boy of 16, he was sensitive and emotionally very mature for his age. He gently placed his hands on Peter's shoulders.

"I know..."

Michael was very conscious not to say that everything would be ok. Peter's breathing was slowing down and Michael could see him calming down. A few seconds passed and Michael hoped he could connect with Peter enough to get him out of the bowl and have a look at his head to see where the bleeding was coming from.

"Let's just get out of here and find some shade."

Michael began to give Peter a little shove to get him moving. Then a voice boomed from the top of the bowl, "You boys ok down there?"

Michael looked up, "Yep, yep. I'm sorting it," he yelled back.

A parent of some of the young boys in the park had been alerted to the chaos but she wasn't that interested and took off.

The boys ended up sitting on a bench under a tree. Peter still had no interest in the blood trickling down his face. Michael knew that Justin had died, he had heard it from some of the other boys that skate at the park on a regular basis, but he hadn't seen Peter since he found out. No words were spoken as Michael reached into his backpack and pulled out a rag, wet it with his water bottle and began to examine where the bleeding was coming from. Peter sat silent and dazed, he didn't even flinch as Michael began to wipe his face. Peter's head hung, "What am I supposed to do, Mike?"

Peter and Michael both used the shortened references for each other. They had spent a lot of time at the bowl but didn't really know much about each other. Justin had been the main instigator of their friendship; he was a person that could talk to anyone, love anyone and find greatness in them. Justin didn't judge people for what they wore or how they spoke, he was a great guy that could just spread the love and find the best in everyone.

Michael felt unqualified to answer Peter's questions but, unfortunately, he had no choice and had to come up with some sort of answer - Peter was desperate. He searched his soul and asked for help to respond. Finally, something came to him.

"Don't think too far ahead, mate. Just one minute at a time, one day at a time, one afternoon at a time."

"I just can't see a future for myself. Every time I feel a tiny bit of normality or Justin is far from my thoughts, guilt gets a hold of me. I should have been with him and this never would have happened."

"I hear what you are saying but you couldn't have stopped anything; you couldn't be with Justin 24/7 to keep him safe. It was an accident, man, it had nothing to do with you."

"I just can't do this anymore, the guilt of being alive is too much," Peter's voice became shaky and quiet, like his will to live had been washed out of his body and he had only the heaviness of grief to pull him through.

"Pete, it is not your fault, it was just a freaky accident."

Michael wet the rag with the cool water from his bottle again and continued to wipe Peter's face. He found the gash that was responsible for the dripping blood and realised that there was no stopping the bleeding with pressure alone, it was too deep he would need to get Peter to a doctor.

"Pete, things will get easier. You will find a way, somewhere, somehow, you will be able to find a way."

Michael knew firsthand about grief because he had helped bury his father three years ago when he had been killed by a drunk driver coming home from work after a late shift. Michael's dad had been his world; he was an only child and he lived with his father after his parents' separation.

"What do you mean when you say it will get easier and I will find a way? How? When? Where, Mike? I just can't do it," Peter's tone became aggressive.

"Listen to me, mate," Michael took Peter by the shoulders, "Look at me." He shook him for a few seconds finally their eyes met, "Pete, just because things move on, doesn't mean you will forget him or he meant any less to you. It is life, it goes on."

Peter's posture was sunken, his face was covered in blood and his eyes were blood shot with dark bags under them. Michael knew that his friend was in a very bad place.

"One minute at a time, mate," Peter reiterated his message.

Blood continued to drip down Peter's face and onto his shirt. Michael took Peter's hand and placed in over the rag on his head to contain the bleeding.

"You've cut your head pretty bad, I think you need a stitch or two."

Peter nodded his head ever so slightly, but without comprehension.

"GRIEF AND GUILT ARE INTERTWINED."

18

MICHAEL - MAKING A CONNECTION

Peter's life went on with no healing and a feeling of perpetual guilt. Every time a glimmer of the old Peter shone through, the curtain of grief came crashing down. A few days after the skateboard incident, Michael decided to visit Peter at home. It took him some investigating to find out where Peter lived but he eventually found out. His hand moved in slow motion to the door, his fingers curled to knock and an element of fear grew inside him as he thought about walking away. Just as he doubted the validity of his visit, the door swung open and a voice spoke, "Hello, young man. How can I help you?"

Natalie was surprised to see a boy of similar age to Justin and Peter standing on her front step because Peter had scared all his other friends off from visiting.

"Oh, hi," Michael hesitated, "Umm... was just hoping to catch Peter, if that is ok? I'm Michael."

Natalie was puzzled as she thought she knew all of Peter and Justin's friends. Michael stood inside the doorway and realised that he knew nothing about Peter's life outside the skate bowl.

"Oh, sure. I haven't meet you before, I'm Natalie," she was

probing for any information so she could place this kid in Peter's life.

"Ah umm, Michael," he replied.

There was a pause and Natalie stood in front of Michael, waiting for a little more information. Their eyes meet and Michael felt the need to explain his visit.

"I just wanted to check in with Peter and make sure he was alright after the other day."

"Oh, right," Natalie looked a bit more puzzled, "You know, when he hit his head? I took him down the doctor's surgery."

"Oh yes, you must be the young man that helped him."

Natalie reached out and pulled Michael into a warm and friendly embrace.

"Thank you so much for helping him, Michael."

Michael stood still like a solider at attention, he hadn't been touched or hugged in over three years. The last time he hugged his father was the morning of the accident before he died. He closed his eyes and drank in the closeness. His own mother was always drunk and abusive, so there was never a warm welcome or any love shared between them. It wasn't that Michael wasn't open to it, it was just that his mother was just so lost in her alcoholism that there was nothing left for Michael.

Michael was wise beyond his years, he had lost his childhood and become an adult at a very young age. He understood the emotions of the people around him, could see emotional manipulation and the spreading of pain and hurt. Alternatively, he could feel love, intensely. Michael didn't have a choice about how he grew up, but he learnt what he needed to survive. He watched and processed everything around him and the interactions between people intrigued him. He learnt more and more about how the human spirit adapts to life.

Natalie stepped back out of the embrace and felt uneasy about what she had just done, hugging a kid that she didn't know, but she was so grateful to Michael for what he had done a few days earlier for Peter. As she stood back, she looked at Michael and saw that his cheeks had turned a little pink and thought that she had made him very uncomfortable.

"Sorry, mate, I didn't mean to embarrass you," she apologised as their eyes connected.

Michael shook his head in disagreement.

"I'm just so grateful that you were there to help Pete."

Michael simply nodded because he was lost for words and the warm feeling in his chest spread across his body.

"Look, I'll show you the way to Peter's room."

Natalie turned and headed up the stairs. She knocked on Peter's door but there was no response, so she opened it and walked in. Peter was laying on the bed with his back to the door.

"Hey, Pete, Michael is here to see you."

"What? Who?"

"I'll leave you boys to it."

Natalie nodded at Michael who was feeling very uneasy about his visit and beginning to think this was a very bad idea. He had no idea what he was going to say to Peter, he had just followed this nagging feeling within himself to see him. Natalie closed the door and Michael stood there in the middle of Peter's bedroom, like an awkward puppet. A few seconds passed.

"Pete... How's the head?" Michael managed to get out a few words.

He wasn't sure how to proceed with their relationship. He was keen to check on Peter's injuries but he was more concerned with the conversation about Peter not knowing how to live without Justin and the guilt he bared. Peter finally recognised Michael's voice and he slowly sat up. For the first time since Justin's death, he felt that he should make an effort with someone and this someone just happened to be Michael.

"Oh, hey, dude."

"Hey," Michael was relieved that Peter had responded.

As Michael assessed Peter's face, he saw the black eye and purple bruises down one side of his face. The stitches made him look like Frankenstein's monster.

"What's happening?" Peter continued the awkward interaction.

"I just thought I would come to see how you pulled up after the other day. You made a good job of smashing your head."

Peter raised his hand to his forehead and felt the lumps and stitches, "I definitely did."

"Did you get out of school?" Michael tried to make light of the situation.

Peter nodded, yes.

"That's good."

The conversation went on like this, awkward and broken. Peter invited Michael to sit down and he thanked him for helping him and apologised for the drama. For the first time in months, Peter was having a conversation with another human being, a conversation that made him feel ever so slightly normal again. The boys made small talk, had a giggle and, eventually, it all began to feel easier. Peter began to forget about his troubles as Michael spoke of skateboards, the skate park and school.

"GRIEF CHANGES."

19

NATALIE - HELPLESS

NATALIE STOOD AT THE KITCHEN SINK AND STARED AT HER hands resting on the edge of the bench. She was tired and her stress levels were maxed out. She wasn't sleeping, continuously worried about her children and overwhelmed by her friends next door and their agony. She was troubled because everything she did to reach out to her son was repelled with hostility, she just couldn't get through to him. She realised that it had only been a few months but Peter was no better off than the day Justin died. She had often forced him to go to school but he stayed home more days than he went. At school, she was told, he stood on the edge of everything, not interacting with the other kids or in classes with the teachers. Before all this, Peter had been a funny child and well-liked by his peers. Now, he just scared everyone away and laid on his bed, day and night. She felt like he was slipping away.

Natalie wanted to help him, but everything she did made their relationship worse. She tried being kind and nurturing, she tried tough love and she also tried somewhere in between. Nothing was getting through. When she hugged Michael a few minutes earlier, it was a gesture of relief and absolute love for the kid that stood before her, wanting to be with her grief-stricken son.

Natalie began to cry but her cry quickly turned into a sob. She raised her hands to her face and began to shake her head. *What has become of us all? Life is unrecognisable, this is all too much.* Her thoughts raced which was becoming the norm for her; racing thoughts that plummeted down a rabbit hole that sometimes she spent days in. Never seeing the light, always lost in panic and sadness. She was tough in front of anyone else, no one knew of her struggle. She was everyone's rock, everyone's go-to person for help. She had managed to keep up her façade until now, but she knew she was on the edge. Peter was pushing her to her limits. It wasn't his disobedience that upset her, it was that he wouldn't let her in emotionally, he wouldn't discuss anything about how he felt or even mentioned Justin's name. This was killing her. Similarly, his father couldn't reach him and his sister couldn't reach him, he had pushed everyone away.

The tears Natalie shed where a sign of relief that Justin had someone persevering with him. He had been so prickly and unpleasant. Since Peter's incident, she had become highly stressed and she felt she didn't know her son anyone. They hadn't had a proper conversation about anything for months and his injuries remained mostly unexplained; he hadn't spoken of how it had happened, why it happened or who had helped him. Natalie wanted so much to help her son, but he had shut everyone out. She was worried about him being on his own and what he might do to himself, but she also worried when he was with other people because his social skills had deteriorated, he had become so unpleasant to be around.

Seeing Michael at the door had given her hope that Peter had let the world in again. Natalie was sad about Justin herself, but she had pushed her own grief aside for Peter. Yet, she felt helpless and disempowered. In the past, she loved having a happy son who shared and loved life, but now she was left with only the shell, an angry recluse that pushed everyone away.

Natalie had terrible thoughts that Peter was going to try and end his life but having Michael there in the house with Peter had given her a second or two of relief from her worry. Even though she knew nothing of him.

Natalie's closest friend was Tina but their relationship was currently nothing but a superficial situation of checking to see that Tina was eating, drinking and sleeping. She felt alone and helpless, her world had fallen apart and was unrecognisable. The only place she felt useful was at work because it was the only place she could forget about her personal tragedy.

James, her husband, had been able to keep an eye on Peter as he mostly worked from home. He also couldn't get through to their son but was keeping close tabs on him.

Sadness overcame Natalie. She was in the middle of a world of pain and had no idea how to progress with anyone in her life. She was still crying when her phone rang. As she turned and looked at the screen, she saw it was work. It was with a little relief that she picked it up because she knew that they would be looking for her help and support. She felt wanted and could forget about her own life for a moment.

"SOMETIMES WATCHING THE GRIEF UNFOLD AROUND YOU IS THE MOST PAINFUL THING OF ALL."

20

KATE - GRATITUDE

After Michael left, Natalie encouraged Peter to shower and try and get some sleep. For the first time in weeks, Peter took his mother's advice. He felt a little lighter and knew he was exhausted so he did as his mother suggested.

The house was quiet but a little brighter after Michael's visit. Kate had already gone to her room to study and James had some work to finish up before the next morning. Natalie didn't know what to do with herself, so she ended up sitting on the couch and began to feel grateful for the little change in their lives; grateful that Peter allowed a visitor, grateful that Michael visited, grateful for the little bit of peace she felt at this unexpected visit. She didn't realise it, but her gratitude was changing the way she was feeling and, therefore, influencing her energy. Natalie picked up a couple of books she had brought months ago, but hadn't yet looked at, which were sitting on her coffee table. She thumbed through them, getting a general idea of their contents. They were New Age books mostly talking in the same vein about controlling your mind and living in the moment you are in. She felt truth in the words she was skimming, so she decided to sit and read instead of doing the usual jobs she would busy herself with at this time of night. The gratitude and new knowledge she was taking in brought her great peace.

Kate had said she was going to study but she was studied out for the day after spending many hours at the library. Instead, she was doing what had become her evening ritual. She hadn't shared anything about what she did with anyone but she found it was helping her digest her life and the pain that was around her. Since Kate had commenced her psychology degree, she had been intrigued by the human spirit and how people cope with life. She had begun to read a lot of alternative literature that focused on living your best life and how your thinking directly effects how happy and content you are. She pulled out her journal and her pen and thumbed through the pages. Over the last year and a half, Kate had developed this little ritual in the evenings before she went to sleep and in the morning when she woke up. It wasn't something she had invented but something she had tweaked to suit her.

Firstly, Kate would write down anything that was troubling her, from being annoyed with someone to feeling unmotivated to having period pain to being stressed from deadlines. However, over the last few months, all that seemed futile and her journaling was filled with the pain she saw in others and how, at times, that became her pain. Actually, more often than not, she was filled with the pain of others. It wasn't the actual loss of Justin but the effect on the people she loved that caused the most pain. She journaled a lot about feeling helpless but, over time, she realised that she couldn't fix grief for another person, she could only be there to support them.

Sally, Justin's sister, and Peter both seemed to have the same reaction to their loss: anger, withdrawal and the placement of a barrier between them and the world. Their barriers were currently bulletproof. Previously, Kate had been close with both Sally and Peter, but now getting through to either one of them seemed impossible.

Kate and Sally had been friends forever so Kate couldn't understand why Sally had pushed her away. For a few weeks after the accident, Sally had spent most of her time with Kate but Kate had come to realise it was out of avoidance because she didn't want to be in a home without Justin.

On the other hand, Peter would simply hide and push everyone away. That was until the arrival of Michael at their front door. After this occurrence, Kate wrote of her relief and the gratitude she felt that Peter was interacting with the world again.

After she journaled, Kate would get into a comfortable position and try her hand at what she felt meditation was. Before she began, she always set an intention to let her pain and worries wash away. She then closed her eyes and relaxed, going through her body parts consciously relaxing each element as she went. Then she would take some slow deep breaths and let her mind go, releasing all her thoughts and using her breath as a distraction from her thoughts. She allowed her consciousness to fall to her heart and she concentrated her energy on the love found there. As the meditation went on, she would spread that love to the rest of her body and, when she felt that she could, she would spread it out to the world. Firstly, to her immediate world, her family, the house, the neighbours, and then on to the planet. This soothed Kate as she allowed her worries to float away, while the love she felt sustained her.

The night Michael visited felt a little different. The preceding few months had been laden with pain and worry. Kate felt complete rejection from Sally and she had almost stopped trying to reach out to her because of the pain it caused them both. Similarly, her brother was inconsolable; he wouldn't talk to her, he basically wouldn't get off the bed, and everything she had to offer was wrong to him. However, following Michael's time with Peter, Kate caught a glimpse of a little healing in the situation. Her brother wasn't laying on the bed and had actually held a conversation with another human being. The devastation and helplessness she was experiencing felt a little lighter. Her meditation had brought her peace.

After her meditation, Kate's night ritual was to make a list of what she was grateful for. She knew this was a very powerful step in her ritual but had struggled with it since Justin's death. Her list was short and focused on very basic gratitudes. She focused on things such as the weather, the warmth of her bed, a soothing shower, something lovely she had seen in nature, food she had eaten that day or simply sleep.

That night, the list was made up of larger gratitudes, like Peter's healing, Peter participating in life, Michael's perseverance, being able to share some love she had created in her meditation with Michael. She thanked the universe for this tiny change in her life, a shift from the stuck nature of how things had become. She smiled as she wrote them down and felt the gratitude sink into every cell of her body. She closed her eyes, "Thank you, thank you, thank you."

A tingling ran down her body as the gratitude she felt energised every cell, and a smile came across her face. In that very moment, Kate realised how powerful her gratitude was.

Kate kept her eyes closed to pray.

> Universe,
> I truly feel so blessed tonight by this
>   tiny shift in energy of Peter and my
>   family. I am truly grateful for this
>   blessing. I ask that you make me an
>   instrument of your divine
>   wellbeing, peace and love and

allow me your grace to spread this
to my world. I ask this with every
fibre of my being.
So be it.

Kate and her family were not religious but her mother especially had raised them to practice kindness, love and peace in their daily lives. She had talked them through stressful times and taught them to forgive easily. They did attend religious schools but their parents had always told them it was because these schools paid special attention to being kind and caring. She didn't really resonate with the whole God thing and Christianity, but she could see the truth behind it all. It was what her parents taught her, to practice kindness, love and peace that had created the person she was.

She used prayer to commune with Spirit; Spirit meaning to her the something that makes the world tick, makes our hearts beat, makes the sun shine and gives life. She didn't like the labels, so she never used the word God or Amen but found comfort in the use of the word 'Universe' which, to her, meant the power that made everything and everyone alive. So, this is how Kate had come to begin her prayers with 'Universe'. She always ended her prayer with 'So be it' because this is what Amen meant (after she researched) and she had decided to say it in plain English to avoid religious meaning. She loved praying to something more powerful than herself, she loved knowing that there is something higher and more powerful than she could ever conceive. She found prayer to be powerful.

Kate had come across a pack of cards in a department store that were entitled 'Inspiration'. She had taken to randomly drawing a card out at the end of her ritual. Each card had a short message that had the power to inspire and inform her. If she didn't feel like using a card, she would reach to her bookshelf and randomly pick something out to read a few pages. She had collected a small selection of inspirational books covering all sorts of topics, including things like autobiographies of great people, inspirational stories and New Age non-fiction.

Kate did the same with her morning ritual, although the last thing she did was sit and be intentional about her day, how she wanted to feel, what she wanted to do.

Kate enjoyed her ritual, it felt good and inspired her. It felt as though she was connecting to a higher power that could help direct her life and fill her with love. She wanted to tell everyone about it but, due to fear of judgement, she kept it to herself.

That night, she drew a card that truly reflected her life. It read:

> *Grief never ends, it changes.*
> *It is a journey.*
> *It is the price of love.*

Reading that the process of grief changes, gave Kate faith that life would shift. She didn't know whether her brother and friend would heal but she was grateful to hear it changes. She was content to go to bed with gratitude in her heart for this.

"GRATITUDE IS THE BEST MEDICINE; IT HEALS YOUR MIND, BODY AND SPIRIT."

21

JANE & SCOTT - HELPLESS

JANE WAS EXHAUSTED, BOTH PHYSICALLY AND emotionally. Spending her days and nights at her sister's house had taken its toll. She had been pushing all her own grief away and focusing on getting Tina's family through each day. She had got the girls back to school and had been attending to the household chores. Jake ran his own mechanical business and had returned to work a few weeks after Justin's death. He was working hard to bury himself in work and often left the house before everyone even got out of bed. He didn't want to know about Tina or consider the housework, so Jane had stepped in and picked up the slack. The problem was that Jane was a wreck.

"You can't go on like this, Jane. You need to get back to your life and Tina needs to work out how she can function on her own."

The frustration had been building in Scott, he could see the pattern of what was happening. Jane was working so hard to save her sister, doing almost everything for Tina's family; Tina's job, according to Jane, was to breathe and get through the day. They were in a holding pattern that Scott didn't care for. He had watched for a few months as Jane had become Tina's carer, as though she was unable to care for herself. Scott had even witnessed Jane instruct Tina to take a shower. Jane was taking over Tina's life and Tina had become like a small child needing instruction to undertake simple day to day tasks.

"What do you mean?" Jane raised her voice and glared at Scott, "She can't function, she needs me, Scott. I can't just walk away and get on with my own life. They are my life!"

Scott could see Jane was getting worked up.

"What do you propose to do, leave your job and spend your days over there nursing Tina like a child? You must allow her to learn how to function without Justin and get back to life."

Jane continued to glare at Scott, what he was saying was unthinkable to her.

"Don't be so cruel. Her son died, how is she supposed to get on with life?" Her lips began to quiver with the frustration of her actions being challenged.

"You have to allow them all to work out a new way of being and functioning. You going over there every day is only prolonging their pain and allowing Tina to remain in shock, she's becoming helpless."

After the accident, Scott had also begun to spend all his free time at Justin's house, trying to be good company for the family, but after a few weeks he realised that they all needed time and space so he had backed off. He had tried very gently to encourage Jane to do the same but she didn't hear anything he had to say.

"You are such an inconsiderate bastard sometimes, Scott. How am I supposed to walk away? Tina is broken, can't you see? Who's going to look after the girls? Jake isn't doing it, Tina can't do it. Someone has to do it. You would be happy to just forget about them all and move on."

"That is not it all! I loved Justin, more than you know, and Jake and Tina are the only family I know but sometimes love is tough. It is not about being their everything and succumbing to their weaknesses, it's about supporting them to adjust to life, not to forget about Justin but to come to terms with a life without him."

He took a deep breath and continued. He had a lot to say because he had kept a lot to himself for so long.

"You haven't had time to process what has happened; your grief, your feelings or how you are going to be now our family has been broken. You need to think about yourself. If you keep on like this, you will be as broken as Tina. I am worried for you and I am worried about you. We have to find a way to live life without reliving the same sad day, again and again."

Jake stopped and took a breath, he knew he was pushing things. A few seconds passed.

"I can see you are losing yourself. You are putting yourself aside and throwing yourself into saving Tina and the girls, but you have to realise that you cannot save them. They all have to work through it themselves, you can't do it for them. You can't save them from what they are feeling."

Scott was trying to be stern but loving. He could see a pattern forming that he believed was not healthy. Jane was turning into a martyr, putting herself aside, and Tina was becoming helpless. There was silence while Jane got riled up at what Scott had just said.

"You are so insensitive and cruel, you just don't love them like I do!"

Scott hung his head and softly shook it, knowing that Jane was hurting and simply didn't want to hear the truth. Jane stormed out of the house and headed over to Tina's house, just as she had done everyday since Justin's death.

Scott was at a loss, he didn't know how to reach Jane. They had a close relationship and Jane had shown him that it was safe to love within their relationship. Scott was very weary about getting close to people, loving them and allowing close relationships to develop. With his mother leaving, his father dying and having no one to call family, it had taken him years to freely love Jane and her family as his own. However, over the last few weeks, he had spent a lot of time alone as Jane was with Tina most of the day and night. He dreamt of days gone by, fish and chips on Friday nights, BBQ's and holidays, the happy times with Justin as the main character. Nothing had felt perfect at the time, but Scott chose not to think that way. He was worried for the future and knew life would never be the same. Scott's mind was getting the best of him, again, churning and mutating his thoughts.

———

JANE ARRIVED at her sister's house and dread came over her as the car came to a stop. She was seething over her interaction with Scott. She had spent the entire car ride hating Scott for what he said. She was doing everything she could to help the situation, to help Tina and her family. She loved each of the children as if they were her own. She knew what they liked, their idiosyncrasies, their favourite things and how they liked to spend their time. She wanted so much to help them through this and take their pain away. Her anger petered out, as the exhaustion of the last few months caught up with her. She had shed a few tears in frustration on the drive over, so she reached up to the mirror and pulled it down to ensure she looked alright before going into the house. She realised it didn't matter anyway as her sister looked straight through her. She pushed hard against Scott's opinion and held on to the idea that she was helping her family.

For Jane, the day progressed as most days had for the past few weeks, gently pushing her sister to partake in life. Tina didn't leave the house and it was a big struggle for Jane to get her to eat and dress, let alone interact with the girls. The house was sad and quiet, filled with pain. Around midday, Jane was in the laundry room organising the washing and Tina had assumed the same position she had for weeks, on the lounge staring out of the window, when a feeling of panic rushed over her Tina. *Am I helping?* Stories and scenarios began to rush through her mind. Things hadn't changed in weeks and Jane realised that Tina was becoming helpless and was slipping deeper and deeper within herself. The panic continued to rise within Jane as she saw flashbacks to weeks prior and Tina sitting in the same spot. Realistically the days had become like ground hog day. The same thing over and over and Tina was not moving forward in life, at all.

The truth of what Scott was trying to get across that morning was becoming clear to Jane. She could no longer concentrate on the washing and stood there with dirty clothes in her hands, lost in panic and sadness. She began to feel helpless, her thoughts began to race, her breathing shortened and her breath became shallow.

What am I doing here? Tina doesn't even acknowledge me. I don't know if I am doing the right thing... Am I helping? Am I just here out of guilt?

Thoughts swirled and swirled in her head. The stress of this escalated her feelings of despair and the pain of the situation was taking its toll. Jane realised that she hadn't thought about herself, or her own life, for a few months. How was the family going to move forward with life? What was she going to do? The current way she was managing life was not actually working or helping. She wanted to help Tina so that she could live her life. A sense of urgency to help was keeping Jane there and pushing her to do everything she could for Tina, but the realisation became clear that she wasn't helping Tina, she was only burdening herself.

As Jane reached this realisation, her phone buzzed which momentarily broke her racing thoughts. Out of habit, she reached to her back pocket and read the screen, it was Scott.

"Can I pick you up and we can go for coffee?"

At that moment, Jane wanted to run as fast as she could from herself and her sister. She replied within a few seconds, "Yes."

Scott responded just as quickly, "I'm on my way."

Scott's guilt from what he had said to Jane that morning was playing on his mind. He knew his wife was fragile but he didn't know what was going through her head. He had reached out to her in the hope she would give a clue to show that she was doing ok but, realistically, he didn't expect a reply. He felt like he had pushed too hard that morning but he could not hold himself back anymore. He pulled the car up outside Jake and Tina's house, anxious about having a follow up conversation with his wife. He had made a promise to himself not to push Jane too far, he simply wanted to show her some love and support. He wanted to let her know he would support her no matter what she decided to do or how she wanted to handle it. He wanted to apologise. He did know, however, that he didn't want to go into the house and deal with Tina. As the car came to a halt, he saw a glimpse of the front door and saw Jane sitting on the front step. Relief washed over him; he didn't have to go into the house and deal with his heartbroken sister-in-law.

In truth, Jane was relieved that she had a reason to escape her sister's sadness. The pain she was witnessing was becoming unbearable. As she saw Scott's car come around the corner, she felt the need to get away, to run away, to be as far from Tina as possible. As far from the pain as possible. Relief came over Jane as she sat herself in the car. She reached over and kissed Scott on the cheek.

"Hi, love," Scott spoke quietly so as not to upset the situation.

Jane responded, "Hey," as Scott drove off down the road.

They ended up at the café where Scott had had his interaction with Joe, the wise homeless man, but these events didn't enter Scott's mind straight away. He just wanted to check in with his wife and make sure that what he said had not caused too much damage. The two of them sat and made small talk.

As they spoke, Scott observed the dark circles underneath his wife's eyes, her pale skin and the clothes she was wearing. Normally, before Justin's death, she was always very well kept, neat, tidy and well groomed. Since she hadn't returned to work and taken long service leave, she had forgotten all about her own life. The only normal thing she did was run. When she came home from a day of doom and gloom at her sister's house, Jane ran on her treadmill, aimlessly wandered the house, ate a small amount of food that Scott prepared and went to bed. Completely avoiding herself, her feelings, her life, her work and Scott. He hadn't been able to get through to her. Life was taking its toll on Jane.

Their conversation was general and the couple spoke of insignificant things until Scott worked up the courage to ask how Tina was.

"She's just the same," Jane choked up.

She wasn't sure why she was holding back the emotions but, in truth, she was losing faith that Tina would ever interact with life again. This was a secret fear she hadn't shared with anyone but seemed a reality for Jane. She wanted to help but, in her heart of hearts, she could feel that what she was doing may not be for the best. She had been having these same thoughts off and on for a few days before Scott said what he had said that morning. She had not come to terms with the feeling of helplessness with regard to her sister, so she fought very hard against the truth and her ego. Jane justified to herself that she was doing her best. She would do anything she could to pull her sister out of her grief. She had to do something because there was no way she could get on with her life if her sister couldn't get on with hers.

"I don't know what to do anymore," Jane continued after a long silence.

Scott was lost for words; she had caught him by surprise, he had been ready for a heated discussion.

"I think I should go back to work and maybe that would make Tina re-engage with life because it seems like she has checked out, but how can I? Who's going to look after Emma and see if Sally is coping? They are all so messed up..."

Scott could feel desperation in her voice.

"I don't know, love, but if you don't give Tina a chance to engage in life now, she never will."

Scott had seen Tina firsthand; she was completely lost and unaware of what was happening in the lives of the rest of her family.

Scott continued, "The catch is, she hasn't had to partake in life because you have taken over."

Tina got defensive, "If I don't shop, wash, clean and prepare meals then who is going to? How would they survive?"

"But maybe they would?"

Scott was trying so hard to be gentle with Jane. He didn't want to upset her but he wanted her to see the reality of the situation. Jane felt a coolness flush over her chest and rush through her heart. What Scott was saying was hitting her hard. Over the last few months, she had been pushing herself to help and try to fix things, to make things as right as she could for sister's family. She had sacrificed her life for them, her relationship with Scott for her sister's family, and it was beginning to feel like it was all for nothing.

"What are you saying, that I've done all this for nothing? I have done all this and I am not actually helping? Are you saying that I am an idiot and can't see that I am hurting them all by helping?"

Jane was getting upset and Scott had no idea how to proceed, so he reached across the table and held Jane's hand.

Scott loved Jane dearly. If he was truthful with himself, for a few days over the last few months, he was resentful of the time she was spending at her sister's. To Scott, it felt like she had been neglecting him and their life together. When he had those thoughts and felt that resentment, the guilt within him was overwhelming. He hated himself for it but not spending time with his wife was taking its toll on him as well. Jane was lost, trying to help her sister's family, and he was lost about how to help his wife. Everyone wanted to fix an unfixable situation.

As Jane and Scott sat in silence, hand in hand, eye to eye, there were no words spoken. Neither of them knew where to go from that point.

A waitress Scott had not seen before interrupted them, "What can I get you?"

"Umm..." Scott responded quickly by picking up the menu, "What would you like, honey?"

Jane shrugged her shoulders and Scott could tell that she was on the verge of tears so he took over.

"We will have two flat whites, the club sandwich and hot chips."

"Ok," the waitress sensed the tension and raced away, without writing down the order.

Scott was beginning to panic as silence again fell over the table when a familiar voice beamed from behind him.

"Hey, Scott."

Scott swung around to see Joe, the homeless wise man he had interacted with weeks earlier. He stood up and wrapped his arms around Joe like he was a long-lost friend.

"Hey, mate, good to see you!"

Scott felt relieved to see him and instantly began to hope that he could help the current situation.

"Who is this pretty lady?" Joe asked as he gestured towards Jane.

"This is my wife, Jane. Jane, this is Joe."

Jane didn't speak but nodded at them both.

"Come and sit with us, we've only just ordered."

"Are you sure? I don't want to interrupt." Joe could feel the tension.

"Of course, mate, sit. I will just get the waitress' attention so you can order."

"That's ok, I ordered on the way in."

"Oh, great! Then sit down, Joe."

Scott had continued to use Joe's breathing technique since their interaction weeks ago to stay present and mindful of his thoughts. Most of the time it worked but he still occasionally got lost in worry and despair for the future.

"So, how's your day going, guys?" Joe started up a conversation.

As they settled into small talk, Scott began to think about how he would explain his relationship with Joe to Jane. Well, he wouldn't call it a relationship, but he would have to admit to their 'encounters'. Panic rose inside him at the thought and the uncomfortable feeling intensified, but he took a deep breath and decided to just let it go. When the time was right, he would tell Jane the truth.

"So, Jane, what do you do for a living?"

"Not much at the moment," Jane didn't elaborate and silence fell over the table.

Scott filled the void, "She's taken some leave from work to help the family regroup."

"I see," Joe nodded.

"What have you been up to, Joe?" Scott wanted to shift the focus.

"I've been spending a lot of time with Lifeline doing some crisis counselling."

Scott was puzzled by Joe's response, A homeless man with a job?

"It's a voluntary position but I spend a lot of time there, it helps me feel useful and gives me purpose."

Scott admired this man more and more every time they met. He seemed to have life together, except for the homeless thing.

"So, what have you been helping your family with, Jane?"

Joe knew that no encounter was by chance and that these two may need something that he could provide.

Jane was taken off guard, "Well... umm..." She paused, "Just helping with house stuff, everyday things."

While Jane was trying to put her recent actions into words, her heart was saying something different. She had been pushing this feeling away over the last few weeks, pushing against everything her gut told her. Her chest began to quiver and she realised that the two men could see right through her. She knew the truth was coming but she was scared.

The waitress interrupted with their food and then their drinks. Jane was grateful for the distraction because she didn't want to discuss the difficult situation she found herself in. Scott split the sandwich and shared it with Jane. Jane sipped her coffee for comfort, calming herself from the anxiety that was building within her.

Half chewing and speaking Joe asked, "How is all the helping working out for you?"

"I didn't think helping was about the helper!" Jane was getting agitated, "I'm helping... I am..."

"I don't know about that. Like I said before, I counsel with Lifeline to help others but mostly it helps me feel worthwhile."

Jane nodded and Scott jumped in to try and show that his wife was a loving caring person. "Her sister is in a bad way. She's the mother of my nephew I told you about?"

Joe nodded while continuing to eat. He didn't seem that sympathetic to the very delicate situation before him. Jane began to wonder who this 'Joe' was and why he knew about Justin. Jane thought she knew Scott's friends.

Joe didn't feel like it was a delicate situation, he thought it was obvious what Jane was doing but realised he would have to explain things. Before he got down to it, he made small talk about Jane and her sister, Tina. Jane began to feel at ease and Scott's apprehension faded. Joe even got a laugh out of the pair and Scott loved to see a smile on Jane's face. Joe knew this wasn't a chance encounter and they were meant to share something, something that would help Jane and Scott with their process of grief.

"How are you feeling about things, Jane?" Joe probed.

"What do you mean?" Jane shot back.

"I mean, how do you feel about your helping your sister and her family?" Joe would not let up.

"I'm glad I can help. They are my family and I love them, plus someone has to do something because they are falling apart."

"I see."

"Do you see? How can you see? They need me to help them because they are hurting and I'm doing my best to take their hurt away and help them through this terrible time," Jane grew agitated, again.

"So, you want to take their pain away and fix the situation?"

Joe continued to question her, he was not giving in. He wanted Jane to see what she was doing. She looked tired and frail and her efforts were clearly having a detrimental impact on her own well being. She was a small lady, underweight, pale and her posture was slumped. Joe could feel her energy; she was depleted.

"Well, I'm not stupid. I can't fix the situation, can I? Fixing the situation would be bringing my nephew back to life," her words were pressured, "I just want to help them back into life!"

"And you think you can do that?"

"I am doing that," Jane shot straight back.

Scott wanted to say something to protect his wife from this difficult conversation and it took everything in him to stay out of it. Silence fell over the table.

"Well, I hope I am helping."

Joe and Jane eyes connected and they held one another's gaze.

"This is a very hard truth to hear but I will share it with you because it's important and I've had first-hand experience with this. You can't fix someone who is broken, you can't fix someone else's hurt. Naturally, your sister's family is hurt and broken up about your nephew dying, but you have to allow them to go through the process of getting back into life because, no matter how hard you try, you will never be able to do it for them."

Joe's tone was soft and Scott could feel the sympathy Joe was showing his wife.

"So, you're saying I just have to walk away and let them sort it out? That's ridiculous! My sister can't do anything for herself right now. Who is going to look after their young daughter? Wash? Cook? Clean? Make sure everyone is ok?" Jane was getting worked up again fighting the need to help and fix the pain of her family, "I have to do something, I have to care, I just can't walk away. That would be cruel for them, but also cruel for me to watch them fall further apart. That is ridiculous!"

"I am not saying that you walk away, that you forget them. I am not saying you stop loving them. I am saying you can't take their pain away with whatever you are doing and you certainly cannot fix them or the situation. You have to allow them to work through their grief and sadness, you have to allow them to find a new and different way to live. It's not your job to try and fix things for them, that's a journey they have to pilot for themselves."

"You are saying that I must walk away and let them live their life and I live mine? But we are each other's lives."

Deep within her being, Jane wanted to help her sister. She did want to fix things, that was what was keeping her alive and moving, her need to be helpful and do it all for them. However, a light was beginning to shine on the situation for Jane, even though it was making her very uncomfortable.

"Everyone wants to help and everyone wants to take the pain away but life doesn't work like that. Your job is to love your family and walk beside them in their grief. You, of course, also need to grieve and process your loss."

Joe paused when he couldn't see a sign of any reaction from Jane.

"Your job is to walk beside them."

Again, silence fell over the table while both Jane and Scott digested this information. Joe knew it was not all going to come together in this moment for Jane, but he had successfully planted a seed for her so that she could begin to see what she was doing in a different light.

"Being busy with work or busy helping is a good distraction from your own pain."

Jane cocked her head and squinted at Joe, she felt like she wanted to lash out at him. She wanted to tell him off for saying and thinking she was just distracting herself from her own pain. As the anger began to bubble, she took a deep breath and a flash of what Scott had said to her earlier in the day became clear. The same information, the same realisation. Jane contemplated, was she going to allow her ego to protect herself in an angry rant or was she going to concede the truth? Seconds seemed to pass by as hours as she processed the situation. Magically, she held back and just sat with the words

> When someone is broken you can't fix
> them,
> You can't take someone else's pain
> away.
> Walk beside them,
> Sometimes love is tough.

The day's events were closing in around her. She had to face the truth; what she was doing was not helping and she needed to back off. She needed to allow her sister and her family to find their way.

Scott reached over and squeezed Jane's hand as Joe concluded, "I can see that you have a lot of love for your family, sometimes you have to be strong and allow them to travel their own healing path."

Jane's breath was laboured as she gave Joe a slight nod in agreement.

"I know it is tough to watch, but you will be there to hold their hands when needed. You have to give them a chance."

"NEVER UNDERESTIMATE
WHAT IT TAKES TO WATCH
SOMEONE YOU LOVE IN PAIN."

- EMMA BOMBACK

22

JANE - WILL EGO TAKE OVER?
THE TRUTH WILL SET YOU
FREE...

JANE TURNED TO SCOTT AFTER A FEW SECONDS OF BEING in the car.

"Who the hell was that guy? How do you know him? I'm sure I have never meet him before."

Jane wanted answers. She was working herself into an argumentative state and Scott knew it. Scott knew he had to come clean about the situation, sooner rather than later. He hadn't told anyone about what had happened, about what Joe had told him and how it had helped, but he realised he had to spill his guts and be honest with his wife.

As Scott began to explain who Joe was and discuss the circumstances of their relationship, Jane became intrigued with the story and lost sight of the issues she had confronting herself. She asked questions about the breathing and about how your life experiences shape you, focusing on the importance of remaining in the present moment. Jane was so enticed with the conversation that she hadn't noticed that they had pulled up outside her sister's house and had spent the last ten minutes stationary.

"So, you see, Joe is an accidental relationship but one that has, and is, helping me. I have been using the breathing to get me through times of unpleasant thoughts, like when I'm unable to sleep. Just knowing he is there with his wisdom makes me feel a little safer," Scott paused, "I'm not sure why."

Jane nodded in agreement with her husband and, as she did, realised where they were and let out a big sigh.

"I'll see you tonight."

Her eyes were set on the front door of her sister's house. She got out of the car and walked towards the house. Scott watched his wife walk off wondering if she heard anything Joe spoke to her about. He was shaking his head with frustration and desperation because she appeared to have already forgotten that she should probably back off.

It had been over two hours since she had left Tina's and Jane had been away a lot longer than she originally anticipated. She expected to see her sister sitting just as she had left her in the lounge, staring out the window, but she found her in the kitchen making herself a sandwich. Jane had struggled to persuade her sister to eat anything over the last few months, so she was blown away by what she saw.

"Hey, how are you doing?" Jane barely whispered.

Tina looked up and glared at her sister. Jane felt very uncomfortable, like she was an intruder.

"What does it look like, sister?" Tina's voice had an aggressive tone.

"Sorry for asking the obvious," Jane took a step back.

"What are you doing here?" Tina shot back.

Jane was taken aback and was not sure what to say next. She finally settled on saying, "Just the usual, I suppose."

"Well why don't you go and do the usual at your house instead of being here, annoying me."

Jane didn't know how to react. She had spent the last few months helping and doing everything for her sister and her family. She thought she was doing the right thing and she truly thought she was helping everyone.

"I don't need you here in my face all the time. I'm a grown woman, I can look after my life myself!"

Jane took a very long, hard blink to hold back all her tears of frustration and hurt, then she nodded her head and backed out of the kitchen, without a word. She was shocked by her sister's reaction. She had hardly spoken since Justin's funeral but here she was being nasty. Without a word, Jane continued towards the front door, picked up her handbag and keys to leave. She felt like she was running for her life; running so she didn't have to hear the bitter words being fired at her from Tina, but also running from the pain of that house.

As Jane opened the door of her car, relief flooded over her and, as she sat herself down in the driver's seat and backed out of the driveway, a small smile spread across her face. With the grin came a flood of tears and she soon realised it was getting difficult for her to see the road. She pulled over only a short distance from her sister's house, wiped her eyes and wondered why she was crying. She questioned herself; was she sad, frustrated, hurt or was she just exhausted? No answer came in those first few seconds, so she reached into her handbag to find a tissue. Jane realised that she felt a little lighter than she had a moment before as she wiped her eyes, blew her nose and looked out into the world. She laughed a little and smiled. She was actually happy that her sister had reacted because, in that outburst, Jane had seen a little spark of who Tina was before the accident. Unfortunately, her relief was short lived and tears began to flow. She felt hurt, she had only been trying to help the best way she knew how.

"Screw you, Tina, you ungrateful bitch," Jane growled.

She threw the tissues she was holding across the car in

frustration, straightened her posture, wrapped her hands around the steering wheel and headed for home.

———

SCOTT OPENED the garage door and, to his surprise, found his wife's car parked inside. He was puzzled because for months she had not returned home until at least 8.30pm. It was only 5.45pm and his mind began to race with scenarios as to why she was home before him. Before Justin's death, Jane has always arrived home before Scott; his job was a little unpredictable but Jane's life was like clockwork, always home by 4.15pm. Scott's intrigue pushed him to move with speed, he wanted to get inside the house to see what was happening. Had Jane implemented the realisation she had experienced earlier that day? Scott had visions of Jane laying on the bed crying or running pointlessly on her treadmill. He hadn't heard from her since he dropped her off at Tina's and she had been in his thoughts all day but, as he entered the house, he found Jane standing over the stove stirring a pot of something delicious. She hadn't cooked at home since the accident so this was a surprising turn of events.

"Hi, Babe."

Jane turned her head towards Scott, "Hey."

Scott wasn't sure what to say next because he didn't want to upset her or make her feel guilty for not being at her sister's. He was lost for words.

"You hungry? I've made your favourite, chicken and mushroom risotto."

"Yes, that sounds great."

Scott didn't know what to say or how to behave, he felt he was walking on eggshells. He was desperate to keep things positive and keep the conversation away from his in-laws. Scott loved Tina, Jake and their kids, but recent events had made him feel consumed by their lives. He had dwelled in sadness and despair and felt as though he was losing his wife to the grief. The relief within him to see his wife in their house cooking dinner was indescribable. He wanted to race over and wrap his arms around her but held back to prevent unsettling the scene before him.

Gently, Scott walked closer to Jane. Usually, they always kissed each other hello and goodbye so he hoped he could do the same in that moment. He leant down to kiss her cheek and Jane turned and kissed him tenderly, then she wrapped her arms around him and Scott felt the warmth of her embrace. There were no words spoken. As they sat and ate dinner together, Scott's conversation was superficial talking about work, the weather and how delicious the dinner was, when, finally, Jane began to drive the conversation.

"I rang work this afternoon and said I would be returning to work on Monday," Jane didn't lift her eyes from her plate.

"Are you sure you're ready?"

"Yes, I am."

Jane wanted to rage about the goings on today with Tina, her hurt and anger had snowballed throughout the afternoon. She needed to explain, truthfully, to her husband why she wanted to go back to work. After a few minutes of silence, the anger came pouring out, "Tina doesn't want me there so I thought I would get back to my life."

"She told you that?" Scott gently questioned.

"She sure did."

"Do you want to have some time off for yourself and hang out at home before you go back?"

Scott thought Jane wasn't ready for work, she had been highly stressed, slept very little and she just wasn't herself. Under normal circumstances, Jane was very committed to her job and was good at it. She worked as a legal secretary for a high-profile lawyer and had done so for the last seven years.

"No, I will be fine. Do you think I can't handle my own life when I have just been running the lives of a whole family?" She glared at Scott.

This was the situation Scott didn't want to create, heated and emotional. He was just worried about his wife.

"No, I know that you are capable but I also know that you haven't been sleeping and you have been neglecting yourself since the accident."

"Neglecting myself? Neglecting myself!" Janes voice was getting louder and louder, "I have been trying to help my sister, my sister who has just lost her son. I can't just worry about myself. Have you seen how they are all suffering? How their pain is eating them all up and how life will never be the same? How the hell can I possibly worry about myself? I'm my last priority," She paused for breath, "It turns out that I've just been wasting my time. Tina told me to go home and leave her to her own life, after I have been there for months trying to help."

Her breathing was laboured and shallow. Quietness fell over the room.

"I suppose that is what Joe was talking about today, you can't fix Tina and her family..." Scott was trying to make Tina see the truth of the matter.

"Do you expect me to just sit back and watch them all suffer while I go merrily on my with my life?" Tina was struggling to let go.

"Not at all, love, but you can't fix them. It's not your job to fix them."

"So, you expect me to just do nothing, not a thing, to help them? Not a thing to fix the situation or distract them from their lives?"

Jane wanted to accuse Scott of being a selfish bastard. She

was so angry at everything and everyone, she literally wanted to reach over the table and punch her husband in the mouth, but, before she did anything that she would regret, she pushed her chair back to leave the dinner table.

"That is not what I meant at all, I just don't want you to neglect yourself or sacrifice your own life for them."

"You don't understand that their lives are my life, without them I am nothing."

Jane got up and walked out of the room. The truth of the matter was that Jane had realised her sacrifice was not helping her family and Tina had devastated her with her cruel words that afternoon. Scott was left sitting there, anxious in the pit of his stomach about the whole situation, but aware that this was a process Jane had to experience to begin her own healing journey, no matter how painful that was.

As he washed the dishes, Scott couldn't think of one thing to say to Jane that might help the situation. She wanted to help her sister and Scott wanted to help his wife. In that moment, he realised that he was, in fact, doing what his wife was doing; trying to save his wife from her grief, from the maladaptive situation she had created. He stopped what he was doing, leant his hands on the sink, closed his eyes and shook his head, *I am doing exactly what I am asking her not to do.* His head continue to shake in dismay. *Joe was right, you can't fix things for others, you can only hold their hand on their journey.*

He heard Jane in the shower and, after a while, he had realised that she had taken herself to bed. It was only early, around 7.30pm, but she probably needed some time to herself. He knew she was physically exhausted.

Jane found herself in bed for no other reason than to get some space. She didn't want to deal with what Scott had said that morning, what Joe had said at lunch time and definitely not with what Tina had said to her. Her mind began to race, trying to prove to herself that she had been helping her sister and her family by being there in their house, helping by doing for them what they could not. She convinced herself that she had sacrificed her life to help and that her sister was being an ungrateful cow.

She lay there for at least two hours before Scott came to bed. She hated him at that moment in time. She hated what he thought, she hated that he had not taken her side and not congratulated her on all the help she had given her sister's family. She hated him for her life and Justin's death and, as Scott slipped into bed, the emotion within her bubbled up to the physical surface and she began to sob. Scott turned the bedside light on, never thinking that his wife had been upset and hurting all alone in their bed. He assumed the physical exhaustion had kicked in and taken its toll and he instantly felt terrible for the neglect. Jane had her back to him and was curled into a ball. He didn't know what to do other than wrap his arms around her. Crying made him feel uneasy and he wanted to make it all better for Jane, take away the hurt. However, in a spilt second, Scott realised that no one person could do that for another. He thought about what Joe's words, *Love yourself and others, walk beside them.* He was trying to do what Jane had been trying to do for her sister for months, fix it and make it better, but there was no answer. He felt tension in every muscle as he desperately wanted to help the women he loved. As Scott laid there, beside his wife, time passed and he relaxed into the embrace.

"Just be there for her."

Scott opened his eyes, to look for someone talking to him, the words he heard were so clear, but no one was there. Then, again, he heard a voice.

"You are already doing it, there is nothing more you can do."

The advice was profound and clear, Scott seemed undisturbed by what he heard, he was consoled by the fact that there was nothing else he could do.

Scott could feel the tremble in his wife's body as she cried. Finally, Jane acknowledged Scott's embrace by placing her hand on his arm that was wrapped around her. Scott felt an element of relief with this acknowledgement. He felt a connection with his wife, more than he had had since the loss of Justin.

———

SCOTT WOKE to find his wife still asleep beside him and he was relieved. The sun was bright behind the blinds and, as he orientated himself, he realised that he hadn't set his alarm and it was a workday. Scott was a hard worker and always on the job by 8.30am but the clock beside his bed read 7.40am. Jane and he must have been exhausted because they were generally early risers. As he laid there, he realised he didn't want to go to work, he wanted to be at home. His work was flexible but he had a strict routine and way of doing things that he knew made him feel safe, so he always kept to the same ways in his life. It drove Jane a little crazy at times but she also knew it kept him sane. However, that day, he didn't have the drive to get up. Instead, he reached for his phone sent a text to his boss to say that he wouldn't be going into work, he was going to stay at home with his wife.

Scott didn't want to push anything with Jane, he simply wanted to be with her and love her. She had been a saint, working to help her sister with no thanks or reward, just operating to help. He could see that she was worn down, unreasonable, short tempered and a little harder than she had been before. So, he made a conscious decision to keep things calm. They ended up in the garden which had been neglected and was in need of some tender loving care. There was little conversation between the couple as they got to work, but they felt at peace helping each other restore their safe haven.

"Look at this mess," Jane finally spoke.

She pulled and tugged at a bunch of weeds and a shrub that had wilted. Scott walked closer to help her but she turned with an angry snarl and growled at Scott, "I can do it, I'm not useless."

"Oh ok, no worries," Scott put his hand up as he backed away.

Jane yanked and tugged and, finally, fell down on the ground, clenching the shrub branches which were still firmly embedded in the ground.

"Frigging thing! Why can't you just come out?" She was raging and continued to pull the branches, "Just frigging come out you bastard! I'm doing the best I can, I am doing all I know how to do!"

Jane's face was red and sweating as she yanked and pulled and kicked the plant. She stomped on it and continued to curse. In her rage, she crushed the flowers and plants around the dead shrub and, eventually, she began to cry in frustration. Scott couldn't watch it anymore, so he walked over and wrapped his arms around his wife. She began to push and shove him.

"Hey, Jane, take a deep breath," he said in a stern voice.

She kept pushing.

"Jane, take a deep breath."

Scott held his wife by the shoulders and tried to make eye contact with her, but she seemed to be lost in her own world. Jane shook her head, tears flooding her red face. Suddenly, she stopped, pushed Scott out of the way and walked into the house.

"Get out of my way," she hissed.

Scott felt sick to his stomach, he knew that Jane was in a bad place but didn't realise it was this bad. He watched as she walked back into the house and slammed the glass sliding door shut. Scott assessed the damage of the rage before him, surprised by the damage Jane had caused. She nurtured her garden, spent hours in it, talking to the flowers and making things look just right. Within just a few minutes, Jane had ruined a large area of her precious garden.

Scott couldn't think of anything he could do for Jane; if he went after her it would only fuel her rage, so he began cleaning up the mess in front of him. He pulled the dead plant out, fairly easily, and began to remove the squashed and damaged plants around the devastation zone, feeling very sad for the plants but even sadder for his wife. Anger seemed to be dripping from every cell of her body and she certainly wasn't letting him into her inner world to work through it.

Scott wasn't thinking about what his hands were doing, where he was or the environment around him. He was so distant from the present moment. He was jolted from his thoughts by a hard wind swooping through the yard. He stood up straight and looked at the mess in front of him. His thoughts slowed and he remembered Joe and their first interaction. The word 'breathe' came to him. Scott could feel his heart beating hard and fast, his breath short and frequent. He took a slow conscious breath in and then out. *Ok, do it. Breathe in 1, 2, 3, 4, 5, 6 and out 1, 2, 3, 4, 5, 6, 7, 8.*

Scott stood there in the yard, staring at nothing and consciously breathing, until he got a hold of himself. It took a solid five minutes and some almighty concentration to keep him centred on his breath. When he finally found some peace, Scott looked around the yard and the mess his wife had made in front of him. Scott questioned himself, *Should I be finishing fixing this mess up or should I go to see if Jane is ok?*

He decided to check on Jane. He followed the loud banging of cupboards and doors and found her in the laundry room, cursing and throwing clothes in every which way.

"What do you want, Scott?"

She wanted to hurt Scott; it was a distraction from the truth of things, only at a subconscious level. Scott was startled by Jane's greeting.

"WHAT DO YOU WANT?" She yelled in his face.

A puzzled look came across Scott's face, he had never seen his wife like this. She was a gentle, loving person with a workaholic nature and a passion for gardening and her family.

"Don't just stand there like an idiot, do some washing. It's amazing that we have any clean clothes at all. You just expect me to do everything. Everyone expects me to do everything, without any thanks."

Jane huffed and puffed as she shoved the washing into the machine. Scott still hadn't said a word and it took all his might not to retaliate to the pain she was inflicting.

"You are so useless sometimes, you can't even wash the clothes."

Scott couldn't think of anything constructive to say. He knew that Jane was in a lot of emotional pain and didn't want to contribute to it. He caught himself and began to breath, *In 1, 2, 3, 4, 5, 6 and out 1, 2, 3, 4, 5, 6, 7, 8.*

He stood and took the abuse from his wife, then, after a few minutes, he responded, "I am sorry. I am so, so sorry. I don't know what to do. I love you and I'm sorry."

Jane turned and looked at Scott. She had never seen him turn away from an argument, he had a quick wit but also a quick tongue. In their lives together, they had only had a handful of shouting arguments and Jane had learnt it was not worth it.

Finally, she was speechless as their eyes met. Scott shared a small but loving smile with her, then turned and headed back to the garden. Jane watched Scott walk away. She wanted to say something but she just couldn't find it in her to let down her walls and let him in. Exhaustion and sadness took over her body as she fought back tears. She squeezed her eyes shut and began to softly shake her head. She was lost in her anger and fear. Her legs began to waver and she plummeted to the ground. She sat and cried as her body began to rock with emotion. Scenes from the last few months ran like a movie across her mind. With every scene, her heart ached a little harder; Justin's battered face, the tubes and monitors, her sister's lifelessness, the cruel comments she had made to her the day before. All the pain came pouring out. Her body began to quiver, her breath to shake.

Jane pulled her knees into her chest and cried as her thoughts overwhelmed her. Her ego had taken over, pain had taken over. Jane was torturing herself.

"GRIEF IS A MATTER OF THE HEART AND SOUL. GRIEVE YOUR LOSS ALLOW IT IN, AND SPEND TIME WITH IT."

- LOUISE HAY

23

TINA - SO MUCH PAIN

TINA WATCHED JANE WALK OUT WITH NO REGRET AND NO apology. She felt like she wanted to walk up to the front door and repeatedly slam it shut. The slamming was to keep the world out and herself away from life. Tina picked up the plate her sandwich was on and threw it hard against the kitchen wall. Then, she picked up the cup she had gotten out to pour herself a glass of water and hesitated for just a second, before launching it against the wall too. She began to pick up the dishes from the dish rack and hurtle them at the wall. After the dish rack was empty, she opened the cupboards and started on the anything she could get her hands on. The destruction stopped when she came across a coffee cup Justin had made her in Grade 2 for Mother's Day. It was worn and well used but she always loved it. She held it and took note of the photo and the little drawing Justin had made of them both holding hands, stick figures with not much detail. You could only tell it was them because Justin had labelled himself and his mum.

Tina started to shake her head in dismay, devastated by her loss. She had so much sadness and devastation festering inside of her. She put the cup back in the cupboard and slammed the doors shut. Her hands rested on the bench like she was building up all her power to punch someone out. She rocked back and forth, her head still shaking, her jaw clenched and her eyes closed. Flashes of Justin's battered face were bright in her mind. She could picture his last breath and then, out of nowhere, Justin's face with his cheeky grin beamed bright. She was caught off guard by the image, love welled in her throat and she began to cry.

"I miss you, beautiful boy, so much," she whispered.

Thoughts of never seeing him again crushed her soul, so much sadness within her. It was like every cell of her body could switch from devastating sadness to insane rage at any time. Sadness overwhelmed her and she collapsed down onto the kitchen floor.

Tina had been pretty numb until a few days earlier. She could feel things changing and, instead of sitting around with an empty mind, her body began to fill with anger for her loss. Tina had been repeatedly asking herself, *Why? Why had Justin died and everyone else lived? Why had such a good guy died when nasty people lived on?*

When Tina's tears finally stopped, she looked up and saw the damage she had made to the kitchen walls; no holes but plenty of dints. She felt disappointed in herself for losing control, but what she didn't realise was that she had experienced a breakthrough. Things had shifted; her outlook was not numb, she was actually feeling again.

A few minutes passed and she looked at the clock, the girls would be home from school soon so she began to clean up the mess she had made. As she swept the floor and wiped the wall, she was happy that her outburst hadn't caused too much damage. She didn't want to have to explain that.

Tina opened the bin to empty the ceramic rubble and found it full. For the first time in weeks, she cared and tied the rubbish bag in a knot. She walked it out the back door and placed the rubbish in the bin. As she looked around, she noticed her car in the garage and realised how long it had been since she drove or even left the house. She hadn't been to work, she hadn't been to the grocery store, she hadn't paid a bill or read a school newsletter. *Had Emma been reading and doing her homework?* She couldn't even recall seeing Sally.

Walking over to her phone to see what day it was on the calendar, she quickly calculated that it had been ten weeks since Justin's death and twelve weeks since his accident. Tina went back inside and surveyed the lounge room. She couldn't remember when she actually last saw this room. She questioned herself, *What's happened to me over these last few months?*

A huge lump formed in her throat, she stared at the ground, her breath rattled up through her chest and anxiety flashed through her body. Everything felt wrong to her; the house, her life and her ability to live her life. She felt guilty that she had just been thinking about life stuff, the girls, the bills. *What sort of a terrible mother and person was I to allow him to float away from my thoughts?* Her face reddened and panic began to build. Panic that Justin wasn't there, panic that she had forgotten him for a second, panic that she wouldn't see him again, panic about how to live. She gasped with pressure and, as she did, the back door flung open and Emma raced into the house, followed by Sally in a slow dawdle.

In a fright, she quickly gathered herself as Emma began to yell out, "Aunty Jane!"

Emma had become accustomed to Jane being in the house most of the time so when she raced around the corner of the kitchen and was confronted by her mother standing there, she was surprised. Emma had gotten used to Tina being absent in her life, just a shell of a person, without any connection.

"Oh, hey, Mum," Emma was thrown off by her mother's presence.

"Hey, Em," Tina quickly responded.

Emma wrapped her arms around her mother's waist which she had always done but hadn't for months.

"How was your day?"

"Oh, pretty dumb. Mrs Pierce made us do so much maths and Tobi wasn't allowed to sit next to me cause Mrs Pierce said we were talking too much... so dumb."

As Emma finished her sentence, Sally walked into the lounge.

"Hey, Sally."

Sally was also surprised by her mother's presence; she took a few seconds to comprehend what was happening.

"How was your day?"

Tina could see the confusion on her daughter's faces, the gravity of the last few months of her emotional absence, becoming clear. It was like Sally had seen a ghost, she was speechless.

"Why don't we get you girls some afternoon tea?"

Both the girls had longed for their mother's love through these desperate times and Emma had persevered, every day, trying to interact with Tina. The rejection had never stopped her from continuing to try, but Sally, on the other hand, had taken the rejection hard. In her own mind and heart, she had ended her relationship with her mother. She had built a considerable wall around her and made a conscious decision no one would leave her again. Instead, she would leave all relationships as a way of protecting herself.

"Yeah, Mum, I am starving. Have we got any crumpets?" Emma chimed.

"I'm good," Sally muttered and headed for her room.

"You sure, Sal?"

Sally didn't acknowledge her mother's question and continued on her way. Tina watched her daughter walk away and the anxiety within her began to build, again. She knew nothing of her eldest daughter's life currently or of how she was coping with the loss of Justin.

Emma began to search for crumpets in the fridge and pantry and Tina joined in with the search. The fridge and pantry were full to the brim with food. Tina wondered who had been shopping for them as she certainly knew it wasn't Jake, he wouldn't know what to buy. "There doesn't seem to be any crumpets, Bub."

"Oh, I must have eaten the last one yesterday."

"What about a glass of milk and these biscuits?" Tina held up a packet.

"Oh, ok," Emma beamed.

Except, as Tina said this, she realised that there was no milk either. There seemed to be everything in their house, except milk and crumpets.

"There doesn't seem to be any milk, Em."

"Oh, yeah, we used all the milk making porridge this morning."

"Who made you porridge this morning?" Tina questioned.

"Aunty Jane, silly."

Tina nodded at Emma and the realisation became clear that Jane had been doing a lot for her family.

"Well, I suppose we should go and get some milk, Mum. We will need it for your cup of tea tonight and more porridge in the morning." Emma grabbed the car keys off the hook and headed for the back door, "Come on, Mum," she encouraged.

Tina couldn't remember the last time she left the house.

"Come on, Mum."

Tina grabbed her handbag and headed for the door. As she

196

got close, she yelled out to Sally, "We're going to get some milk, Sal. We will be back in a minute."

————

As THEY GOT to the grocery store checkout, Emma selected which lane they would go through, making a preference for Peter's.

"Look, Mum! There's Pete, let's go through his one."

As Tina caught a glimpse of Peter, she was confronted by the loss of Justin. She hadn't seen Peter for months and knew nothing of his life either. Peter was like a second son to Tina; she had probably seen him every day of his life, until Justin's death. Anxiety began to build again.

"Hey, Pete. We ran out of milk," Emma beamed as she plonked her crumpets down on the checkout.

Tina slowly placed the milk on the conveyor as she studied Peter's face. Peter was taken aback by the presence of Tina. His mother had pushed him to go back to work to get some routine and normality back in his life, but her presence made him feel uncomfortable and guilt overcame him for being at work and getting back into his life.

"Hey, mate," Tina greeted Peter.

"Hi, Mrs P," he responded.

Tina could see how uncomfortable Peter was so, as he grabbed the milk to scan it, Tina reached out and touched his hand. She gave it a little squeeze in the hope that she would reassure him that it was alright for them all to be together. Their eyes met. No one else would have noticed the significance of their interaction, but it was heart felt and no words were necessary.

As Tina looked back in the rear vision mirror of the car to

reverse out of the carpark, she caught a glimpse of herself; she was pale and there were black circles under her eyes, her lips looked white and her hair was dishevelled. She stopped the car and brushed her hair down with her hands. She couldn't recall the last time she looked at herself in a mirror.

As they drove home, Emma nattered away to her mother. Tina was only half listening as she was trying with all her might to hold herself together. Seeing Peter working and living his life had made her anxiety rise. She didn't know how to feel. An element of relief came as she drove into their driveway, at least at home she could keep the world out.

Tina reorientated herself to the kitchen as she and Emma set to work making the crumpets. She couldn't seem to recall the most obvious things, like where the plates were or what container did they keep the butter in.

Later that evening, they watched the TV and decided on spaghetti for dinner. Sally never came out of her room, which was unusual for her as she was a sociable person with so much to say.

Emma heard Jake drive in the driveway, "Yeah, Dad's home!"

She was bouncing up and down in the lounge when Jake walked through the door. It had become a habit that Emma met Jake at the backdoor with great excitement, so Jake was surprised she was not there. Jake placed his bag on the kitchen bench as he walked through the house looking for Emma, wondering if she was even home. He had noticed that Jane's car was not parked out front and thought, maybe, Emma and Jane were out together.

"Hello, Daddy!" Emma beamed. "Come sit with us. We are watching cartoons, they are so funny."

Emma didn't want to leave her mother's side because she

hadn't been with her like this for months and wanted to keep it alive.

"Hello, ladies," Jake walked over to the lounge and sat down.

Tina realised she had no idea what Jake had been doing to keep himself together since his son's death. He was obviously going to work as he had his uniform on, but she couldn't recall if they had even spoken since. Her anxiety began to build again. Emma wrapped her arms around her father's neck and snuggled into him.

"Mum and I went to the shop and got some crumpets and milk. We saw Pete there, Dad."

"That's nice, Em. You do love crumpets, hey?"

"I do."

"Anyone seen Sally this arvo?"

"Briefly, when she came home, but she went straight to her room."

Tina and Jake's eyes met and Tina's anxiety rocketed, her heart was beating so fast it felt as if it was going to jump out of her chest.

"Sally!" Jake called out, "I'm home, time to come down."

Jake and Jane had made Sally promise that she would come out of her room when her father came home, at least until after dinner, because she had become a recluse hiding herself away. Secretly, Sally liked that her father had noticed her behaviour as her mother was nowhere to be found, emotionally, since her brother's death. Sally had begun to feel cheated by life, by her brother for leaving her and by her mother for emotionally abandoning her. However, she couldn't help but be intrigued by the change in her mother's behaviour and the absence of her aunt so headed downstairs to join her family.

"Where is Aunty Jane today, Em?" Jake asked.

Emma raised her eyebrows and responded, "I don't know, I haven't seen her".

"Jane went home to sort things out at hers."

Tina didn't want to elaborate because she was ashamed of what had gone on between them. Jake found it difficult to look at Tina. She had been so absent from life and everyone had gotten used to her just sitting on the couch staring out the window. As Sally came down the stairs, she could see the back of everyone sitting on the couch.

"This is weird," she whispered to herself, "So weird."

As she reached them, Jake stood up and embraced his daughter. This was also an agreed upon act between them; time out of her room, a hug and at least some chit chat about the day.

Similarly to Jake, Sally too couldn't make eye contact with Tina. She had become used to her mother not being a part of her life and she resented her. Before the accident, Sally and Tina had been close and Tina had been a very attentive mother. She cared about all the small things like what they all ate and the big things like what was happening at school. Sally had felt abandoned after Justin's death, lost in the grief of the house. At the beginning, she spent a lot of time next door but that soon came to an end when her grandmother returned home. Sally also avoided Kate as much as she could, as Kate began to challenge her state of mind.

Tina sat and listened to her family talk about their days. Well, mostly Emma. She noticed that Jake and Sally both looked like shells of themselves. Jakes posture was humped, he looked like he had lost a lot of weight and he had dark circles under his eyes. Sally looked as if she had gained weight since Tina had last noticed her and that she seemed emotionless.

After a few minutes, Tina excused herself to make some dinner and Emma jumped up to join her. Life seemed a little normal and routine seemed to resume, at least for the few moments while they cooked dinner. Emma set the table as her mother requested while Jake and Sally watched television together. However, Tina did have an ever-growing level of anxiety within. Remembering Justin being around the kitchen, looking for dinner, made a lump form in her throat, but Emma kept bringing her back to reality quickly.

"Dinner is ready, come and get it."

This was a common statement shouted in the Point house for the last ten years or so. Jake started doing it when Sally was about eight years old and Justin was about six to get the kids to come to the dinner table quickly. Emma said it automatically, not even considering that their world was not automatic, it was not normal. It put Tina on edge. *Should we really be doing what we used to do?*

Jake appeared at the doorway to the kitchen and, as he caught a glimpse of Tina, he realised that she was struggling. He shooed Emma out of the kitchen, picked up the meals and took them to the dinner table.

"Come on, Sally. Up at the table, dinner time."

Sally was surprised because they hadn't sat at the dinner table together since the accident. She raised her eyebrows and dragged herself off the couch to sit at the dinner table, waiting for everyone else to sit down. Jake returned to the kitchen to see if he had given Tina enough time to gather herself. She was wandering around, not sure what she should be doing, and Jake could see she was visibly shaking.

"You coming, love?"

Jake hoped that a prompt from him would snap her out of it. It appeared to work because Tina turned, lifted her hand to push the hair off her face and she nodded at Jake.

"Ok, let's go together."

Jake and Tina had hardly spoken since the funeral. Jake had pushed himself into work, doing busy work to keep his mind off the reality of his life. It had also helped him avoid his wife.

Jake was relieved to see his wife interacting with the world. He wanted to support and encourage her as much as he could. As they all sat down and began to eat, Tina could see Justin's seat in her peripheral vision. She was trying with all her might to not enter into the thought that it would be empty forever. Every time her mind wandered, she tried her best to listen to the conversation at the table. Jake was working hard to keep things alive when Emma interrupted him.

"Dad! Dad, you will love this story. I can't believe I forgot to tell you before, but you know Timothy in my class?"

"Yeah, the little fella that threw pinecones at you and Nicole the other day?"

"Yeah, him. Well, today we were sitting on the carpet and Mrs Harper was telling us all about this science thing that we are going to do tomorrow. We're going to grow these seeds or something. Anyway, we were sitting there and Mrs Harper stopped talking for a second and Timothy let the biggest fart you have ever heard go, bigger than your farts Dad!"

Before Emma could finish telling the story Sally, Jake and Tina were laughing. As the laughing got louder, Emma started to make fart noises and lift her leg, mimicking Timothy. Through the laughter, Jake asked, "What did Mrs Harper say, Em?"

"She didn't say anything, she was laughing her head off. Then, before everyone stopped laughing, Timothy got up off the floor and took a bow, like they do when they do stuff on a stage. That made everyone laugh more. It was the funniest thing."

They all had a great laugh. As the laughing at the table died down suddenly, Tina's laugh turned into a sob. After a split second of fun, guilt came crashing down on her. How could she possibly be happy? How could she laugh and enjoy things? She was devastated by the happiness she felt, thinking it was an injustice and dishonour to Justin.

Sally looked at her mother and Justin's empty seat and tears welled in her eyes. Emma saw her mother crying, so she got out of her seat and walked over to her.

She embraced Tina and said, "Mum, it's ok, Justin would have laughed too."

Emma squeezed her mother tightly while Jake reached over and squeezed Sally's hand. Pain filled the room. Something so simple had triggered their pain and even more suffering. Except for Emma, she seemed ok with being happy.

"GRIEF REARS ITS HEAD WHEN YOU LEAST EXPECT IT!"

24

SCOTT - HE FOUND HIS HEART

OUTWARDLY, SCOTT LOOKED LIKE ANY OTHER PERSON working in his garden. Inwardly, he felt like his heart was breaking, helpless and alone. He had found himself out in the yard, cleaning up the mess that had erupted earlier. Scott wondered how Jane was doing inside but knew that by checking on her it would only exacerbate the situation. As he was working, Scott found that his mind wandered to replaying recent events, but each time he noticed he was able to bring himself back to the present. *Breathe in 1, 2, 3, 4, 5, 6... and out 1, 2, 3, 4, 5, 6, 7, 8.*

Unexpectedly, visions of his father's last breath came to mind, of the man that he loved unconditionally and lost when he was far too young. Although he continued to love his father, Jane had replaced him as a person to love in life. *What would he be without someone to love and someone to love him?* Scott kept picturing Jane floating away from him and the subsequent panic caused him to hyperventilate and made his chest ache.

Unconsciously, Scott placed his hand on the centre of his chest and began to rub in a circular motion. As he focused on this, rubbing and breathing, his pain began to dissipate.

I am breathing in 1, 2, 3... I am breathing out 1, 2, 3...

It was soothing and began to comfort him.

Then he began to say out loud, "I am letting it all go, I am breathing in 1, 2, 3... I am breathing out 1, 2, 3... I am letting it all go, they are all just stories."

Scott continued this for a few minutes until he calmed down. He stopped rubbing his chest as the pain had dissipated, but he continued with his conscious breathing.

Breathe in 1, 2, 3, 4, 5, 6... and out 1, 2, 3, 4, 5, 6, 7, 8...

He laid back on the grass and looked up at the sky and the tree branches above him. Scott began to notice the beautiful blue of the sky and the deep green leaves of the trees. They were so beautiful that it distracted him from the counting and he just admired their beauty. He felt a shiver rising up his body, beginning at his feet then flooding every inch of him. It felt wonderful, like someone had wrapped their loving arms around him. He continued to look at the sky and managed to stay present as his chest began to feel warm, almost glowing. Scott knew he wasn't actually glowing, but it felt exactly how he thought glowing would feel if he could imagine it. He had only felt remotely like this once before, the lightness and freedom within him was inexplicable. He recalled the few minutes he spent with Justin alone in the hospital room and the love he felt. This experience was similar to that, but ten times more intense. It was like he was being bathed in pure love, directly from the heavens. He surrendered to the feeling and a smile spread across his face, he recalled the love Justin shared with everyone. He lay there for much longer than he realised relishing in the feeling.

———

THE AISLES of the shopping centre were crowded and Scott began to quickly feel overwhelmed. He didn't normally shop, at most he would push the trolley for Jane while she selected all the items they needed for home. He looked around, hoping to locate some familiar food he could throw in the trolley so he could get out of there. The results of his peaceful, loving experience in the back yard earlier that day began to fade. Finally, he made it back to the car and began to think about going home. Dread rose within him, thoughts of having to deal with his wife and her anger wasn't an appealing prospect. It was 6.05pm and he hesitated to start the car, for the first time in his married life he didn't want to go home. He felt stifled, he couldn't do anything to help Jane and he felt he couldn't live life either. Scott sighed and decided to drive the long way home, passing by Joe's stomping ground and hoping that he would see him. He wasn't sure why he wanted to see his new acquaintance but he just wanted some connection with someone and, maybe, Joe could impart some wisdom.

Scott drove around Joe's neighbourhood aimlessly, not knowing how to find him. Exhaustion finally overcame him and, after looking for Joe for 20 minutes, he decided to head home. The night progressed in silence and Jane only grunted or had one word answers for Scott. She made no eye contact and only came out of the bedroom to grab dinner and take it back to hide. Eating in the bedroom was something neither of them had ever done. This certainly was not how they lived prior to Justin's death. Scott was lost, not knowing what to do. He knew that he couldn't let this behaviour continue, so he loaded a movie on the television and ventured to ask Jane if she wanted to watch it with him.

"Hey, babe, want to watch a movie with me? I've got the new Tom Hanks movie ready to roll."

Jane's eyes didn't even lift off the pages of the book she was reading, "No."

Normally, Jane was a polite, loving and caring person so

Scott was growing concerned at the change in personality, but he didn't want to let the way Jane was talking to him go. Before he could response, Jane looked up at him.

"You can go now".

"Really?" Scott paused and a few seconds passed, "Really, Jane? Is that how you are going to talk to me? We have never spoken to each other like this before. Why would you think that I want you to talk to me like that now?"

Janes head didn't move but her posture slumped and silence fell over the room. Scott walked over and sat on the bed beside her.

"Just because Justin died, doesn't mean we have to stop loving each other. Why are you so angry?"

There was a long pause and Jane rubbed her forehead, she could feel the tension rising. Scott began to feel uneasy. Had he just opened a can of worms he didn't want to deal with? He reached out to wrap an arm around his wife in comfort but, as he did, Jane lashed out and pushed him in the chest.

"Get out, get out, get out!" Jane screamed in Scott's face.

Scott felt his heart begin to ache with the rejection.

"Jane." Scott said in a firm voice he was extremely surprised by Jane's physical outburst.

"What, what do you want from me?" Jane continued to yell.

"I don't want anything from you. I'm just reaching out to you to show you that you're not alone!"

"I am alone. We are all alone. We are all just left behind and forgotten."

"What do you mean?" Scott was puzzled.

Jane sobbed in anger, "In the end we are alone. Your closest loves will leave or let you down and push you away."

"It might feel like that now but that's not the truth. Things will change. You will feel differently as time passes."

"What? That's a stupid thing to say. I can't move forwards and we can't go back to how it was. I can't help anyone, I can't fix things for anyone, I'm useless. Do you realise life has ended for us all? It will never be the same. I hate it. I hate that things have changed; I hate that everyone is broken and I hate that Justin is gone. I loved him like my own son, I loved him, Scott."

Jane's gaze dropped to her lap and tears of frustration flowed.

"I hear you, Jane. Life will never be the same."

Scott rested his hand on Jane's and she didn't push it away. He felt like he might be getting through to her a little.

"Just because Justin is gone, doesn't mean we have to stop loving him," Scott spoke very quietly and hoped his words would soothe her pain. "What you feel is natural. We all want to help, we all want to take the pain away, but you have to allow it to happen naturally for everyone. They have to deal with their own grief in their own way. All this grief you are feeling is the love you have for your family and Justin. You feel like you can't give it anymore, right, but what if I said you can? Just love them all, regardless of how they are feeling. It is no sin to spread unconditional love."

Jane leaned forward, rested her head on Scott's chest and cried. She wrapped her arms around Scott's neck and they embraced warmly. For the first time since Justin death, Scott felt as though Jane was actually beginning to process her grief.

"It's so hard though. I feel cheated and taken for granted," Jane responded, "My heart is aching. It's aching now, like someone has taken a knife and jammed it into my chest."

Scott moved his right hand to Jane's chest and placed it over her heart. He began to breathe deeply and count, hoping that Jane would follow his lead and focus. He hoped that she would find the same relief that he had earlier in the day.

"Only love is real. Breathe in slowly, and out slowly, and think of only that."

Scott guided Jane to lie down, keeping his hand over her heart and counting aloud to her. Eventually she began to relax and, after a time, she finally fell asleep as exhaustion kicked in.

"GRIEF IS LOVE WITH NO PLACE TO GO."

25

PETER & MICHAEL - THAT IS WHAT LOVE IS...

MICHAEL BEGAN A RITUAL OF VISITING PETER AT HIS home. He also continued to go to the skate park, hoping each time that Peter would show up and hang out, except that this never happened. Each day, when Peter didn't show up, Michael would skate a bit and then head over to check on him. Over the last few weeks, Michael felt that some days Peter was softening to their friendship and then other days he was closed and resistant. Michael could feel things that he didn't tell anyone else. He could feel the energy of people's emotions around him, and Peter was prickly. He wasn't sure what was pulling him to keep in contact with Peter, to check on him and persevere with their friendship, but he kept on going back.

On the other hand, Peter had pushed all his mates away. He barely knew Michael so the resentment he felt for everyone else was lost on him. Michael seemed to be a clean slate for Peter, so he felt no pressure to be happy or as he was before Justin's passing. Peter felt Michael had no expectations for him and that is why he allowed their relationship to continue.

Everyday that Michael had stopped in at Peter's house, he had found him lying on his bed. One particular day, Michael knocked on the door and, to his great surprise. Peter opened it.

"Yo, hey," Peter greeted him.

"Hey," Michael was surprised.

"Come in. You want a sandwich? I'm just getting something to eat."

Michael didn't know what to say but wanted to encourage Peter's interaction with him. Michael noticed how much weight Peter had lost over the past months and how, every time they had interacted, he had to push the conversation. This was a big change that he wanted to embrace, so he accepted the sandwich offer.

The boys ate and watched the television which was a major step forwards in their friendship; in the past, they had mostly sat in silence. At first, it had made Michael feel incredibly uncomfortable, but he was so driven to keep up the relationship that he had accepted it for what it was. However, the shift to a normal interaction made him feel uneasy. They didn't speak, but just sat together munching on their sandwiches and watching some mindless trash on the television.

The boys had been hanging for at least an hour when Natalie came rushing in from the back door. She was wrestling with shopping bags and gave a shout, "Boys, are you there? Can you help?"

The 'boys' she was referring to were Peter and her husband, James.

"Hey, boys?"

She could hear that the television was on, an unusual occurrence recently, so she poked her head around the corner of the lounge room and was surprised to see Peter and Michael. Michael had turned in the direction of her voice.

"You two will do, come and help me with the groceries."

Peter had been very unhelpful and mostly ignored his mother and father since Justin's death and he appeared to be ignoring her now. Michael, however, jumped to his feet to help. Peter didn't move.

"Yo, mate, come on."

Peter looked up.

"Come on and help your mum."

Peter had become desensitised to his mother because she was always pushing him to return to life.

"Are you coming?" Michael encouraged Peter as he walked towards the kitchen to see exactly what help Natalie needed.

As Michael walked past him, Peter finally got to his feet and followed Michael into the kitchen.

"Hey, boys!"

Natalie's eyes were cemented on Peter, astounded by his presence. She was even overjoyed by the food crumbs on the kitchen bench, knowing that Peter would be the only one to leave such a mess. Natalie had been very worried about Peter's weight loss and loss of appetite. Actually, she had been worried about every aspect of him. She was puzzled as to why Michael continued to visit her son but was so grateful that he did.

"The boot is full. Could you bring all the stuff in? I'll unpack."

The boys went back and forth to the car, hauling the groceries in without a word spoken to each other, while Natalie flittered around the kitchen from cupboard to cupboard putting all the groceries away.

"Thanks, boys."

Natalie was overjoyed by this event as Peter and Michael returned to the couch. This was the first time since Justin's death that Peter had done anything around the house. Before life was turned upside down, Peter had chores to do and there were rules; how many hours of TV he could watch, homework was to be done after dinner, when he had to be home if he was going out. He also had to work for pocket money. However, since the accident, all he had done was go to school, occasionally work and lay on his bed. Even his personal hygiene had taken a downward spiral. He didn't watch TV, he barely ate and didn't really speak to anyone. Michael seemed to be the only interaction with the real world he permitted.

James opened his office door and could hear the television on, his eyebrows furrowed. The house had been so quite since the accident, unnervingly quiet. In the past, he often had to come out of his office while he was trying to work and quieten the visitors down. On this day, however, he was intrigued. As he walked into the lounge, he saw the back of two boys' heads and was a little shocked as he reorientated himself. It wasn't Justin, he recognised Peters head but knew it couldn't be Justin. He was just so used to seeing and having Justin around the house. Michael had met James but they had barely spoken.

"Hey, boys."

James was keen to see who his son was spending time with. Michael swung around and greeted James but Peter didn't flinch. James headed straight for the kitchen.

Michael felt uneasy. He hadn't really interacted with Peter's family; he had only been greeted at the door and said a quick goodbye if he saw anyone on his way out. His life had been rather solitary since his father's death. His only interaction with his mother was limited to checking if she was alive and taking her drunken abuse, if she wasn't in a drunken coma. He had friends but he kept them at arm's length because he didn't want to explain his family situation. Peter didn't ask any questions about his home life and Michael liked the company.

"Hey, boys," Natalie poked her head out of the kitchen. "Do you want to stay for dinner Michael?"

Natalie wanted to encourage Michael and Peter to spend time together. Peter's eyes didn't leave the television screen.

Michael didn't have anything to go home to, no one cared if he was there or not. He came and went as he pleased and spent most of his time alone in his room. He had nothing to lose.

"Sure," he responded.

The boys chatted and watched the television. James kept looking in on them, checking to see if what he thought was happening was really happening. He had tried and tried to reach Peter over the last few months, without any result. It was like a pressure had been lifted from him, seeing Peter and Michael together. Someone had reached Peter and he thanked God for it.

Peter hadn't eaten with the family for months. Natalie had taken his meals to his bedroom because he had simply refused to come to the dinner table. She didn't want to push it that evening, so she delivered the boys' food to them in the lounge.

As James and Natalie prepared the dinner table for the rest of the family, Kate came bursting through the front door.

"Sorry, Mum!" She yelled, "I'm here, I got caught at the library."

Kate had digested Justin's death better than anyone around her. She saw the pain her family was in but she had a different outlook on things. Kate was in her second year of studying psychology and had taken a special interest in grief. Preparation, if you will, for what was unfolding in her life. She had a tight relationship with both Peter and Justin. Her own hurt was deep from losing Justin, but she was coping with it in a healthy way. Kate dumped her bag on the table and walked over to the boys.

"Hey, Michael"

She bent down and wrapped her arms around Peter so that their cheeks touched, relieved to see her brother out of his room.

"Hey, bro."

Peter actually responded to greet her which was a huge step forward for him. Kate and Michael acknowledged one another. They had met on a few occasions at the house but they hadn't really had a decent conversation.

Michael watched the interaction between Kate and her parents intently. Kate wrapped her arms around her mum as soon as she saw her. Their embrace was heartfelt and Michael observed the love between them. He could feel it.

"Hey, sweetheart," James said as he also turned to hug his daughter.

"Hey, Dad, how was your day? Another exciting day in the world of engineering?"

Kate was being facetious, she thought that her Dad had the most boring job in the world.

"Actually, it was."

Their embrace ended but Michael couldn't take his eyes off them. For so long he had longed for love and for someone to take an interest in him, seeing that it was possible gave him hope.

Peter pushed his food around his plate, he had no appetite, while Michael ate every bite. Michael watched as Kate and her parents chatted about their day at the dinner table and longed for the familiarity and connection he saw.

As the meal ended at the table, Natalie began clearing the dishes and Michael collected both his and Peter's plates and took them into the kitchen. He wanted to help because he had really appreciated the meal. James and Kate continued to chat as Natalie went into the kitchen to begin to clean up.

"Thanks so much for dinner."

"That's my pleasure."

Natalie turned and looked at Michael. She was so grateful for the boy's friendship with her son. She couldn't help herself as she reached out and wrapped her arms around Michael in a warm embrace.

"Thank you, mate, thank you so much."

Her chest tightened as she fought back the tears. He was surprised by the embrace but he closed his eyes and drunk in every bit of the physical and emotional connection. He hugged Natalie right back. After a few seconds, Michael realised he was confused by her gratitude. Natalie had fed him and welcomed him into her home, yet she was thanking him.

"Thank you for what?"

"For spending time with Peter when no one else could."

Michael left it at that. He didn't think he deserved the thanks because he hadn't thought what he was doing was anything special. They were still in the embrace when Kate walked into the kitchen to help with the clearing up.

"Oh my gosh, Mum! You can't help yourself. Sorry, Michael, she has a problem on the hugging front. You know she loves to spread the love."

Natalie let go of Michael hesitantly and he smiled when he saw the tears in Natalie's eyes. Suddenly, he found himself being hugged by Kate.

"I may as well get in on this, too."

Kate knew why Natalie was hugging Michael, she knew he was helping Peter in a way no one else could. Kate had felt so hopeless and helpless with regard to her brother's situation. She had tried to get him to open up and return to normality, but nothing she did helped. Seeing Peter downstairs watching television was a big deal.

James entered the kitchen and found Kate and Michael in each other's arms. Michael had a grin from ear to ear; he hadn't felt love like this for a long time and was relishing in every second of it. He really didn't understand why he was being showered with gratitude.

"What are you two doing?" James walked over and wrapped his arms around them both in a bear hug, "I feel left out, I need to get me some hugging too!"

Michael began to laugh as he was overwhelmed by the physical contact and the affection. James finally let go.

"Sorry, we are a weird bunch, aren't we? I'm betting Natalie started this."

The family had no idea what a special gift they had just given Michael, they were only aware of the effect Michael was having on Peter. When the embrace finally ended, Michael began to help clean up the kitchen but Natalie stopped him.

"You're alright, mate, we can do this."

"Are you sure? I can help, you cooked dinner."

"I am so sure," Natalie reassured Michael as she much preferred the idea of him spending time with Peter.

Peter remained staring at the television with no idea of what was happening in his kitchen. He was completely distracted from his reality, his loss, his sadness, his anger and his pain. This was something he had been unable to do since Justin's death. Somehow Michael was helping him cope, but he didn't realise the magnitude of it.

After a short while, Michael skated home with a smile on his face. He had enjoyed being in Peter's home, being part of the warmth and friendliness of his family. He didn't even dread going home for once. When he arrived at his house, the television was blaring and his mother was asleep on the couch, beer bottles surrounding her. He covered her with a blanket, turned off the television and went to his room where threw himself on the bed. Michael was still smiling and relishing in the evening at Peter's. He had longed for love and connection with someone for a while but didn't realise just how much until that night. *So that is what love is, I remember now.*

"THE POWER OF LOVE…"

26

EMMA - HOW IS SHE COPING?

Jake was putting Emma to bed, but he felt unsettled. Laughing at dinner and sitting at their dining table had shocked Jake into realising the gravity of what his family had lost; their wholeness and connection to each other. It was like no one knew how to be, how to act, how to behave or what would be accepted by everyone else. Were they allowed to be happy? Were they able to move forward? Or did they have to stay in misery and pain?

Jake tucked Emma into bed, making sure her blankets were straight and checking that she would be warm throughout the night. He was kneeling beside her bed when Emma placed a hand either side of his face.

"Dad..." Emma made direct eye contact with him.

Jake didn't say anything.

"Dad?" Emma repeated.

"Yes, Bub?"

"I want to tell you a secret."

"Oh, really?"

Jake was slightly amused and got closer to Emma as if she was about to whisper to him.

"But you have to promise to keep it a secret, a real secret, you can't tell anyone."

"Why so much secrecy, Missy?"

"I don't know, it just seems like we shouldn't tell everyone."

"Ok, promise I won't tell anyone."

Jake was deliberately being a bit silly and childish to compliment Emma's seriousness.

"Are you ready to hear this?" She paused, "I've been talking with Justin."

Jake was taken aback by Emma's words. Emma watched her father for his reaction but he remained silent. She paused for a few seconds but then she continued as she couldn't hold it in any longer.

"He told me that he was happy and felt incredible love in heaven. When he was talking to me, I felt so good because I knew he was telling the truth. I know Justin would never lie about something so important. He said everyone is so happy and well looked after there. He also said there was so much fun there in heaven and that the care and peace they all shared was bigger than planet earth."

Jake could barely keep up with what his youngest daughter was telling him.

"Hang on, hang on, Em. Say that all again. You were talking to Justin? How were you talking to Justin?"

"Dad, stay calm. I knew I shouldn't have told you. You're freaking out, aren't you?" Emma had a look of regret on her face.

"No, I'm not freaking out, that was just a lot of information. Let's just go slow."

Jake wanted to hear every detail, true or not, because in that moment, when Emma was talking about him, he felt close to Justin. Since his death, everybody had been hesitant to talk about Justin, worrying they would upset things, so it was almost refreshing to have this conversation. Whether it was true or not, he wanted to hear every detail of what Emma had to say.

"So, tell me, Emma, how and when did you talk to Justin?"

"Well," Emma wavered, "It was when I was asleep... but it felt like I was awake."

"Could you touch him?" Jake questioned her. He wanted to see how far Emma believed this was real.

"Dad, he was a spirit or something, maybe a ghost, but not in the scary way. He held my hand and we walked around heaven."

Jake raised his eyebrows and assumed that Emma had had a vivid dream about Justin. Emma began to whisper, "Dad he said to tell you that he's fine. He loves you and Mum so much, he will always love you. He also said don't be sad that he is gone, it was his time and we will all meet again."

Jake was silent, drinking in every word that came from Emma's lips. He stared at Emma as a wave of relief rippled through his body, beginning at his toes and ending at the tip of his fingers. What she had said brought him some peace, it felt like truth.

"Dad? Dad?" Emma waved her fingers in front of Jake's face.

"Sorry Em," Jake shook his head.

"Dad, did you hear me?"

"Yes, yes, I heard every word, Little Miss."

"Do you believe me? If you were me and you got to walk around heaven with Justin, you would believe me. Justin is ok. Actually, he's great. He wants you to be ok and great too. Don't you see? We have to be happy. Death is sad but Justin will never be gone, he lives with us every day. Dad, do you believe me?"

Emma still had her hands on either side of Jake's face.

He hesitated then answered, "Of course I believe you, Em. You must feel so lucky that Justin visited you."

"Well, actually, he comes all the time. He comes and visits you too, but he said you can't see or hear him. But I always see him."

"He tries to visit me, you say?"

"Yeah, he sure does, but like I said you are not ready."

Jake nodded at Emma. He was secretly longing for this all to be real, he would give anything to talk to his boy.

Jake quickly grabbed Emma in a warm and loving embrace, "I'm glad you were ready, Bub."

"Oh, Dad, when Justin visits me it feels like I'm floating. It feels so good and I am so happy."

"You make me so happy, Emma."

"Ok, now I've finally told you what Justin asked me to, can we read my book?"

She threw herself back on the bed like her admission to Jake was a tiny and insignificant thing. She didn't know the magnitude of peace Jake felt from it all.

"Here, Dad, let's read this one."

She handed him a book they had read at least fifty times. Jake smiled, lay down beside his daughter and began to read. Love welled up inside him, he had never felt so much love.

When he closed Emma's door, after lots of kisses and cuddles, Jake realised he finally had the answer to a question he had been asking himself for weeks, *How was Emma ok with everything going on?* He couldn't put it into words, so he simply smiled to himself and continued down the hall.

"DEATH IS NOTHING TO FEAR,
IT IS ONLY ANOTHER
DIMENSION."

- DR. WAYNE DYER

27

JAKE – GRIEF IS THE PRICE YOU PAY FOR LOVE?

Jake's attention was drawn to the door of Justin's bedroom. Instead of turning and walking down the stairs, he walked over and opened the door. The darkness that confronted him was unsettling. Jake had no reason to go into Justin's room since the accident, he wasn't sure why he was there. Listening to Emma talk about Justin, really made Jake realise how much he missed his son; their banter and fun, their jokes and pranks.

He closed the door behind him and walked over to the bed to sit down. A streetlight shone through the window, lighting the room enough so that Jake could see. Memories of Justin wandered through his mind. His body felt heavy and weighed down, he was tired and worn down by his life situation. He had allowed work to consume his thoughts during the day and, when he had been home, he had successfully distracted himself with the girls and household chores. He knew it was getting the better of him because he was having trouble sleeping and sadness plagued his nights. He had always had a drink or two at night with Tina, just a light beer, but he had taken to drinking heavily when everyone had gone to bed. He was reluctant to admit that he needed alcohol to get any sleep. It helped him get to sleep initially, but he would wake after a few hours. He had justifed the drinking by telling himself that a few hours sleep was better than no sleep at all. Jake was becoming so anxious at night that, about a week ago, he thought that he had been having a heart attack and he was happy about it. He had hoped to die.

Jake's drinking had begun to worry him. His secrecy about it and how, in the evenings, he was longing for everyone else to go to bed so he could begin his ritual of escaping his mind, was reason for concern. Jake had never been the best sleeper but, since the accident, things were getting out of hand. The worst part was that he didn't know who to turn to or how to take control of the situation. Every morning, he was ashamed of himself, embarrassed and he would tell himself that he wouldn't do it again. Except, when the night came and his thoughts were too much to bear, he would go out to the car where he had been hiding a bottle of bourbon and the cycle would begin again.

That night, he sat down on Justin's bed and recognised the love he felt for his children, noticing Justin's things and remembering little stories about them all. His football was sitting on his desk which reminded Jake that Justin's priority certainly hadn't been schoolwork. There was a photo of Justin and Peter from about eight years ago, swinging upside down in big gum tree in the backyard. Jake remembered that day clearly; he had been trying to mow the lawn and rake the leaves but the boys had been running around like crazy, getting in the way. It was frustrating but, deep down, he had loved seeing them being silly and having fun. Remembering happy memories of Justin was helping Jake to see things differently. He realised that Justin's main purpose in life had been to have fun and he had managed to fit so much into each day. Jake had tried, on many occasions, to counsel him to slow down a bit and to think things through before he acted, but it had had no effect. Jake thought about how much Justin really had loved life. *Justin and his antics,* he thought.

Jake lifted his hand up to his heart and felt a glow. He closed his eyes and relished in the feeling; he couldn't remember the last time he felt any sort of lightness within himself. He was overwhelmed and amazed that he could feel this way after so many months of despair. Fear of being sad had stopped him of thinking of Justin. He had been barely holding himself together, so he had deliberately blocked Justin from his mind and his heart, as much he could.

At least half an hour passed before Jake left Justin's room. As he opened the door to leave, Sally was walking towards the bathroom and saw him. They both felt a little uncomfortable and Jake didn't know what to say. It was like he had been caught doing something he shouldn't. Sally had a strange look on her face.

"Hi, Sal," Jake finally got out.

In secrecy, Sally had been spending a lot of time in Justin's room. Some nights she even fell asleep in there. She felt a little violated that her dad had been in Justin's room without her knowing. She kept walking to the bathroom, trying not to show her surprise. In reality, she didn't want anyone to touch anything in his room or even look at his stuff. It comforted her to think that she was the only one that would go in there.

Jake decided that the encounter had been bizarre so he headed into Sally's room and waited for her to return so that he could talk to her. It wasn't long before Sally walked into her bedroom to find her father sitting on her bed. The sight of Jake stopped Sally in her tracks. Her family had mostly gone their separate ways since Justin's death when, before, everyone had been very open and sociable. They used to go in each other's bedrooms all the time, watch TV together and they often went out together. Things were certainly very different since the accident and seeing someone, other than Emma, in her room was weird.

"What's up, Dad? What are you doing in here?"

"I just wanted to talk to you, see what you are up to."

Sally wasn't angry or sad, she wasn't irritated or frustrated, she was just numb. Since Justin's death, she had become a recluse, avoiding the world and every single person in it. She tolerated Emma but she had cut everyone else out of her life. She had become sick of everyone's sympathetic faces and having to endure the same stupid questions, people asking her if she was ok. Most of all, she was confused about how she should behave, act or be without her brother. As a result, she had simply hidden herself away, not allowing anyone to get close to her and doing her best to avoid interaction with the world. Yet, here her dad was, in her room, probing her and wanting to talk.

"Am I in your way?"

Jake jumped to his feet, he could sense the tension in the room building and they were clearly both feeling uncomfortable. Jake didn't know what to say to Sally, so he started with an apology.

"I'm sorry things have been pretty strange around here, Sal. I think we are all struggling."

Sally was silent but she walked over to sit on the bed, her eyes remaining on the floor the whole time. The silence was deafening so Jake continued, "Are you ok?"

Sally wanted to scream in her father's face but, instead, she remained silent and continued to stare at the floor. Jake sat beside Sally on the bed and wrapped one arm around her, pulling her close to him.

"You know I love you hey, Sal? So much more than you know."

Sally didn't say anything, she wasn't letting anyone in.

————

Jake found himself, alone, in front of the television when everyone else went to bed. He contemplated having a drink, but it was only a fleeting thought. He continued to flick through the commercial television channels. He paused on one channel to hear the words, "Better to have loved and lost, than to never have loved at all."

Everything around him went faint as he digested these words. He had fought so hard to not think of Justin since the accident, but he had finally stopped fighting and surrendered to the happiness that his son had brought into his life. Memories flowed and the external world was washed away as a smile came over his face and his heart grew warm.

About 20 minutes passed before Jake came back to reality and the gravity of his loss became clear. His life would never be the same and his relationship with the world had shifted. He was a light-hearted man and had created a good life for himself and his family, but now he was losing his faith in what it had all been for. He felt his energy shift and looked at the clock, wondering how he would get through the night. In that moment, the house was quiet and he felt lonely. His body was fatigued and felt heavy, so he lay down on the lounge and closed his eyes. He purposely left the television on so that he didn't feel so alone.

In the early hours of the morning, Jake woke in a cold sweat. He had been having a reoccurring dream that he was falling but never reached anywhere. He sat straight up and looked around, trying to work out where he was. His breathing was short and laboured and beads of sweat began to run down his face. Anxiety and panic rose within him.

The unsettled energy made him stand up and race to the kitchen. Jake had no idea what he was looking for, but he switched on the light and scanned the kitchen. He leant on the counter, not knowing what to do with himself. The panic was rising as his mind flickered between worries; his girls, the bills, Tina, life without the normality he had appreciated since he got married, how he could ever have a happy life again, why restful sleep evaded him. The thoughts kept rolling in and he had no control over them.

Before he knew it, Jake was in the garage, looking for the only thing he had found that could dull his thoughts. The bourbon was hidden under the passenger side seat of his car. He cracked the lid and began to gulp it down.

"YOUR MIND CAN TORTURE YOU OR NURTURE YOU, IT IS YOUR CHOICE!"

28

TINA – WAKING UP FROM NOWHERE

Tina had taken herself to bed and left Jake to settle Emma, she was spent and felt overwhelmed by her day. As she stood in the shower and the water ran over her body, Tina felt unsettled. Showering was something she ordinarily loved to do but, to her recollection, she couldn't remember when she last took a shower. Her mind traced back over the last few months but she couldn't recall much, except what a terrible person she had been that day. Tina had experienced an awakening, she had gone from her zombie-like being to checking back into reality, but it had been a very rough ride.

Tina recapped her day in her mind and recalled the moment that had snapped her out of the protective cocoon she had created for herself.

———

Earlier in the day, the doorbell had rung and Tina had simply sat there and listened to it. After a brief pause, the visitor rang the bell again in an aggressive manor with three sharp rings. Tina ignored it, again, telling herself that whoever was at the door would go away. Then, the doorbell went again with the added extra of someone banging on the door. She heard the door handle rattle and someone shout out.

"I know you're in there, Tina! Get your arse off that lounge chair and come and let me in!"

Bang, bang! Bang, bang! Bang, bang! The doorbell sounded again.

"Tina, I am not going anywhere."

More banging on the door and ringing of the bell. This went on for a good few minutes before it got the better of Tina and she snapped. She marched over to the front door and threw it open with all her might.

"Finally, Tina, I thought you would never come." Natalie was red faced and flustered.

"What the hell are you doing, Natalie? Banging and ringing like that, what is the matter with you?" Tina was visibly annoyed.

"I am not apologising, Tina."

Natalie pushed through Tina to enter the house and ordered her friend to take a seat. Natalie had been incredibly patient and comforting for Tina, they were the best of friends and had seen a lot of life together, but this had been building for a while and things had to change.

"What is wrong with you, Natalie? You are so worked up."

This was the most conversation Tina had had in months.

"I am worked up, I am. I've been stewing over what I have to say for a few weeks now and I have to say it because things have got to change."

Natalie had witnessed her very bright, loving and intelligent friend turn into a shell of herself. No matter how much she prodded her, or what she said, she couldn't connect or even have a meaningful conversation with Tina. She was ignoring her girls and her husband and Natalie was watching Tina's family grow further and further apart and become disconnected. She had watched as Jane tried to manage the situation but had seen that she was drowning and things were not getting any better.

That day, Natalie had been watching out the window for Jane to leave the house so she could get some time alone with Tina. Finally, after hours of peeping through the window, she saw Scott pick Jane up and leave Tina behind. As soon as she saw this, Natalie marched over to the Point residence to try and crack the hard outer shell Tina had placed around herself.

"Now, listen to me, Tina. It has been months since Justin passed away and I don't think you have left the house or moved off that couch. You have ignored your girls and neglected Jake and, on top of all that, you have allowed Jane to shoulder the responsibility of your entire life. I can't sit back anymore, you need to reengage," she paused for a breath. "Everyone is pandering to your every move so that we don't upset you."

Tina stared at Natalie as her eyebrows furrowed and her lips pursed, anger was beginning to steam up inside her.

"Can you at least change one thing about what you are doing? Sitting on the couch and staring out the window isn't healing!"

Tina began to feel anger burning in the pit of her stomach. Natalie was still talking at her but she was seething and didn't hear a word that was being said.

"Are you even listening to me, Tina?" Tears began to run down Natalie's face, "I don't know what to do anymore. What is it you want from me? How can I help you move forward? This is killing both our families... It's killing me to watch this, there has to be some movement."

Natalie slumped down in the chair opposite Tina. She thought that Tina hadn't been listening. Tina looked at her broken friend, the anger swirled inside her and she exploded.

"What the hell do you want me to do, Natalie? Scream and

shout? Cry and beg for Justin's return to me?" She yelled at Natalie, "What do you expect me to do? To just get on with my life like Justin's death doesn't matter? Do you know my son is dead? Do you? He's dead, he is never coming back, and you want me to get on with living? How the hell do I do that? It's ok for you, you have your own kids so you don't have to work life out without him. What the hell am I supposed to do? How dare you come in here and tell me what to do. What gives you the right?" Tina's face was red and sweaty, she was wild with anger.

"Don't you think I am sad? Don't you think I am trying to work out how to live through this? Justin was like a second son to me, I loved him with all my heart and soul." Natalie's voice was hard and she glared at Tina, "Our lives have been thrown into despair."

"What are you saying, that because you are out of your house you're grieving better than me?"

"All I am saying is, I understand a little of what you are going through. I feel pain, so much pain," Natalie became distraught with tears and sadness, "I feel like I just need to slap you to wake you up from your current state!"

"Go on then, Natalie, Slap me, slap the crap out of me! Slap me slap me! You don't have the balls and you have no idea what I am going through, or how I am feeling. You are pathetic thinking that your opinion or intervention here means anything to me. Get out of my house. I hate you for thinking I need to be different. Get out, get out!"

Silence fell over the room. It was not how Natalie thought the conversation would go. With tears of frustration dripping down Natalie's face, she got up and gently shook her head. As she did so, Tina also got up and they were face to face.

"You meant nothing to Justin, absolutely nothing," Tina scowled, the hate was palpable in the room.

With that comment, Natalie lifted her hand and slapped her best friend across the face. Tina's face turned away and Natalie cried harder, she couldn't believe what she had done.

"Just get out, Natalie."

Tina found herself sitting back in the same spot she had been sitting for the last few months, staring out of the window. She was feeling depleted and shocked by what had just happened. Her hand rested on her cheek, feeling the throbbing from the slap. She didn't recognise the pain from the slap but she did recognise the pain in her heart. She had been numb for so long, numb from the shock, or maybe overwhelmed from the extraordinary pain from her loss. She sat there, fuming with anger that someone would come in here and tell her she wasn't moving on, that she was neglecting her family. She stewed and stewed on the anger.

After a time, and for the first time in months, Tina began to notice the room around her. Her house appeared perfect, clean, and everything was in its place. She wondered how it got to be like that. The last thing she remembered was the mess that was left across the room after they took Justin's body away. Tina looked down at her hands and inspected her fingernails, they were long and unkept. She took note of her clothes and realised that she didn't remember putting them on. She slowly, although reluctantly, realised that Natalie had been speaking the truth. A feeling of unrest began to rumble in her gut as she recalled what she had said to Natalie. Terrible, hurtful things that she had meant, purely from the pain of hearing the truth. She got up and walked around the lounge room, looking at all of the photos of her family, realising that Natalie, James, Peter, Kate, Jane and Scott were in a significant portion of them. The smiles and the love she saw between them all made what she had said and done even more painful. She knew that she had to go and speak to Natalie and explain.

Tina knocked on Natalie's door and waited patiently. Finally, Natalie opened the door and, as soon as she did, Tina wrapped her arms around her friend in a desperate embrace to thank her and apologise without words. Natalie was still sobbing from their last encounter. Tina stepped back, took Natalie's hands in hers and gave her the slightest smile. She turned and left Natalie standing in the doorway. Tina couldn't speak or explain properly but she did know that she wanted to apologise.

> *"Sometimes it takes a lot of love to reach out to someone in an honest way.*
>
> *Love is not just about being kind, it is about truth and that can be painful."*

THE WATER WAS STILL RUNNING down Tina's back. She was exhausted and longed for peace. She desired forgiveness from Natalie and Jane; she knew that she had been unjust in her reactions to them and was just lashing out from the pain she felt. She was too ashamed to talk to anyone about it or to even repeat what she had said and done. As such, the incidents were never spoken of again.

"SOMETIMES IT TAKES A LOT OF LOVE TO REACH OUT TO SOMEONE IN AN HONEST WAY.

LOVE IS NOT JUST ABOUT BEING KIND, IT IS ABOUT TRUTH AND THAT CAN BE PAINFUL."

29

TINA & NATALIE – MOVING FORWARD

Tina had risen early, she was sick of lying in bed, tossing and turning, plagued by her sadness and memories. She found her husband asleep on the couch in his work clothes - a common occurrence that Tina had barely noticed. It wasn't something she had the mental capacity to digest. Before losing Justin, Tina and Jake were mostly happy. No marriage is perfect, but they did care about each other deeply. Since their loss, they had hardly spoken and had absolutely no idea how the other was doing, it was like they only had the capacity for their own pain. Tina had been in her cocoon and Jake was just getting through life, busying himself as much as he could.

The sun was beginning to rise and Tina decided to make a cup of tea, sit on the front steps and watch the day break. Tina and Jake had a pretty house and a lovely sunrise view over the surrounding houses. She had always been an early riser and loved the peace and stillness the early morning brought with it. The cup was warm in her hands, the air was crisp and the sun was just peeping out from the horizon which made a spectacular scene. She pulled her dressing gown up around her neck with one hand, appreciating the warmth it gave her, and sipped her tea, loving how it was warming her from the inside out. Life felt good for a few seconds. Staying in the bliss of the present felt good for Tina because she was in awe of the beauty that was being created in front of her. Nothing else entered her mind. Admiration for the beauty and the light filled her; she thought how if she was to die in that moment, she would die happy.

However, the thought of death floating across her mind reignited her sadness and her stomach dropped as if she was plummeting from a big height on a roller coaster. The guilt of not feeling sad for those few moments plagued her.

How could I possibly be happy? How could I possibly let Justin out of my thoughts?

Her mind closed to the world in front of her as recollections of the trauma of the last few months rose up and the pain began to swirl, again. Tears of sadness built in her eyes but, as she blinked them away, she noticed her garden and how the sun shone on it; it was beautiful. The more she appreciated the garden and how it looked, the more her sadness melted away and, eventually, a tiny little grin even reached her face. A memory of Justin trying to help her plant a garden bed sprung to mind. For a spilt second, it was a happy memory, but then it turned to a tragedy. Tragedy that he was gone. She started crying at this memory, holding her hand over her mouth to stop her verbal distress from escaping.

To her great surprise, Tina felt a warm embrace as someone sat down next to her on the top step. She opened her eyes with a fright and saw it was Natalie. Natalie had walked out of her front door to head off for her morning walk and spotted Tina sitting on the step. She decided to test the water after yesterday's train wreck and join her friend.

"What am I going to do, Natalie? What am I going to do?"

Tina rested her head on Natalie's shoulder. Natalie was lost for words. She had found the last few months incredibly hard but had been living by the mantra, *just live one minute at a time, one hour at a time, one day at a time.*

"There is no magic answer, my love, one foot in front of the other."

Tina had a good sob in the arms of someone she loved and felt safe with. The pain from their encounter yesterday was healed.

Amazingly, Tina had learnt the power of being present in the moment, but would she recognise its power?

"ONLY LOVE IS REAL..."

30

TINA & JANE - UNSPOKEN FORGIVENESS

Guilt was getting to Tina because, as time went on, she heard and saw all that Jane had done for her family since the accident. Stories Emma told of her aunt and how her cupboards and laundry were arranged were all clues of how much her sister had stepped up. After their argument, Tina didn't know where to start with asking Jane for forgiveness. Every time she thought of her sister, she felt ashamed of herself. She knew Jane would be hurt but she just didn't know where to start.

Jake walked in the back door as Tina was contemplating her woes at the kitchen sink.

"Hey," Jake greeted Tina. He was startled by Tina being in the kitchen but he continued, "James rang and invited us over to a BBQ at theirs this afternoon. Natalie's got everything under control, we just have to show up at 4.30."

"Oh, ok," Tina responded, not really thinking about what Jake had said.

It was currently 4pm so Tina didn't have a lot of time to find a decent excuse why not to go. The thought of going next door without her whole family was anxiety provoking. She immediately became unsettled at the thought.

Later that day, Tina found herself settling in the neighbours' back yard. As she looked around, she could see everyone was looking uncomfortable. The doorbell rang and Peter went to answer it, while everyone else continued to make small talk. Scott and Jane then walked into the back yard, something common pre-Justin's death, but certainly not something that Tina was expecting. Similarly, Jane wasn't expecting to see her sister there, engaging with the outside world. Tina grinned at Jane as a peace offering, but Jane refused to make eye contact. Jane was hurt but Tina knew she deserved the rejection after what she had done. Tina wondered if she had pushed their relationship too far.

After dinner, Tina followed Jane into the kitchen to help wash up. It was just the two of them but Tina was lost for words and an uncomfortable silence began to grow.

Jane broke the ice, "How did Emma do with her science experiment?"

Tina searched her mind to recall what Jane was talking about; she wanted to connect with Jane, even if only on a superficial level.

"Yeah, good, she said hers sprouted but died the next day."

"Oh ok, she was pretty excited about the whole thing."

Jane decided to let things go and relax into Tina's company, she always did because she hated conflict and was a forgiving person. The sisters chit-chatted about everything except their grief and the altercation they had had.

Forgiveness, on Jane's part, happened without an apology or explanation. She had been brutally wounded by her sister but knew she had to let it go, she had to let her sister off the hook. She also had to stop torturing herself. As the conversation went on and they both relaxed into it, a weight lifted from both of their shoulders.

Tina turned to her sister, "I am so sorry, you have done so

much for us," she paused and their eyes locked. "Thank you, little sister."

Forgiveness flooded Jane's heart as she let it all go. The sisters embraced each other; all was forgiven.

"HOLD NO GRUDGES AND
PRACTICE FORGIVENESS.
THIS IS THE KEY TO
HAVING PEACE IN ALL
YOUR RELATIONSHIPS."

- DR WAYNE DYER

31

JANE - SHE THOUGHT SHE WAS DOING OKAY

Jane had been back at work for a week and was struggling. She struggled with life moving forward, she struggled with her exhaustion, she struggled with the work she did. Jane was successful in her job role, she was highly valued and she did believe that her job had purpose, but her heart ached. At every turn, she was reminded of the sadness that was swallowing her family and herself up. She wasn't coping.

Her colleague and friend, Lori, had been keeping a close eye on Jane, knowing that she was fragile. It only took Lori to walk up to her desk and Jane lost her composure, she began to silently cry. Lori walked around the desk, took hold of Jane and walked her into the conference room where she shut the door behind them. Lori wrapped her arms around Jane and clung on.

"I thought I was ready for this, for work, but I don't think I am. Actually, I don't think I will ever be ready for this job, not anymore."

"I understand."

Lori was sad for Jane and felt empathetic to the situation her friend found herself in. She felt like she knew Justin herself because Jane's family was often a common topic of conversation between them. Lori worked hard to console Jane and, by the end of the conversation, it was decided that Jane would go home and take a break for a few weeks. Jane hadn't processed the accident and her grief fully, so Lori thought that more time out of the office would help.

Jane left work and, as she reached the car, she rang Scott.

"Hey," Scott answered.

Jane was silent, she couldn't talk because she was too upset.

"Honey, are you ok?" Scott had a hint of panic in his voice, "Where are you, Jane?"

"In the car," she sobbed.

"What are you doing?"

"I don't know. Going home, I suppose."

"But it's 11.45... Aren't you supposed to be at work?"

"I can't do it, work I mean, so I'm going home. Is that alright?"

"Of course, that's ok. Yes, go home."

Scott knew that Jane hadn't been ready for work but there had been no convincing her.

"I don't know what to do, Scott. I can't seem to do what I did before."

"It's ok, you don't have to know right now. Just go home and I will meet you there for lunch."

Jane spent the next few days at home, working hard to quieten her mind from all the grief and despair around her. She was fragile; anything that caught her off guard which reminded her of Justin brought her to tears. She walked and gardened often. She went about her daily activities slowly with routine, but a reoccurring thought kept creeping into her head, Am I happy? Do I love life? This made her uneasy. She had avoided herself for months, keeping busy with Tina and her family. Over the last few years, it was a thought that had hounded her but she had reassured herself it would be fine, work was good enough and life was good enough.

Preceding Justin's death, she had spoken to Scott about her unsettled feelings which he had reciprocated, but they seemed to be able to placate each other that things would be alright. Years had passed by where Jane had thought about a shift of career and about their decision not to have children. She wasn't unhappy, but she wasn't happy. Justin's death had pushed all these thoughts and feeling aside but, since returning to work, they had been awakened and were troubling her.

———

Scott walked into the house wondering what he would find; would his wife be in denial about their situation, an emotional wreck or happy and pottering around? He found Tina sitting on their back deck, staring at the garden. She heard Scott walk out behind her and turned to greet him. It was getting late because Scott had been showing a house to a client after work hours.

"Hi, love," Scott spoke gentle as he analysed the situation. He leant over Jane from behind and kissed her cheek.

"Hey," Jane squeezed out, "How was your day?"

"Busy, busy," Scott was more interested in what Jane had been up to and how she was coping today. "How was yours?"

"Are you happy, Scott, like really happy?"

Scott was startled by the sudden shift in conversation, it was a big question.

Jane continued, "You work so much, long hours, and you don't do much else."

There was a short pause and then Scott spoke, "Well, I love

you and I love coming home to you. Does it really matter what I do?"

Silence fell upon them, again, before Jane spoke out, "I don't like my job. I'm good at it, it comes easily to me, but I'm sick of other people's troubles and the cruel nature of humanity. People fighting each other, mostly for money. I don't want to be a part of it anymore."

Jane had spoken about this over the years but had always reconciled herself to stay put and do what she had always done. However, the unsettled feeling was beginning to grow.

"I've been thinking... Justin's death has made me think that life is not supposed to be like this. Shouldn't I love what I do? Shouldn't it bring me joy and peace?"

To Jane, most of the time, life seemed to be about just going through the motions, getting enjoyment from the thought of things in the future, like food, holidays, outings, but never about being happy in the moment. Yet, recently, she was becoming frustrated by her normality. To the outside world, it looked like she was driven, organised and always on a mission. Whereas, in reality, she was trying to get through things so she could then find a true happiness. Except this never happened because every instance where she found time for herself, she filled it with busy work that she found no joy in.

For the first few months following Justin's death, these uncomfortable thoughts were repetitive in Jane's mind, they could not be ignored. It wasn't that she denied their truth, it was that she didn't know what to do with the information or how to remedy it without knowing what would fulfil her. She complained to herself about lack of motivation in life, kicked herself about not doing things that were good for her and belittled herself for not living the life she was destined for. The problem was, she didn't know what she was destined for and that was the real issue.

Scott interrupted Janes thoughts, "I don't know about joy and peace. What really are they? Does any job bring them?"

Scott wasn't sure what else to say, he had not been prepared for this avenue of conversation. He had readied himself to try and persuade Jane to remove herself from Tina's house 24/7, but he was not ready for these big questions. He wanted her to realise that there was nothing she could do to ease the pain and suffering of others and, instead, she had to accept it for herself. Life was different now and there was no going back.

"I can't go back. I have to find something that I look forward to doing each day."

"These are pretty big questions, Love. What sort of job do you think you want to do?"

"I'm not sure, just something that I can connect with people, where it's light and I can just be happy. In my job, now, I feel like I have to always be sombre and respectful of our clients' circumstances, meaning no laughter and limited happiness. I don't need this anymore."

"There's nothing stopping you from quitting, you know."

"What do you mean there is nothing stopping me from quitting? We have bills and responsibilities. What am I going to do, just sit at home until I find a spreader of 'love' job?"

Scott hesitated, "Well, yeah, my pay can cover all our bills for now and you know that I will be happy if you choose never work again. I will take care of us."

Jane reached over and squeezed Scott's leg, "You're sweet but I would never ask that of you."

"What do you mean? If I was in your situation, you would do exactly the same for me. You would tell me to take it easy and work things out. Why is it different if I do it for you?"

Scott was offended that Jane didn't take up his offer, he

wanted to help her. *There it was again, the need to help. I can't fix this, I just have to be there for her.*

"You are right, Scott. I just mean I want to do something other than what I am doing, not sit at home."

"Oh, ok. Well, don't panic, you will find your way."

Silence fell over them and, as they sat there quietly, they were just with one another.

"You will work through this, Jane, and I will support you with making the change."

"Thank you."

"You know, I thought that this would be harder with you."

"Really? Why?"

"I couldn't say, maybe it was just my projection of the situation and not the reality."

Silence, again.

Scott had been contemplating something which he had not yet told anyone and wondered if it was the right time to discuss his thoughts with his wife. However, after some consideration, he decided to leave it until a later date. Jane was still fragile and Scott was acutely aware of that.

"You know," Jane began to get emotional, "I feel like, for me, Justin's death was a wakeup call." She paused and tears ran down her cheeks, "A wakeup call to get real with myself, to make a big change and do what it is that I truly desire."

"What is it that you truly desire?"

"To be light, without a work burden, and happy. I have been such a serious person, filled with doubt about who I am and what I can share with the world," she sniffed and wiped her face. "Do you think that Justin could have saved me?"

Scott and Jane looked directly at each other but, before Scott could answer, Jane spoke, "I do."

They sat there together in silence as they both reflected on their beautiful memories of Justin. The love they had for him was real. Jane's chest ached hard as she cried, held her husband's hand and remembered.

That night, at dinner, Jane brought up their encounter with Joe. They had not spoken of it since that day, but it had been playing on Jane's mind, a lot. The wisdom they shared had really helped her to let go of her need to fix her sister and her family's lives.

"You know Joe, that fellow we spoke to that day you picked me up from Tina's?"

Scott knew exactly what day Jane was speaking of because he had often thought of it too. He had thought about all of his encounters with Joe, repeatedly. Scott felt peace and solace with Joe and longed to see him again.

"Yes, sure,"

"I want to talk to him again. Do you know where he lives or how can I get in touch with him?"

"I don't really know. I have only talked to him at the coffee shop I took you to. I don't actually know that much about him."

"It's pretty weird, isn't it, that a stranger offered so much?"

"It is, but I see it as an answered prayer, however weird it is."

"I agree. I would definitely like to talk to him again."

"All I can suggest is to head down to the coffee shop and look for him. That's all that I have done. If you want to go together, we can."

Jane wasn't sure about this suggestion, but nodded in agreement, for now.

As they sat there, Scott re-evaluated his decision not to bring up something that Justin's death had raised for him. He wanted to get it off his chest, so in that moment, he gathered himself and talked Jane through the feeling that he wanted to be a Dad and he wanted to see her as a Mum. He had realised that Justin's death had given him a glimpse of loving as a Father and he wanted that on a permanent basis. He truly loved Justin and the girls and had come to understand that this was what was missing from their lives, love of his own children. Jane sat and listened. She didn't agree or disagree with Scott; it was a lot for Jane to take in.

"DEATH CHALLENGES LIFE
FROM MANY ANGLES."

32

PETER – HE MISSED HIM
EVERYDAY

PETER SIMPLY WENT ALONG WITH LIFE AS MICHAEL dragged him around, whether he wanted to or not. There wasn't a day that went by without Peter thinking of Justin, some days with sadness about what he missed and sometimes with love about what they shared. Michael was Peter's saviour; he had picked up where Justin left off and Peter did appreciate his new friend, however, whatever Michael did, it wasn't the same. It wasn't that Michael was trying to replace Justin, it was just that Peter expected certain reactions or actions out of familiarity. It was never the same, he knew Michael would never replace Justin.

Time passed, Peter's relationship with Michael grew. Their relationship was very different than Peter and Justin's but it was still a good relationship, a healthy relationship, that was helping them both to heal.

One day, the boys were hanging out in Peter's room after a skate at the park. Peter still didn't get into the skating that much himself but enjoyed the commentary he provided to the group of boys that seemed to be meeting up at the same time each day. Sometimes, Peter would sit back on the park bench and watch, even though the boys always pushed him to have a skate or to joke with them. Each one of them knew what had happened to Justin and they all knew what Peter and Justin's relationship was like. It was like they were all trying to help Peter to heal. Michael knew he had to get Peter to the park to interact. As Michael walked around Peter's room, he noticed a picture torn out of a magazine of two young adventurers that were sitting on what looked like a desert cliff. The picture had written in black marker 'Our Trip' with the number '1' in a circle. He then noticed there was a picture of a massive skate bowl with a '2' in a circle and, next to that picture, was a picturesque scene of beautiful blue water with a rock jutting straight up out of the water with a '3' in a circle. Michael was intrigued, he had never noticed these pictures before.

"What is this all about, Pete?"

Peter looked up to see what Michael was referring to. He slowly got up and walked over to view the pictures. Michael could see that he had asked a hard question of Peter.

It took a few seconds of Peter digesting each of the three photos before he responded, "Justin and I were planning a trip for when we finished school because we would both be 18, a trip of adventure." He pointed to the first picture, "This is Kings Canyon in the USA, we wanted to hike around it." He pointed to the second photo, "This is the biggest and best skate bowl on the planet, we wanted to ride it. Then this is Ha Long Bay in Vietnam and Justin wanted to sail and kayak through it. I haven't thought about this in a long time..." Peter turned to Michael, "Dumb, I suppose, to think we were going to do it but Justin was so enthusiastic. We both had savings accounts and we told our parents of our plans. You know, Justin would check every week that I was putting some savings in my adventure account... It's never going to happen now."

Michael was shocked by even the mention of Justin's name - Peter had never spoken about him before - he felt uneasy and was unsure how to handle it. Peter stood there, silently, looking and remembering fond memories of Justin's delight while they planned their adventure, and a grin spread across his face. Peter felt a brief rush of joy remembering Justin and he liked what he felt.

"Well, let's hit the skate park," Peter abruptly changed the subject and headed for the door, Michael followed but thought it was weird that Peter suggested to go back to skate, he never really showed that much interest. They raided the fridge on their way out the door.

As they skated along the street, eating and nattering, Peter felt more peaceful than he had felt in a long time. It was nice talking about Justin and what he had been like.

"Hey, you know, I know I am no substitute for Justin but want to take me on your adventure? We could do it for Justin and celebrate at each place, just as he wanted to."

Peter was silent for only a second before he responded, "Let's do it, I will fill you in on the details, Michael, but I think that would be so cool."

Michael smiled a big booming smile; he felt great to be a part of something with Peter.

The boys skated at the park for a while, but Peter was a little distracted by the conversation he and Michael had had regarding Justin's adventure. He recalled some scrap pieces of paper that Justin had written down their plans on. Plans with not a lot of detail as far as Peter could recall, but some information just the same.

Within Peter and Justin's relationship, Justin was the doer, the mover and the planner. Peter had always had input but Justin was the ideas man. That was probably why Peter was so lost after Justin's death, his ideas man had gone AWOL. He was keen to get home and look for the papers, to see just what Justin had written. He prematurely ended the skate and walked up to Michael with his arm stretch out with a fist. He didn't say anything but Michael knew what he was doing so he fist pumped Peter. Peter nodded and began to skate home.

Michael stood there and watched Peter skate away. Peter had never done anything like a fist pump that would demonstrate any form of familiarity with Michael. Michael was smiling on the inside; he felt a spark of genuine friendship between the two which was great because he still hadn't been completely convinced that it wasn't one sided.

Hope I didn't rock the boat too much with the suggestion of the trip or adventure. He wanted his friendship to continue but he thought that he may have pushed past their boundaries. *Nothing I can do now, just have to see if he comes around.*

Peter raced through the door, up the stairs and started pushing things around his desk, pulling out draws and books in a frenzy. He wasn't mad or sad, he was just eager to see what they had written because, for the first time since Justin's death, he felt some sort of purpose. He felt like he was keeping their friendship alive. Truthfully, Peter liked Michael and their friendship but it was making him feel guilty that maybe he was disrespecting Justin. However, this adventure they had planned shot a bullet of zest and connection into his relationship with Justin.

Finally, he came across two pieces of paper. One had Justin's messy handwriting on, outlining the trip. Peter was amazed by the details because he didn't remember it all. Justin had detailed the duration of each part of the trip and had outlined what they would do each day. For Kings Canyon, he even had the name of the accommodation and the tour group to trek with. Justin had researched more than Peter had given him credit for. Peter had been saving with Justin and he had listened and agreed with his chitchat about this adventure but it had mostly gone over Peter's head. At the time, he thought that they probably wouldn't do any of it. The A4 page was covered from front to back.

Peter turned over the second piece of paper and saw an agreement that Justin had drawn up that they had both signed:

I, Justin Point, and Peter Wood, do declare that we will embark on our journey of adventure as stated in other document. We will save every week until our departure so we are cashed up and journey ready. We will undertake this journey at the completion of graduating high school, no matter what happens, who happens or who says we can't.

We are doing this thing, no matter what!!!

Peter looked hard at the exclamation points and the messy signatures underneath, he barely remembered the day when they made the promise to each other. The only thing that popped into his mind was how Justin had grabbed him by the shoulders and shook him while he said, "You gotta mean it, Pete. We gotta do this, no matter what. Swear you will do this, you gotta swear."

Justin's face filled his whole vision and Peter got a fright seeing his face with such vivid recollection. He had fought off remembering what Justin looked like or sounded like. It was too painful and he tried to avoid the pain as much as he could. He backed up and sat on the bed with the scrap pieces of paper clenched in his hands, staring up at the pictures of their adventure which were stuck on the wall. A feeling of relief flowed over him as he realised that doing this, fulfilling his promise to Justin, was a must. It was a non-negotiable.

Since Justin's death, Peter had gone through so many emotions. He was trying to get past the guilt of doing and being while Justin was no longer there. At first, the guilt completely stopped him from doing anything and he found himself praying for death. He prayed and wished he had died instead of Justin or that he was with Justin and they had both died. Peter couldn't work out how to live without him. He knew exactly what he was doing when he pushed everyone out, everyone except for Michael. Everything he did or anyone he interacted with was only on a superficial level. He had gotten sick of his mother hounding him to get out of his room, shower, go to school, smile, live, eat and so he went through the motions simply to get her off his back.

From the outside looking in, Peter looked like he was ok but, from the inside, it was actually torture for him. He hated everyone for Justin being taken away from him. He was annoyed that he couldn't see anyone else mourning the tragic loss he had experienced. This had lasted a long time. He hated Michael at first, but Michael's perseverance had grown on him and he didn't know what would have happened to him that day he went to the doctors if Michael hadn't been strong enough to talk him through it all. His heart definitely softened a little with Michael but it had taken many months. Peter wasn't over his grief but because he went through the motions, day after day, loathing life, the routine helped him to slowly assimilate.

Peter sat on the bed and read through Justin's handwritten pages again, reading every detail and note. He felt a burning desire building up within him to confirm these plans with Michael, he was the person that would make this thing happen. He needed a promise from Michael, it would give him peace of mind. It would give him confidence that he could fulfil his promise to Justin. How could he ensure Michael was on board? A signature was needed. He grabbed his skateboard and headed for the skate park, with the pages squashed up in his hand. As he approached the park, he realised that he couldn't see Michael and panic began to rise within. He realised that he didn't even know where his friend lived. He skated towards the bowl and started panicking about what he could do.

"Yo, you're back, Pete!"

He looked up and saw another lad from the skate park, Matthew, standing before him.

"You seen Michael?"

Peter held his breath hoping that Matthew knew where he was.

"He headed home a few minutes ago, you could catch him there."

"Do you know where he lives, Matthew?"

Peter was desperately hopeful Matthew could help him, he felt like he wouldn't be able to rest until he worked this all out.

"Yeah, he lives on the street next to mine, Grand Street, in the blue house on the corner."

Peter turned to skate off. He raised his hand and called, "Thanks, mate."

———

PETER SKATED FOR HIS LIFE. He wanted to confirm with Michael that he was being sincere about his offer to take the trip for Justin. He had never skated so fast and, as he turned the corner, he scanned for the blue house and caught a glimpse of Michael walking through his gate.

"Hey, hey, Michael!" Peter screamed.

Michael turned around and saw Peter flying towards him. He stood still and cringed at the thought that Peter might find out about his life.

"Hey, dude," Michael tried acting calm and cool about Peter's visit.

Peter came to a screeching holt. While Peter caught his

breath, Michael questioned him, "What are you doing here? Are you ok, dude?"

Peter reached his hand out and produced the now screwed up crumpled pieces of paper. Michael took them and began to straighten them out.

"I found these," Peter huffed and puffed.

Michael presumed that Peter wanted him to read them. A few seconds passed.

"See, we have to do this, Michael. I don't have a choice, I made a promise."

Michael digested the writing on the paper. He looked up at Peter, "Sure, mate, I suggested it. I am keen."

"Yeah, but I need you to be solid. I need you to promise me, are you solid?"

"Yeah, yeah, I am solid."

Michael could see that Peter was frantic about their agreement and he hadn't seen him like this before. He wasn't like this the day Michael had found him in absolute despair at the bottom of the skate bowl, he was frantic, he was jittery, red and sweating. Michael took a deep breath and took him by the shoulders. Peter's mind flashed back to seeing Justin's face, making him promise about their adventure.

"Mate, it's ok, I said I would."

Michael was trying to calm Peter down but he wasn't sure why he was so worked up.

"Are you sure?"

"As sure as I can be. We only spoke about it an hour ago."

"But I need you to be sure!" Peter's desperation was not dissipating.

"Look, let's sit down and have a proper look at this."

Michael ushered him over to the gutter to sit. There was no way he was going to let Peter into the house, he had no idea what they would find.

"Ok, yeah, let's look at what Justin wrote and see if this is do-able."

Michael guided Peter to the gutter and then he began to read aloud the hand written scrawl. Peter nodded along as he read.

When Michael had finished processing the words, he questioned, "So what do you think, Pete? You reckon you can do all those things? It is a big list and it would be a long trip. I'm thinking that it would take us six to eight weeks and it's going to cost a fair bit of money. Not to mention the guts to travel on our own."

The whole time Michael spoke, Peter was nodding his head and agreeing.

"Yes, of course we could do it! But will you do it with me?"

Peter took the paper out of Michael's hands and he pointed to the signatures and the words, "See, I made a promise. There is no question, I have to do this."

A screaming voiced boomed from behind them, "Hey, Mikey, you coming in? I need you to do something in here!"

Michael froze. He recognised the voice and he didn't want to have to explain about his home life to Peter, but knew his cover up was over. Michael hadn't gotten too close to anyone in his life since his father passed away and he didn't want people to know how he had to live.

"Michael, get in here!"

Without looking at Peter, Michael got up, "Be back in a minute."

Peter turned and watched Michael walk towards the front door. He saw the woman that had screamed for attention. She looked dishevelled and he heard her ask, "What the hell are you doing out there? Don't sit out in the gutter like a homeless person. I need you to go to the shop, NOW!"

Michael and the woman both went inside and the door

slammed behind them. Peter could see inside the house before the door closed and he had noticed the mess and the fact that the lady was holding a can of lager in her hand.

Peter was shocked. Michael was so friendly, kind and well-kept. As he sat in the gutter listening to the muffled yelling coming from inside the house, he realised that he knew nothing of Michael's life. He had never asked him anything and he never spoke of anything. Peter began to feel uneasy and guilty for their relationship being so one-sided. The original selfish reason why he wanted to find Michael began to fall to the back of his thoughts. The yard appeared clean and tidy, so Peter had had no reason to think that Michael's life was any different to his. He shook his head in disbelief. As he sat there, thinking back over their friendship, he couldn't find a single clue that Michael was living badly.

A few minutes passed before Michael came out of the house.

"Sorry about that, Pete, but I have to go down the shops for my Mum. Can we talk about this tomorrow?"

Peter stood up, bewildered by the events. Michael's mother opened the door again and yelled, "Hurry the hell up, son!" She tripped a little and was leaning on the door to hold herself up.

"I've gotta go!" Michael started to skate away.

Peter was left standing there, not knowing what to do with himself. He thought about how embarrassed Michael must be and he wanted to let him know that their friendship was solid. He grabbed his skateboard and caught up to him. They skated side by side.

"I'll come with you."

They skated in silence all the way to the shop. Peter waited outside while Michael gathered what his mother wanted, paid and headed for his skateboard to get home. Michael held two bags and immediately Peter grabbed one and began to skate back the way they had come. Michael sped ahead of Peter, trying to avoid any conversation about his home life, but Peter wanted to break the silence.

As Peter caught up, Michael beat him to it, "Sorry about that, Pete. Sometimes my Mum is a lot to take," he paused, "You don't need this in your life."

Michael felt he had just become a burden that Peter didn't need.

"What do you mean, I don't need this in my life? We are mates, aren't we?"

As the boys got back to Michael's house, Peter handed Michael the bag.

"I will just put this stuff inside, I'll be right back."

Michael opened the door, hoping that his mother had calmed down. He had no idea why recently she had been so angry and he hoped that the alcohol had put her to sleep so he didn't have to deal with her. The door opened and all he could hear was the television. He saw his mother in a drunken sleep on the couch. He was relieved and quickly stuffed the shopping in the fridge and cupboards, before he went back out to Peter who was sitting on the edge of the gutter, waiting patiently.

"Before you say anything, Michael, I want you to know how sorry I am that I don't know anything about your life. I have been a really shitty friend. I have been so self-centred."

"Don't feel bad, Pete. That's how I wanted it. This is all too much to explain."

"Well, no explanation is necessary for me."

There was a long pause before Michael spoke again, "Let me tell you a little. Mum and Dad separated years ago now, when I was about nine years old and I lived with my dad because, as you can see, my mother is an alcoholic. Except, when I was twelve, my Dad was killed."

"What? Man, I am so sorry," Peter couldn't believe what he was hearing.

"He was killed by a drunk driver and I had nowhere else to go, so I had to live back with my mother full time. Look, it's not as bad as it looked today."

Michael wanted to hide his misery, he didn't want to burden anyone and he felt ashamed and embarrassed. Michael longed to be like the other boys he knew, part of a normal family. When he was with Peter and at his house, that was how he felt.

"I am really sorry about your dad, I had no idea."

Michael nodded, "There is nothing for you to be sorry about."

"Yes, there is. I am sorry you have to live without your dad."

Michael nodded in acknowledgement of Peter's concern for him. The boys sat there in silence and watched the world go by for a few minutes.

Michael broke the silence, "Give me another look at that stuff Justin wrote about the trip."

Peter pulled it from his pocket. He hadn't thought about Justin or the trip since Michael's mum appeared at the front door.

They ended up chatting and laughing about all the details Justin had included in the plans. Peter and Michael both found some peace sitting there in the gutter talking of their adventure. They both had a lot to escape from.

"YOU NEVER KNOW WHAT PEOPLE ARE GOING THROUGH, SOMETIMES, THE PEOPLE WITH THE BIGGEST SMILES ARE THOSE STRUGGLING THE MOST."

33

PETER & MICHAEL - PLANS ARE UNDERWAY

Michael knocked on Peter's front door. He had been keen to see Peter after school as he had an idea how he could set Peter's mind at rest over his commitment to fulfil Justin's adventure. There was no answer from his knocking, so he sat on the top step and waited. The boys didn't attend the same school and Peter's was a little further from home. Michael heard Peter's skateboard coming down the footpath and was eager to chat. As Peter headed up the front stairs, he was caught by surprise that Michael was waiting for him.

"Yo, hey!" Peter was pleasantly surprised by the early visit.

"Hey," Michael replied, "I was just thinking about all that adventure stuff and if you want me to, I can sign Justin's agreement."

Peter stood and stared at Michael, he pondered over the suggestion and then exploded with excitement.

"Yes, yes, definitely! Then we have both made a promise to Justin that we are bound to keep."

Michael was pleased that his idea made Peter so happy; he wasn't sure how it would have gone down with him but it was just what they were both looking for.

"Let's go and do it now."

Peter grabbed the keys from his school bag, opened the door and raced through the house.

"Come on, I have to find it."

In fact, Peter knew exactly where it was in his room. The night before, he had painstakingly flattened the paper out and placed the two pieces of paper under three heavy textbooks. He pulled them out and rifled through his desk draw to find a pen. Then, with only a second of hesitation, he handed the pen to Michael.

"Before you sign it," Peter took hold of Michael's shoulders, "You have to swear that this is something that we will do together, we will plan it, save for it and make it happen. Every little detail, right?"

"I swear and promise, Pete." Michael felt special being part of Justin and Peter's plans.

"Ok, then sign away."

Michael did exactly that.

———

WEEKS PASSED and the boys spoke of their planned adventure, every day. It gave them both hope for the future.

One particular day at the skate park Peter wanted to approach a subject that had been playing on his mind, "I have $1993 ready to fund this adventure, how are you going? You got any savings?"

Peter had been considering Michael's home situation and he was concerned that Michael might be eager to go but be unable to fund it.

"Yeah I will be fine, I got it covered."

"Are you saving each week?" Peter had been putting all his pay from his part time job away to save.

"Yeah, don't worry about me, I have it covered."

"But we will need at least six thousand dollars each."

"Yep, I will be fine," Michael persisted with his reply, hoping that Peter wouldn't probe him any further.

"But mate, if we are going to make this happen, we have to plan."

"Look, I already have the money," Michael finally shot back.

"What do you mean, you already have the money? Where did you get it?"

"Look, man, I have it. How many times do I have to tell you?"

Michael had never been anything but friendly with Peter, so Peter realised that he had struck a nerve. He didn't mean to upset his friend, it was just the pressure to fulfil Justin's adventure had pushed him to continue with the conversation.

A few minutes passed and Peter broke the silence "Sorry, I didn't mean to make things weird. I just feel such pressure to make sure we do this thing, it's the only thing I can do for Justin."

Michael didn't make eye contact, "Look, I have the money because my dad left me everything, including his money. That's how I know I will have it. My dad left me everything and the day I turn 18, I can access it. Besides that, I have $2876 saved from working and we still have 16 months before we leave. I will have it covered."

Peter nodded, again. He had been thinking a lot about Michael and how well adjusted he seemed to be in such a terrible situation. He lived with a drunk and his dad had been killed. He wanted a little bit of the peace that Michael seemed to have because he was often tormented by his hate for the world over Justin's death. Often, he had tried to bring himself to ask the question but had always chickened out. Finally,

Michael had brought up the subject of his father, so Peter realised that the topic was for open discussion.

"I have been wanting to ask you, how you are so normal after your dad has been killed? I struggle everyday with Justin's death and it was just a stupid accident."

Silence fell and Peter began to wish he had never said anything. Michael rubbed his head. "You know, I was angry for a long time. It all happened over five years ago, although it feels like yesterday. I'm not sure that I will ever accept that my dad was taken away from me, but someone told me once, I don't remember who, that 'time heals' and I supposed that is what has happened for me. I suppose that I have just got to a place where I can live with it. Anything I do cannot bring him back, so one day I decided to just get on with my life. I started hanging out at the skate park, went to school consistently and got myself a job. It got me out of the house and it distracted me from my pain."

He shrugged his shoulders and he noticed that Peter was looking at the ground.

"You know what? God has a plan. I don't know what that is for me but there is a plan." Another gap in conversation. It wasn't what Peter had been hoping for, he wanted a secret trick thing that he could use to feel normal again.

"Are you a religious nut or something?" Peter was a little frustrated.

"Not at all, but doesn't death make you realise that there is a power beyond us that is so powerful and we are just along for the ride?"

"Can't you just tell me what to do so I can feel normal again?"

"This is the new normal, Pete. You will never be the same person you were before Justin died and you are not supposed to be. Death changes people. The way I see it, you can let it warp you with misery and pain or you can become a better person."

"I was already a better person, Michael. I didn't need to change."

Peter got up, grabbed his skateboard and began to ride off. He was angry.

Michael had no inkling to chase him, he just yelled, "You think that now, but it is not the truth!"

Michael stayed at the skatepark, thinking about his father. He was thinking about how much he loved him and how much he missed him but, mostly, he thought about what a different person he had become. At the beginning, when his father had died, he was numb. He didn't remember much about the funeral and moving in with his mother. However, this soon changed and he became so sad for himself, sad that he had no one to love. He adored his father and they had had a great relationship. He was the one that told Michael over and over that, "God has a plan for you, you don't know it, but it is important to surrender to it."

A lot of the time, when he asked his dad for advice, he would say, "Just let go and let God."

Michael was not proud of how he had acted after his father's passing. He would play up at school, if he went at all, swore at the teachers, threatened other kids, stole things from any shop or any person he could and vandalised whatever he could find. These were not his proudest moments. He remembered one Saturday afternoon when he was caught smashing the windows of the janitor's shed at the skate park; the police had picked him up and, luckily, they hadn't charged him but his mother had to pay the bill for repairs. One of the policemen returned to his house every afternoon for two weeks at the same time, 3.20pm, to talk to him. At first, Michael was hostile towards him but, by day three, Michael had begun to like the police officer because it was the first time anyone had been truthful with him since the death. He would take Michael for a walk and ask him about his life and his dreams for his own life. In those discussions, Michael found himself saying exactly what his father had told him, "There is a plan for me, God has a plan for me."

The police officer had responded, "You must listen to the plan and be guided by it."

Michael thought long and hard about those conversations while he sat at the skatepark. They had changed the whole trajectory of his life; being arrested had changed his life. Sometimes the worst thing that happens to you turns out to be a good thing. Michael had realised that being a good friend and a good person is not always about being kind, instead it is about being honest and being truthful.

Michael remembered something else that the police office had said that changed the way he looked at things; just because his dad had passed away, it didn't mean that he had to stop loving him. This stranger, who had become Michael's friend for these two weeks, had changed everything. He had been harsh with him at times, but he had spoken the truth and been totally honest with him.

Michael realised that he had to take this approach with Peter if he was to be a good friend.

"LOVE NEVER DIES."

34

PETER & MICHAEL - BEING
HONEST AND TRUTHFUL

A COUPLE OF DAYS HAD PASSED AND MICHAEL HADN'T heard from Peter. It finally got the better of him and he went to visit Peter at home. He knocked, hesitantly, not knowing what reception he would receive. The door opened with Natalie on the other side.

"Hi Michael, good to see you."

"Hi, Mrs Wood, is Pete here?"

"Actually, you just missed him. He's gone down to the skate park."

"Ok, thank you. I'll go find him there."

"No worries. You coming back for dinner tonight, mate? I am making your favourite, spaghetti and meatballs."

Michael grinned, "Yeah sure, Mrs Woods, thanks."

He turned and walked down the steps. Dining at the Woods' had become a regular thing but he did catch himself thinking, *If Pete and I are still friends.*

Michael scanned the skate park but he couldn't see Peter and he was in no mood to skate alone so he decided to head home. As he got closer to his house, he saw someone sitting in the gutter at his front gate. It was Peter.

"Where have you been, man? I've been waiting," Peter spoke as if nothing was wrong between them.

"Oh, I have just been at yours, looking for you."

Peter nodded at Michael to acknowledge what he had said.

"Want to go skate?"

"Sure, why not?"

The boys headed down the road towards the skate park and Peter led the conversation with chitter chatter about nothing of real interest. Michael knew he had to be honest and truthful with Peter, but he knew he had to time it right. They needed each other and they both knew it.

"HONESTY IS OFTEN VERY
HARD.

THE TRUTH IS OFTEN
PAINFUL.

BUT THE FREEDOM IT CAN
BRING IS WORTH THE
TRYING."

- FRED ROGERS

35

JOE & JANE - FINDING PEACE, WHAT DOES YOUR SOUL WANT?

DAYS PASSED BY AND JANE REMAINED FRAGILE. SHE CRIED a lot, was sad often and she was truly troubled by the wakeup call that Justin's death had caused.

I need to find something more meaningful and fun. Something that makes me happy. I can't stay miserable like this.

To an outsider, Jane's life would have seemed full of contentment and opportunities. She was financially sound, had friends and family around her and a good husband. However, she never had contentment and happiness within. Fleeting happiness occurred in her life; a night out, a material purchase, a visit with a friend, a BBQ with the family, but it never lasted.

A new job, a different direction in my life, and I will be happy. Jane's thoughts raced, *I can't waste my life, what am I going to do? Do I want a baby?*

Finally, she decided to seek out Joe to offer her advice. She got in the car and headed for the coffee shop near Tina's house. She burst into the vicinity of the shop while scanning for Joe. She walked up and down the lane, looking around at each person she came across. For a few seconds, she thought that she had forgotten what Joe looked like. She shook that thought off quickly as she was desperate for some advice. Her breathing began to quicken as she marched up and down, looking and looking for someone that was not there. After 15 minutes of looking, Jane decided to give up and she sat down at the table she and Scott had sat at when she first meet Joe, a last-ditch effort. Her coffee cheered her up. She sat and drank it slowly, enjoying every last sip. The world around her drifted away as she lost hope of getting some advice.

There were only a few outlets around the coffee shop and, when Jane noticed them, she thought they looked interesting and walked over to inspect further. All her worries melted away as she enjoyed looking at all the bits and pieces in the shops. As she walked out of the gift shop that had consumed her for at least half an hour, she turned to say goodbye to the shop assistant and walked straight into Joe's trolley.

"Hey, hey, are you ok?"

Joe moved closer to Jane to check for injuries as she had hit the trolley with force. Joe flicked through his recent encounters in his mind before he remembered her name, "Jane, are you ok?"

Jane couldn't believe her luck. She didn't even feel the pain in her knee or hip from the collision, she was focused only on Joe.

"Hello, Joe. It is so good that I've found you."

Jane wanted to get everything out of her head; she wanted to blurt it all out and have him solve all her problems. She secretly wanted him to tell her exactly what to do and fix her head.

A puzzled look came over Joe's face, "You found me? Did you come here looking specifically for me?"

"Umm..." She hesitated, "Well, yes."

"Well, let's get down to business then, let's go and talk."

Jane was thrilled that Joe was willing to talk with her. She followed him back into the coffee shop and she settled into her seat.

"So, what you looking for a crazy trolley-pushing man for?" Joe joked.

Jane was lost for words and there was an uncomfortable silence.

"Let me start." Joe broke the silence, "Are you feeling like life doesn't work quite like how it did before Justin's death? That things just don't fit together anymore?"

Jane nodded, bewildered that he knew why she was there and what she was going to talk about.

"There is nothing easy about moving forward after a great loss like you have experienced. I think that you can sometimes lose control of your mind and of all the memories and scenarios of moving forward without that person can torture you. You lose connection with the actual world and, when that phase passes, you question everything in your life."

Jane nodded, "You are absolutely spot on. My mind is running ten to the dozen, spinning thoughts of scenarios and possibilities, sadness and panic, about how life will go on without Justin. The guilt of living while he is gone is tremendous."

Anxiety began to rise in Jane and she felt her insides begin to tremble as she felt the impact of what she was saying.

"I completely get what you are saying and it is not an easy path to tread." Joe paused to gather his thoughts, "It's like I told you last time, it is your thoughts that torment you the most, the continual talking in your mind that runs story after story, scenario after scenario and possibility after possibility. Also, second guessing every decision you make. Controlling your mind, which is your ego and not the real you, is the ultimate key to gaining clear direction, reaching your soul and finding the real you. Control."

"That is exactly what is happening to me. It was like this before Justin died, but with my exhaustion and deep sadness, everything seems to be exaggerated tenfold. I weep all the time; it comes out of nowhere and I just can't reconcile with the loss. Why does a young boy have to die? Why does such tragedy have to strike my family? I feel so ripped off that my life is now shredded apart." Her lips quivered and her voiced stuttered, "My life feels wrong. It feels like all of this is a wakeup call for me, to face many things that I have been pushing away. I feel like my job drags me down, but I don't know what else to do. I keep having nightmares that Justin is disappointed in me for not waking up which makes me feel anxious and restless."

"Oh, Jane, I know you feel broken right now. Honestly, I think that you are, but you will rebuild yourself for the better. You will grow and feel a connection to your spirit and that will bring so much peace and joy with it. I know, right now, life is hard for you."

Jane partially smiled and squeezed her eyes shut to hold back her tears. She thought that Joe really did understand and that was enough to give her some relief.

The waitress walked over to them, "What can I get you?"

Jane jumped in to try and distract the girl from her tears, "I'll have a flat white, please. What would you like Joe?"

"I'll have my usual breakfast please, Annie. You want something to eat, Jane?"

"Maybe, I might. I haven't had breakfast yet. Have you got a muesli and yoghurt type thing?" Jane had no idea what was on the menu.

"Sure do," Annie replied cheerfully, "I will get that happening for you."

Joe observed Jane and he could sense that she was living on the edge of sanity and insanity. He sympathised with her; he had been there.

"I'm not sure what 'control' means, Joe. How do you control how you feel? You feel what you feel."

"Great question, your feelings are something you can change. The key to it is catching your mind as it creates stories and circumstances that evoke the unwanted emotions."

Jane nodded, enthralled by Joe's words.

"Tell me about your sadness and your weeping, Jane. How does it begin, go on and end?"

It took Jane a few seconds as she recalled her morning, "Well, this morning, it began with my husband leaving the house to go to work. I started thinking about him being killed in a car accident. These thoughts started because Justin popped into my head and how we couldn't see the accident coming. Then, I was thinking about how it can happen to anyone and I just lost it over the thought of losing my husband and I fell apart."

Joe interrupted Jane, "See what I mean about the stories that your mind creates? Your mind applied the death of Justin to your husband. It made you panic and become distressed, even though your husband was safe. There is no sense in that. You became distressed about something that wasn't real, hadn't happened and was very unlikely to happen. When you think about this rationally."

Jane contemplated these words carefully, "So, you are saying these thoughts about possibilities of life events are made up and that I shouldn't listen to them? Would that be right?"

"Mostly right. Peace is found if you don't think of these stories in the first place or if you stop them before they explode into emotional connections within you."

Jane nodded at Joe, "I understand what you just said, like I was making up a scenario that wasn't real but made me upset anyway."

"Exactly."

"But what about when you are living a terrible event that is happening? Because what led me to thinking about my husband being killed, was that Justin is actually dead, never coming back. He is never able to grow up and live his life. The pain that causes our family and friends is real."

"Now, that is a little more difficult," Joe paused he looked at his feet and many memories of his own losses flooded his mind. He quickly scanned his thoughts to find the answer, "What I do in those circumstances, is I work to release my thoughts by finding something I am grateful for out of the situation."

"Grateful for? That is ridiculous, Joe. How can you be grateful for anything in the death of another?"

"You would be surprised. There is always something to be grateful for, even if you go to the most basic things in life. Like the sun is shining, the colours around you, the air you are breathing, your clothes, that you're warm. There is always something. For you, it could be that you had Justin in your life. What would life be like if you never had him? It could be for the time you spent with him, maybe you can think of something he taught you or a laugh you shared or a meal. There are so many things. We think of death too much as a punishment for who is left behind, rather than a celebration of what we had when they were alive."

"This is so hard to swallow, Joe. It is so hard to believe that switching your thoughts to gratitude can actually make you feel better about something tragic."

"You can use a code or phrase if you like, to help realise what you are doing. I don't want you to think that this is a scam to avoid yourself and how you feel, because if you really go into your feelings and feel them then they will dissipate and lose their power. It is not about being afraid of them, it is about feeling them and releasing the need for them to arise in the first place. When my mind gets out of control, I breathe slowly and deeply whilst counting my breath and telling myself to release. After that, I go into the feelings without fear. Our society fears feelings and we are under the illusion that negative feelings are bad. What if I told you that they are just feelings and that when you relax into them, they will go away as quickly as they came? You will be surprised. Finally, I drop my energy or awareness into my heart. The heart is the centre of your universe and has all the answers, so I always like to be there feeling my heart beat."

"You make it all sound so easy, Joe," Jane paused, "Justin's death is making me feel like I need to live differently, be light and loving, and to do that I need to change jobs."

"I am not sure 'easy' is the right word, Jane. It takes practice and dedication to connect with the peace, rather than the chaos, of your mind. Your thoughts about not being in the right job or place are good thoughts to have, if you try and understand them. You are unsettled and you would like a change. It's good information, but if you torment yourself with this idea and panic over the outcome, then you have achieved nothing. You are still in the same place, just with added panic and discomfort. You have achieved nothing but self-torment. What if you tackle things differently? You have identified you need a change and to open yourself up to possibilities. You don't have to push and panic. Keep calm and, most importantly, keep an open heart. Be present in daily life and be aware of what you are doing, at all times. Your mind will quieten down which will mean that you allow yourself to be guided!"

Joe reached over and held Jane's hand. Jane found immediate peace from Joe's touch.

Joe closed his eyes and took a slow and conscious breath. Jane watched him, wondering what was happening. Joe did it again. He took a very slow breath in and, as he began to breath out, Jane instinctively followed suit. She closed her eyes and listened to Joe's breathing, following his pattern. Her mind was quiet and the tension went from her body.

Joe quietly whispered, "Drop into your heart."

Jane had no idea what Joe meant, he said it again, "Drop into your heart, breathe through your heart."

Jane allowed her attention to settle at her heart centre and with every breath she allowed her heart to expand. She felt so peaceful, all thought was abandoned. She felt removed from her worries.

After a few minutes, Joe squeezed her hand to bring her attention back to her surroundings. "See, peace comes from within. It is not brought to you from something outside of you, you find it within."

Jane just nodded at Joe, she had no words. Everything Joe has said to her felt like truth, she felt as though she was speaking to a wise man. It all made sense and brought peace within her. A spark of empowerment spread though her body and her posture straightened a little. Joe could see that she got it, she understood. He could feel her peace and he wondered whether she would use this advice and integrate it into her way of being.

"Jane, if you quieten your mind you will be able to hear which direction to go."

"YOU CANNOT ALWAYS CONTROL WHAT GOES ON OUTSIDE. BUT YOU CAN ALWAYS CONTROL WHAT GOES ON INSIDE."

- DR. WAYNE DYER

36

TINA – ONE FOOT IN FRONT OF THE OTHER

Tina's life became a battle of putting one foot in front of the other. Some days, she got through the whole day not knowing what she had done and where she had been. Justin inundated her thoughts and it was all the things she would miss out on with him that broke her heart.

One Tuesday morning, she was collecting washing from around her house and automatically opened the door to Justin's room. She had walked in with the intention of picking up washing but she was startled by the neat and tidy state of his room. Ordinarily, Justin's room would be a nightmare of dirty clothes, school books and junk laying around. She was always asking him to clean up and have some respect for his belongings. She stopped in her tracks when she realised her mistake, then slowly walked around his room, looking at all his stuff, and sat down on the edge of the bed. She had rarely been in his room since the accident, or even opened his door, because it was too painful for her. As Tina sat there, she recalled Justin's nature. He was always busy and filling his days to the brim with activities and interactions.

On some level, had he known that he wasn't going to be on this planet long and had to make the most of it?

She shook her head in disbelief that he was gone and a heaviness came over her. As she took a deep breath, the phone began to ring which startled her. Tina quickly got up and walked into the hallway to pick it up. She was glad to be free of her thoughts and the time in Justin's room. It had been painful and she had been triggered to think about things she didn't want to think about.

Tina picked up the phone to hear Natalie asking if she wanted any shifts at work. Their work was linked; Natalie was the Clinical Nurse Educator and Tina was one of the Clinical Nurses at a small private hospital, only five minutes' drive from where they lived. Tina worked in the maternity unit, while Natalie worked all over the hospital in her position. Natalie thought it might have been a good idea for Tina to start back at work to remove herself from the pain of her life. It was proving difficult to convince Tina, but Natalie kept trying. "Let me think about it, Natalie."

It was the first time that Tina had even entertained the idea of returning to work. Natalie was very surprised and didn't know what to say so remained quiet.

"Well, I mean, I should just get on with it. I have to do it, I can't hide here forever," Tina sighed.

"I think it would be good for you, just to break your routine and get out of the house." Natalie hoped she wasn't forcing things too much.

"What days do you want, Tina? How many a week?"

"Umm... I haven't really thought about it."

"How about you just try two days and see how that goes?" Natalie knew that Tina only worked three days a week prior to Justin's death, but she wanted her friend to feel needed.

"Yeah, sure."

Tina wasn't really thinking about what she was agreeing to,

she was only thinking about putting one foot in front of the other and a huge part of that was to get back to work.

"Ok, starting this Thursday, early shift. Does that suit you?"

Tina finally agreed.

"Ok, great! I will add you to the roster."

"See ya, Natalie," and Tina hung up the phone.

Tina had realised that she was hiding away from life, but she kept hearing within herself, *You don't have a choice. You either curl up or you get on with it, one foot in front of the other. Life goes on.*

It brought tears to her eyes because she didn't want to know a world or a life without Justin in it. She felt like life shouldn't go on, she shouldn't go on, but she could see around her that life does and life was moving forward, whether she wanted it to or not.

The stress Tina was feeling was interrupted by the cyclone that was Emma, flying into the house from school. Sally followed her in but not with the same enthusiasm. Tina was sitting on the top of the stairs trying to reconcile going to work with getting on with life.

"Mum! Mum?" Emma shouted.

Before Justin died, Tina was often not home when the girls got back from school because she had been at work, but Emma had quickly got used to Tina being there. Emma loved it and always found an excuse not to leave her mother's side, except for going and being with Sally.

Tina quickly got up and walked down the stairs towards Emma's voice, her arms filled with dirty laundry. Tina was really trying to hide her grief and sadness by going about life as normal; cooking dinner, cleaning, washing, things that were just busy work really to avoid getting back to life.

As Tina got closer to the girls, she could only think, *One foot in front of the other, that is all I can do.*

"LIFE GOES ON…"

37

SALLY – PUSHING, PUSHING, PUSHING

SALLY PUSHED PAST HER MOTHER AND WALKED DIRECTLY up the stairs. Tina watched her disappear into her room while Emma continued to talk her mother through her day. Sally was all too much for Tina, she didn't know what to do with her as she was barely hanging on herself. She had no energy to even think about Sally's troubles.

Sally didn't want contact with anyone. She didn't want to talk and she especially didn't want to answer any questions about how her day had been. She hated everyone around her and wanted to push every single person far away; being on a deserted island on her own wouldn't be far enough away from people. Hate was all she could see when she looked at her mother and sadness seemed to be all she could feel. Teachers at school had been wanting her to see the counsellor, or just even talk to any adult or friend, but Sally had hidden within herself so no one could get close to her. The day Justin died in their lounge room, was the day she stopped feeling life and she stopped living life. It was the day she began to hate the world.

Justin and Sally had a friendly and supportive relationship. They were brother and sister, but they were also true friends. Surprisingly, they didn't really fight or annoy each other like other siblings that were similar in age. They were both kind and gentle people, as were their parents, but the love they had for each other could be seen through their interactions. Of course, they had their spats but nothing of significance.

Sally had other friends, including Kate from next door who she had grown up with. Kate had tried and tried over the months following the accident to reach Sally, but Sally would not let her guard down and let her in. She tolerated her dad trying to love her, but she would not even entertain the idea of her mother raising a question concerning her wellbeing, schedule or agenda. Hiding out in her room became her favourite pastime.

Emma slammed the door behind her as she burst into Sally's room and jumped on the bed, ready to dissect her entire day. Emma was a bright and uplifting little soul and she and her big sister had always had a connection. Sally always looked after her little sister and, when her mother wasn't at home, Sally was her little sister's care giver. Justin had been a fun brother, but Sally was always the one to keep Emma safe.

Except, the tables had turned in their relationship. Emma had become the voice of reason while Sally was being unreasonably stubborn and egocentric. Reaching out to her sister had become a lost cause for Emma, but she had learnt that Sally would always soften when Emma pulled her into her own life. So, this had become the pattern in their relationship. Emma would discuss every aspect of her day with Sally and Sally would be present, interested and supportive of her little sister.

The bond they had would never be harmed as Emma was the only one Sally could count on. It wasn't factually correct, but Sally believed it because she just didn't want to open up and love other people who could potentially leave her at any point in time. The feeling of abandonment and rejection kept her tightly locked in her shell which was fast becoming the most impenetrable barrier you could imagine. The only thing Sally was keeping hold of was the bond and sense of connection she had with her little sister. The reason she allowed and kept this feeling alive was that these feelings and the connection was equivalent to what she had had with Justin. The love and connection she shared with her siblings was special, and she had realised that she had taken Justin's love and company for granted, but for now, the reciprocated love she had with Emma was keeping her alive.

Sally lay on the bed with Emma curled up beside her, nattering about her day. Sally engaged with every word and responded appropriately.

Suddenly, Emma sat up in the middle of a story and gave her big sister a shake by her shoulders, "You gotta get back into life, Sal. We can't just be in your room all the time."

"Really, Little Miss? What if I told you that there is nothing for me outside this room? I am not interested in anything that the world outside of this room could possibly offer me."

"What do you mean? The world will only offer you what you offer it."

Sally paused and tried to digest what her little sister had to say.

"How did you get so worldly and understand the ways of life?"

Sally was confused and partially annoyed by her little sister who was only eight, yet here she was, telling her what to do.

"Do you really want to know?" Emma paused and looked deep into her sister's eyes, "Actually no, you are definitely not ready."

Emma wanted to tell Sally everything that Justin had whispered to her in her dreams, but she was reluctant because she felt her sister's anger and knew that she was stubborn with it.

"What do you mean, I am not ready? Not ready for what? And how am I not ready? What the hell are you talking about?" Sally's blood was beginning to boil. She had been very quick to anger recently when anyone challenged her emotional state. Her intolerance to life was rising every day. Emma was young but she felt it and she knew not to rock Sally's boat.

"I don't know, Sal," Emma hugged her sister to try and distract her from their conversation.

"Let's watch those funny cat video's on my tablet, they make me laugh so hard."

Sally knew that Emma had more to say but she let it go. She also knew she didn't want to hear anything that challenged her routine of locking the world out. She felt safe being sheltered from her pain. She hugged her little sister back. She had an urge to push Emma away, but held back as she knew she shouldn't.

"WITH EVERYTHING THAT HAS
HAPPENED TO YOU, YOU CAN
EITHER FEEL SORRY FOR
YOURSELF OR TREAT WHAT
HAS HAPPENED AS A GIFT.
EVERYTHING IS EITHER AN
OPPORTUNITY TO GROW OR
AN OBSTACLE TO KEEP YOU
FROM GROWING.

YOU GET TO CHOOSE."

- DR. WAYNE DYER

38

SALLY & KATE - DETERMINED NOT TO LET ANYONE IN

THERE WAS A KNOCK ON SALLY'S FRONT DOOR WHICH TOOK her by surprise. She opened it with huge reluctance because she didn't want to talk to anyone and she was instantly annoyed.

"What?"

Sally didn't care who was there; she wasn't interested in anyone, or in their conversation, so she was as rude as she could be. Kate was standing at the door and she was shocked at the reception she received. Generally, the Point front door was unlocked and Peter and herself could come and go at their own leisure. They were always welcome, so this reception made Kate's heart curl up inside itself.

"Oh, umm... Hey, Sal."

Sally almost interrupted Kate, "What? What are you doing here? I'm not interested."

"Oh, umm..."

Kate didn't even get through a complete response before Sally shut the door in her face. She was left standing there in disbelief. In the past, the girls had a tight relationship and there had been a truly great love between them. Kate had felt Sally was pushing her away since the accident and she was making a real effort to look past all the hurt and rejection and remain a constant and steadfast friend. So, this was a lot for Kate to take. She wasn't sure what she should do next. She shook her head, turned and headed down the steps, truly hurt by the rejection. Her hand found itself on the centre of her chest as her heart ached. Kate just couldn't understand why Sally wouldn't let her in.

They had been through a lot together; they had shared their secrets, their joys and their pain throughout their whole lives. Kate wanted to reach out and help her friend to heal a little. Kate had heard from other friends that Sally had put a barrier between herself and every person she knew. She had been cold and distant and, to Kate's knowledge, she wasn't connecting with any other person on the planet.

After Justin's death, Kate comforted Sally and tried to help her reconcile her thoughts and feelings about the loss of Justin. Sally had been fragile and Kate had nurtured her through a very rough time. Kate felt there had been a shift in Sally when her grandparents left to go home to their own lives, interstate. The girls had almost formed a routine with Sally spending all of her free time with Kate, in Kate's room, away from her own house and the pain that was present there.

Grace, Sally's grandmother, had taken the lead with Emma. She had worked hard to keep her out of harm's way, out of the family's grief, sheltering her. Grace was an observant person and had picked up on Sally's coping strategy of avoiding life and avoiding her family. Over time, Grace had become concerned that Emma was being left alone while Sally was always next door, with Kate. It was alright while Grace was there, but she was to leave and she knew that Sally had to get back to life at her house and that Emma needed her.

As Kate walked down the path and into her house, she

made a promise to herself. She promised that she would just keep trying with Sally, she would never give up. Kate imagined that things would get easier as time went on.

"Time heals," she spoke out loud, as she walked into her bedroom and picked up a book to distract herself.

"TIME HEALS."

39
SALLY & GRACE - TIME TO RECONNECT

Before Grace left to return home, she knew she had to connect with Sally, somehow.

"Hello, my sweet Sally," Grace caught Sally just as she was heading to Kate's, before she could escape the house.

"Hi, Grandma," Sally looked puzzled.

"Let's just go out here," Grace opened the door and directed Sally outside, "Let us sit for a while."

Grace sat on the top step and waited for Sally to do the same. Sally hesitated but finally sat down. Sally and her grandmother were not close, they had only really gotten to know each other following Justin's death.

"I wanted to talk to you because your grandfather and I are leaving in a few days. I want you to know that Emma really needs you." She paused, "I know you have been spending a lot of time next door, I assume with Kate, and I'm happy for you that you have such a lovely friend."

Grace rubbed her hands together, as if they were cold. Sally didn't make eye contact, but the pit of her stomach began to ache because she knew what was coming; she knew she was going to be asked to be at home, a place she so didn't want to be. Sally had learnt how to feel safe with Kate and she had created a life where she was not challenged, surrounding herself with the predictable. Sally's breathing began to quicken as her stomach ached.

"I was just thinking, maybe you would be able to spend some more time with Emma, at home, here?"

There was deathly silence. Sally wanted to get up and run a million miles away, she hated it at her house. She hated the constant questioning, asking if she was ok, if she was hungry or if she needed anything. Most of all, she was haunted by the memory of her brother at home. Everywhere she looked, there was something that reminded her of him and it made her heart ache. It made her sad and scared for herself for the future. She continually asked herself how she was going to live, what she was going to do, stirring something deep within her that she didn't want to feel. So, she had removed herself completely and, next door, she felt loved and like no one challenged her. She had found her safe place. Sally couldn't bring herself to respond to her grandmother. She wanted to scream in her face, but something stopped her.

"Emma truly loves you and, more than that, she needs you."

Tears welled in Grace's eyes. The whole situation had broken Grace. She had spent her life always doing the right thing by others. She had supported her husband and his career, which had led them all over the country and had put a great distance between her children and her. It had all been for the greater good of other's. Now, she had realised that she had missed out on relationships with her grandchildren and her grown children, for no reason other than doing right by others. She was disappointed with herself and it had prompted her to talk to her granddaughter about keeping the love alive between herself and her little sister. Grace wanted to explain to Sally the importance of what she had missed out on herself, but she also wanted to make sure that Sally didn't make the same mistake that she had and let important relationships slip by.

"I know it is hard at your house and I understand why you don't want to be here." Grace was getting nothing back from Sally, so she thought she would use her personal experience to try and connect with her, "You know, I distanced myself from the people that were most important in my life... I suppose I did that for a number of reasons. I was supporting your grandfather's work but, also, I have always found it easier if I don't get too close to people. You see, I am scared to be too close."

Grace hadn't spoken much before about what she was telling Sally; it was new territory for her.

"You see, when I was about 13 years old, my dad left my mum and we never saw him again. Apparently, he left my mother a note saying that he didn't want to be married and he just left us all. I still remember the devastation I felt... What I have realised, in these last few days and weeks, is that that event in my life changed me as a person. I became distant with my family and my friends and I tried so hard to be the 'perfect person.' I didn't want to give anyone an excuse to leave me. I was, and I still am, scared that I will be abandoned or left behind, so I just do what everyone else wants."

Sally still didn't acknowledge that her grandmother had been talking to her, so Grace continued.

"I know, now, that I want to be with my children, my grandchildren and my friends. I am sick of leaving everyone."

A few seconds passed and Grace shuffled herself along the step to get closer to Sally. She wrapped her arm around her granddaughter and pulled her close.

"I don't want you to push everyone away and be like me. Emma needs you. Your mum and dad need you."

The pain that had been simmering in Sally began to rise

within her. Grace gave her another squeeze and Sally rested her head on Grace's shoulder.

Finally, Grace thought, *She is hearing me.* She realised that Sally was crying. She hadn't really seen Sally be anything other than angry and dismissive.

"Oh, my love. Emma especially needs you. I know Aunty Jane will be here, but she will always go home and you will be Emma's constant."

They sat there for a few minutes, in silence, before Sally wiped her tears away with the back of her hand and promised, "I'll do my best."

"Well, your best is all I can ask for."

Grace had been relieved that the girls would be together, but what dominated her thoughts was the feeling that Emma was, in fact, going to save Sally. She would bring Sally back to life, she would hold her up and she would love some healing into her big sister.

"LOVE IS ALL THERE IS AND IT IS THE ROOT OF ALL PEOPLE'S DESIRES."

40

JAKE – ANGER BEGINNING TO BUBBLE TO THE SURFACE

JAKE CONTINUED TO DROWN HIMSELF IN WORK. WHEN Justin was around two years old, he made the leap of faith that he could open his own mechanical workshop. He was proud of what he had accomplished but, since Justin's death, he had made work consume his thoughts and his time. He used to be organised and efficient, so he could get home to his family and enjoy their togetherness, but now he allowed work to fill his everything until the last possible minute he felt would be acceptable to go home. This was his ego protecting him from the pain of what home held.

Jake was hurt by the death of his son and he was becoming angry with the situation. One evening, he picked up the spanner lying beside his right hand and pelted it across the workshop. It hit the wall, bounced off and crashed into a pile of crates holding new stock. The noise was so horrific that he scared himself.

Jake whispered to himself, "That felt good."

With his teeth clenched hard, he screamed a bellow of anger, so loud that it echoed through the workshop and out the open shed door.

Why would a God, that is supposed to be loving, take my

son? Justin was a good boy; he never did anything that would warrant death. He was a good boy. He was my good boy. He was kind and loving and he was my boy.

Jake's head began to shake and tears of frustration ran down his face, "He was my boy, he didn't deserve to die."

He wanted to smash the whole workshop to pieces. He stood and imagined himself smashing the windows, feeling them shatter everywhere. Then, he imagined smashing the cars parked inside the workshop, smashing their shiny bonnets and roofs. The pain was too much and he could feel his heart pounding. A hatred for God flooded him, he was so angry. He picked up a bolt that was within his reach and threw it hard against the wall. It bounded back and rolled across the concrete floor, back to his feet. He picked it up, again, and threw it even harder at the wall. The bolt ended up back at his feet, so Jake squatted down and threw it again. With tears of frustration still running down his face, the bolt rolled back to his feet. As it rolled to a stop, anger bubbled and hatred simmered and Jake shook his head in disbelief. *What the hell is going on here?*

He gritted his teeth and bent down to examine the bolt, wiping his eyes to clear his vision, when a voice within him spoke, "You will keep getting the same back as you give."

"Go screw yourself! You stole my boy from me, I will hate you forever!"

Jake waited for a reply, but none came.

"Screw you!"

He walked over to his car, dragged the bourbon bottle out from under the front seat, unscrewed the lid and did something he had never done before; he slugged the bourbon directly from the bottle.

"You will keep getting the same back as you give," the voiced beamed louder.

"Screw you!" He slugged another gulp, "Screw you!"

Jake took the bottle, sat on the floor and leant against the wall of the shed. He drank his way into a drunken coma.

It was 5.45pm and, normally, he was home by now, but it had gotten to a point where he just could not bear to go home, to be in his house or to talk to his family. He was feeling ripped off by life. Justin had been taken from him, unnecessarily.

Jake's earlier conversation with Emma, about Justin being happy and that his time on earth had rightfully come to an end, was a distant memory. It gave him no peace and anger plagued him.

James, Jake's neighbour and friend, walked into the workshop. As soon as he had pulled up outside, he had known that Jake was inside because the door was up and the side door was open. Since Justin's death, Jake had become distant and James had noticed that he was drinking a lot when they would see each other. Something wasn't right.

James had been sent to find Jake because it was 8pm and no one knew where he was. Things were starting to get stressful at home with the panic and fear of another accident. He found his friend leant up, against the shed. James assumed that Jake was asleep, but he was stinking of alcohol and the lights were off, so James turned them on to properly assess the situation. There was a pile of vomit on the floor beside Jake and a mostly empty bourbon bottle. After checking for the rise and fall of Jake's chest to ensure that he was still alive, James reached into his pocket to make the call to Natalie. He wanted to let them all know that he had found Jake, although he didn't think it was a good idea to bring him home.

As the phone began to dial, he reached down and shook Jake a little to see if he could rouse him. Jake lifted his hand and pushed James away. James had no idea what to do and it made him feel uncomfortable. He wanted to run as fast as he could to get away. The problem was, he was the only person there. James wasn't good with emotions and he had coped with the whole Justin situation by just not thinking about the loss they all had endured; when he saw the grief and sadness around him, he had simply removed himself from the situation, where possible. He had not dealt with any of it, but now he couldn't get away. Natalie instructed him not to leave Jake and to stay with him to ensure he was safe. She would let Tina know that Jake was with James and not to expect them home any time soon.

James pulled a chair out of the office and dragged it in over to sit beside Jake so that he could keep a close eye on him. He knew that Jake was conscious and breathing and Natalie had said it was good that he had vomited a lot of the bourbon up. He lent forward and took a long look at his friend. He had known him for many years and they had been through many major life events together.

Man, he looks old. James squinted his eyes to get a better look at Jake. *He looks like an old man. Life has really taken it out of him.*

James' eyes dropped down to Jake's body and he noted that Jake's belt was just about hanging on his hips, pulled into the smallest hole. Jake had been a big strong fellow, wide across the shoulders with strong muscled arms. For the first time, James noticed the physical change in Jake. Guilt began to flood James and his eyes stared at the rise and fall of Jake's chest. He realised that he had been avoiding Jake.

When James was twelve years old, his infant brother had died. He had only been six months old. James was devastated by the loss, but watched his mother and father continue with life like nothing had happened. James had helped his mother a lot with taking care of his little brother, even changing nappies when required. His other three siblings were not that interested in little Brock but he, for reasons he didn't understand, loved him dearly. He never knew the exact cause of death, but he knew that Brock had been rushed to the hospital after having trouble breathing. His mother shed a few tears in public for the first couple of weeks post his baby brother's death, but he didn't see one change in his father. The family simply got on with their life with only a brief explanation to the family that Brock was gone. Any conversation about him never held up in the house.

James hadn't thought about his little brother for many years but, since Justin's death, memories of Brock had been coming back to him. Memories of the gut-wrenching pain he felt after Brock's death had been troubling him. Natalie didn't even know that he had had a little brother who had died.

James recalled how it felt when no one spoke to him about Brock following the death and how no one had helped him digest his loss. He could never understand how his little brother could die, without warning, and yet he was lucky enough to be alive. James had become emotionally dismissive as a result. He was able to emotionally remove himself from any uncomfortable situation with ease.

All he had wanted as a 12-year-old boy, was someone to talk to and help him digest his loss. Someone to tell him that Brock was real and that they had shared a lot of love and that, someday, they would meet again. Sometimes, as a young adult, James had questioned whether Brock was actually real or just a figment of his imagination.

As James looked at his friend, guilt plagued him. Seeing Jake alone in this drunken coma made him realise that he had abandoned him. He hung his head in shame and shook it from side to side. He squeezed his eyes shut and his heart physically ached. He stood up, deciding to find a bucket, detergent and paper towels to clean up the vomit. Jake slept through the clean-up.

As midnight passed, Jake stirred. James watched as he realised where he was and tried to recall his afternoon.

"Yo, mate," James tried to sound light and upbeat; the last thing he wanted was for Jake to feel embarrassed.

Jake struggled to his feet and stumbled over to James, "What are you doing here?"

"The girls were looking for you, so I thought I would find you for them. You know, to stop them worrying."

"What time is it?"

"Just after midnight."

James didn't want to alarm Jake too much. Ordinarily, Jake was a responsible and diligent human being, but times were changing and James knew it.

"That is late, hey?" Jake continued to stumble around, "Just need to go to the toilet."

Jake was wobbly, glassy eyed and dishevelled. Guilt rose within James, again. He had managed to let it go earlier in the night by distracting himself, but now it was bubbling up.

James watched the toilet door praying to himself that Jake would get himself out ok. James wasn't good at this. As Jake stumbled out of the toilet, James directed him to the little couch that was in the office. Jake sat down and James sat directly opposite him so that they were looking directly at each other.

"What is happening, mate? I'm not used to seeing you like this."

Jake shrugged his shoulders.

"I know you are going through some tough shit, but this isn't you."

Silence fell over the room. The crickets' chirps echoed through the workshop.

Jake stretched back on the couch, lifted his right hand up to his eyes and began to rub them.

"I don't know, I don't know. What the hell am I supposed to do? I hate life, I hate living!"

He slammed his hand down on the couch, "Am I supposed to just live as I was before?" His words were slurred but heartfelt, "My son is dead. Do you know what that means, James? I have lost a whole part of life. My boy is gone and I have nothing to show for it but a massive hole in my life."

Jake leant forward with his elbows on his knees and began to sob. He hadn't shed many tears because he had been drinking them away. James got up and sat beside his friend on the couch and wrapped his arm around his shoulder. James didn't say a word, they just sat together and he allowed Jake to cry. He couldn't say that it would be alright, he couldn't say things will get better, because he didn't know if it would be alright.

James was choking back the tears himself. He had lost his little brother, but it had been like someone had clicked their fingers and life had just gone on. That is how he had dealt with Justin's death but, for the first time in his life, he was feeling the full effect of his grief.

Justin and James had had a great relationship. He had bantered with the Justin, but he also kicked his butt if necessary.

Jake shook off his tears, "Ah, what am I supposed to do?"

James was lost for words. Sorrow was filling him up, sadness was filling him up. He had nothing to offer his friend. Finally, he said, "I don't have any advice for you, mate. I don't know what you should do."

Jake jumped up from the chair and stumbled quickly back to the toilet. James heard the heaving as Jake began to vomit. A few minutes later, James heard the water run as Jake washed his face. He walked back out of the bathroom and just stood there, without any words.

"I just don't know how to do this without him!" Tears welled in Jake's eyes.

"Who said you have to know?"

James hugged his friend who smelt of vomit and alcohol. There was so much sadness in the room, from both men.

———

JAMES DROVE them home while Jake slept, and he realised that he had been a selfish and neglectful friend. He had been avoiding Jake because that is how he dealt with loss, just forget it and move on. He thought about his own family and realised that he was doing the same; he didn't discuss Justin, he avoided the issue. Although he was aware his family were grieving, he didn't partake in the process. As he drove, memories came back to him of his baby brother; the little giggles, pushing him in the pram, holding him while he slept. James also recalled that he had had very little to do with his own children when they were babies. He began to understand why.

James looked over at Jake and a lump formed in his throat; the reality of life without Justin began to hit James hard. For the first time since Justin's death, James was experiencing the loss, the gravity of his reality was becoming real. As the realisation settled in, it became too painful to bare. James shut himself down in that moment and became indifferent, as he always had been.

As weeks passed by, James became more and more unsettled within himself. He didn't like the pain he felt and was uneasy, morning, noon and night. He dodged any uncomfortable conversation and became more and more indifferent about life. When he was asked anything by anyone he loved or was close to, he was indifferent. He couldn't bring himself to connect with anyone and went on with life as if everything was ok, just as his family had done when he was a child. He never changed, never grew and was never truly happy or at peace.

"HOW CAN YOU SUPPORT ANOTHER, WHEN YOU ARE BROKEN YOURSELF?"

41
TINA
WORK WORK WORK

Months passed and Tina always looked like the living dead with deep bags under her eyes and a permanent frown of sadness on her face. She was pale and gaunt. When Tina first went back to work, everyone walked around her on eggshells, never knowing what to say or how to act. Tina knew that and she liked having that over everyone; it felt good that everyone should be quiet and have no joy. It was just the way she thought everyone should be, everyone deserved to be punished because Justin was dead. If she had to endure life, that is what she wanted everyone around her to do. She wanted everyone to be miserable.

When Tina started back at work, it felt good to be distracted, however, it triggered her to see busyness as a distraction. She began to fill her life with things to do, places to be and people to see – nothing of real value. Emma was either dragged along or forgotten about and Sally was lost in the busy schedule. Tina didn't realise that she was simply filling her days so that she didn't have time to think about the reality of her life. She neither enjoyed nor even really experienced what she was doing or who she was interacting with. It was worse at night time; terrible thoughts played in her mind and sadness overcame her. To combat these feelings, she either stayed up most of the night doing things, busy work, or she drugged herself until she was comatose.

Tina and Jane's relationship was fast becoming one that was only made up of things to do and places to be. There was no connection or soul to soul conversation ever held between them; Tina was all business. If Jane didn't want to be part of that, Tina found another person that would do what she wanted or be where she wanted them to be. There was a deep and dark hatred just under the surface of Tina, simmering away, and it would pop out with a sharp and hurtful tongue. She wanted to hurt people around her so that they would hurt for a second or two, just as she was hurting. Tina would feel a little relieved after lashing out, but it quickly passed and guilt began to settle in. But the guilt never stopped her.

Tina pulled up in Jane's driveway, she turned the ignition off and her hands fell into her lap. She wasn't sure why she was there. She felt panic inside and didn't know what to do with how she felt. Tina couldn't put her finger on why she felt so panicked, but the uneasiness pushed her to try and reach out for some help, advice or anything else that could take away her discomfort. In a split second, she pushed the car door open and jumped to her feet. The quicker she moved, the more she felt some relief. She raced to the front door and rang the bell. She did reach for the door handle to open the door but it was locked. Tina stood there for a moment, puzzled where her sister could be because she was always so predictable. She needed her. Anger started to build, the plan was not going her way. The doorbell caught her attention and she began to press it, endlessly. She started banging on the door, as hard as she could. When she had worn herself out without any result, Tina walked over to the front step, sat down and burst into tears. She was crying out of desperation for someone to save her from her herself and her pain. Howls of pain escaped from her lips and she began to rock as she wrapped her arms around her waist. Just as she became hysterical, Jane pulled into the driveway. Jane noticed her sister's car and was surprised by the visit. Tina had not been to her house since a few days before Justin's accident, almost a year at this point. Jane had come to realise that Tina would never be the same and she certainly wouldn't be interested in her life again. She saw Tina on the front step and wondered what she was doing and, as concern built within her, she raced to Tina's side.

Jane didn't speak to Tina, she just wrapped her arms around her. She didn't speak because she didn't know what to say, but also she was so uncomfortable by the display of pain that she didn't want to exacerbate it. At first, Tina was resistant for Jane to hold her, but she eventually surrendered to the embrace. For the past year, she had held herself together by keeping everyone at arm's length, with no talk of Justin or her grief. She had wanted to reach out to her sister but something had kept Tina from doing so.

Jane had so wanted her sister back, back to the sharing friendship they had previously, but she thought that it was never going to happen.

When Tina had stopped crying, Jane finally spoke, "Why don't we go inside for a cup of tea?"

Tina nodded in agreement. Jane rattled through her keys and fumbled to open the front door. She had been nervous around Tina for the last few months; she had big news, life changing news, but she was hesitant to share it with her. Jane didn't want her sister to know she was moving forward with life, but she had a secret that she couldn't keep much longer.

Justin's death had made Jane realise that her life needed to change, a change in career and a change in family. Justin's death had shocked her from the life she had been living. A life where she had been feeling empty but didn't want to admit it to herself or her husband, Scott. As a result, Jane had quit her job as a legal secretary and found herself a new job. She had chosen to train and work as a barista at a coffee hutch, only a few minutes' drive from her house. She loved it, talking to people and spreading cheer. It was a happy place and she loved the light hearted nature of her new role. The most rewarding thing was when people loved their coffee. Her customers liked it that she knew their names and their orders and she enjoyed spreading the love. However, there was something else in her life that she was longing to change.

Jane put the kettle on, opened the back door and suggested they sat on the back veranda in the garden. She loved it outside and thought it might help Tina feel a little better. As they sat and made small talk, the mood lightened a little. Again, Jane wasn't sure she wanted to know exactly why Tina was so upset but, in her heart, she knew it was time to tackle Tina's pain.

"What's upset you so much, Sis?"

Jane made eye contact with Tina. She noticed the dark circles under her eyes and her pale complexion. Jane could feel Tina's resistance to share.

"If you can't share with me, Tina, who can you share with? I am your sister, you can trust me, I love you and you know I would do anything for you."

Tina's silence continued as she gazed at the floor. Jane wasn't sure what to say, but she took a deep breath and concentrated her energy on her heart. Another deep breath, and then another.

"You know what I have found the hardest since the accident, Tina?" She paused to see if she had the strength to continue, "The most gut-wrenching thing is that it seems as though the world has moved on without him. I thought the world should have fallen apart and mourned our loss forever. It didn't feel right that life was moving without him."

A tingle rattled down Tina's spine. She knew that she should talk to Jane but Tina had made the armour around her very strong.

Jane continued, "I miss him, I miss our family and our lives without him. Life is so sad at times. I don't know how to live, or even interact, anymore. You know, the way I have come to reconcile all this is that I would rather have known and loved Justin than not have had him at all." Tears welled in Jane's eyes and she was determined not to cry, "Justin was so funny and light and had a real passion for life and doing what was right and just. More than once, he made me see we should always choose kindness and always choose love."

Tina took an enormous breath of relief to hear these words from Jane. She had loved Justin so much and missed him every day, so it was so good to hear that someone else was experiencing something similar. It gave her hope that, maybe, she could begin to move forward with life.

Words eluded them both. Jane's breathing was the only thing that filled the space. It was hard and heavy, like she was trying to get something out but it wasn't ready to come.

Finally, she said, "We can still, and always will, love him. When I get lost in my thoughts and grief, I try to find the love I have for him and feel how lucky I was to be his Aunt."

Jane was reluctant to continue but she had been holding herself back from her own truth for long enough. She thought if she spoke to Tina and the situation exploded, then at least she had said her piece and it was out there.

Joe had been helping her to find peace, a peace that she had never felt before. Peace with death, peace with living. Sharing it with her sister was something she felt compelled to do. Their relationship had become one of superficial interaction, but Jane longed to share.

"I miss him!" Tina finally broke down and spoke, "I am haunted by the fact that we turned the ventilator off. What if he could have recovered but we killed him?"

Jane jumped straight in, "Now, that is just crazy talk! You know that there was no way Justin could survive with his injuries. You're torturing yourself."

"It all haunts me, truthfully, day and night. I wake in a cold sweat of panic as I recall the last days with him in the hospital and the last hours at home." Tina began to sob.

Jane stood up to walk around and sit beside Tina. She reached out and held her hand, "You are torturing yourself. You had no control over the situation, what happened or why it happened. You couldn't have stopped it or prevented it. It just happened."

"But what if I stopped him from going to the skate park that day? If I had looked for him earlier, maybe his injuries may not have been so bad."

"It is what it is. What happened, happened. I find some peace in the idea that God has a plan and that plan is something that you can't control. We can only get on the rollercoaster and ride the ride of life."

Tina retaliated, "Don't talk to me about God. There is no God! The God I thought there was, wouldn't do this to a child, wouldn't do this to a family." Tina pushed Jane's hand away, tears of frustration flowed.

"I know how you feel, I know this is tough. But do you think Justin would have wanted you to be so tortured by his death and absent from life?"

Tina didn't respond she just continued to stare at the floor.

"It doesn't have to be this way," Jane continued.

"What would people think of me if I just got on with life? I deserve to be sad and miserable."

"What do you mean, you deserve it? You don't deserve to be tortured and miserable. Yes, Justin died. Yes, he is not with us on this earth anymore, but I am 100% positive that he is with us in spirit and he would want us all to be happy. He would want us to remember our love for him and keep loving him. That love is what makes his life worth it. It is what makes having him in our lives worthwhile."

"I do love him and that is why I have to mourn him forever."

"What if you just loved him forever? No self-punishment is required of you. Let us celebrate his life and the love we all shared..."

Silence fell over the conversation, yet again. As Jane looked at Tina, she felt that what she was saying was beginning to sink in.

After a few seconds, Tina nodded, "I so want to feel the way you feel, I just want to feel the love and no guilt."

The sister's eyes met and Tina actually initiated an embrace with Jane. They held each other tight. In that moment, Jane felt a relief that she had longed for and hoped for. She felt like she had finally gotten through to Tina. Jane knew that Tina would never be the same but she now held hope that Tina might start to heal.

The sisters sat on the veranda, drank their tea and made small talk. Eventually, Tina's gaze fell into Jane's lap and, as she looked, she noticed that Jane had an unprecedented belly bump. Her sister was a fitness freak and had always been trim and fit, so this surprised her. She raised her eyes to meet her sister's and an uneasy feeling rose within Jane; she knew her secret was out. Both sisters were lost for words. In that instant, Tina realised that she had stopped life, she had stopped the flow. She had been completely absent from her sister's life and consumed by her own torture and grief. The sadness had stopped them sharing and living life together, just as they always had. The reality and truth of their conversation hit Tina, hard. Guilt filled within her. She knew why her sister hadn't told her and it hurt.

"So, you're having a baby?" Tina managed a tiny glimpse of a smile.

"GRIEF CAN MAKE YOU
ABSENT FROM LIVING
IN YOUR LIFE."

42

JAKE - DOWNWARD SPIRAL, READY TO STOP

JAKE WAS STILL IN THE SAME HOLDING PATTERN OF working hard and drinking hard and Tina had had enough. The girls had gone to the park and Tina was ready to explode. She had organised for Jake's mother and father to come over and all three of them were going to talk to Jake about his choices. Jake's father, Tom, had noticed Jake's heavy drinking and he had given his son some slack, understanding that he was going through a tough time, but things were getting out of hand.

Following Justin's accident, Tom and Grace had moved back from the other side of the country to live one suburb away from Tina and Jake. Grace had pushed for the move since the day they returned home following the death. It had taken her over a year to make it happen, but she was determined that Justin's death was going to make her change her life for the better. For her, his death was a wakeup call that, if she ignored, she would regret it for the rest of her days. Grace wanted to be a part of her family's life. She wanted to see them grow, she wanted to be there for them whenever they needed her. She wanted to be loved and to love with all her heart and not hold back. She felt like Justin's death had saved her.

Jake walked through the back door and Tina yelled out, "I am in here."

Jake grabbed a beer from the fridge and heading into the lounge room. He cracked the lid and guzzled half the bottle and, instantly, relief flooded over him. As he turned the corner and caught a glimpse of the lounge, he was startled by his Mum and Dad's presence.

"Hi, Son," Tom got to his feet and reached out to embrace Jake.

"LOVE IS HAVING THE
ABILITY TO BE TOUGH
AT TIMES, SAY THE
HARD THINGS AND DO
THE HARD THINGS."

43

PETER & MICHAEL - JUSTIN'S ADVENTURE

THE TIME FINALLY ARRIVED AND THE BOYS WERE boarding a plane heading to America. Peter found great relief that they were actually doing it, fulfilling Justin's dream, and Michael felt pure bliss that they were embarking on their 'adventure'. They had come a long way and were ready to take on the trip that they had been planning for months.

They settled into their seats after take-off and Michael was fiddling with his television when Peter interrupted, "I know this was Justin's adventure and we are doing it for him, but I think we should do it for your dad as well."

"What do you mean, do it for my dad?"

"Let me start at the beginning... Remember that day you helped me at the skate park when I busted myself up?"

"Yes, absolutely."

"Well, I think you were following God's plan, God's plan to bring us together."

"You think?"

"I really do because I had successfully pushed every single person away from me and I was an arse to be around, but you persevered. You had to have been following something because no one else would have put up with me."

"You weren't that bad!"

"I know I was. I feel like your dad has helped me through tough times, through you. You made me get on with life, you made me realise that I could keep my friendship with Justin alive. I understand what you said to me that day in the skatepark, that I would become a better person, and I feel like I have."

Michael nodded in agreement.

"So, I think we should dedicate this adventure to both Justin and your dad for making us both better people."

Michael was moved by Peter's words and it made him remember what a great person his dad had been, and he liked that. He fist pumped Peter in celebration; it was all he could do as he was lost for words.

———

AFTER FOUR DAYS of their adventure, having already met so many people and experienced so many things, they arrived in Kings Canyon. They were due to head off the following day on their three day hike to climb the highest peak, but Peter was planning a little hike of his own for sunrise. Peter had surveyed the area and had chosen a peak not far from their accommodation. He woke at 4am, climbed out of bed and grabbed his jumper. Peter had found a photo of himself and Justin, which was taken only a short while before his death, and he had also found a little skateboard keyring that Justin had given him for his last birthday together. He put them in his pocket, along with his phone and a torch, and headed to the spot he had scoped out the day before. This was something he had to do alone, something he felt would be cathartic for his own healing.

Peter climbed up to the ledge and sat there, waiting for the sunrise. This was something that Justin had wanted; he had always wanted to see a sunrise at Kings Canyon and Peter intended to show him. After some time, the sun started to rise and the excitement of fulfilling Justin's desire flooded Peter.

"Hey, mate. I did it, I made it. A lot of heartache and missing you but I have made it."

He was happy that he achieved this dream but with a sigh, he said, "But, mate, I have to leave you here. I have to let go of this pain in my chest that has sat there since the day of your accident. You know I was so pissed off with you for leaving me, but since you left, I have realised that God had a plan for you." He paused and took a deep breath, "You have made me a better person for knowing you."

He watched the sun rise a little higher and smiled with glee as the tears ran down his face, "I love you, man, but I have to leave my hurt here. It is too heavy and I don't want it to drag me down for the rest of my life."

Peter reached into his pocket and pulled out the photo of himself and Justin. He admired Justin's smile while he recalled the day it was taken. He placed the photo on the dirt in front of him and started shifting small rocks and placing them on top of the photo. Every time he put a rock over the photo he spoke, "Thank you, my friend, for all the laughs, thank you for fun, thank you for the skating, thank you for the footy, thank you for all those camping trips, thank you for the fishing, thank you for your company, thank you for our familiarity, thanks for being my brother from another mother. I am so thankful that I knew you and that we got to spend so much time together." As he reached for the skateboard keychain he continued, "Thank you for this pain I feel because, without it, I would never had known the love we shared, bro. I will love you forever."

Peter placed the keyring on top of the pile of rocks and

closed his eyes, "I am leaving this pain right here, man. I will take the happy times and the love with me."

A cold shiver ran down his body and, in that moment, he realised that Justin would always be with him. The shiver was a sign that he was right there with him, in that moment.

Peter took a few deep breaths and felt the burden he had been carrying leave his body, his eyes closed and he felt a cool breeze float across him. The sun grew brighter by the second and, when he opened his eyes, he saw the most spectacular scene.

"God's really putting on a show for us, Justin. Here's to you!"

Peter stood up, selected a small rock and threw it over the ledge with all his might. It was exactly what Justin would have done if they were together.

Peter had found some healing.

Take the love and the happy memories with you forever.

Peter walked back into the boys' hostel room.

"Mate, there you are! I was starting to get a bit worried."

"It's all good. I just had to do a thing but I am all good now."

Peter felt exhausted but so much lighter. Michael didn't probe Peter for any further information because he figured that his friend had been doing something that he thought he should do on his own, otherwise they would have been together.

"Right then, let's do this thing, Pete. Let's tick off the first thing on our list, Kings Canyon."

"Can we have breakfast first?" Peter joked.

A FEW WEEKS LATER, the boys were floating through a cave in Ha Long Bay, Vietnam, when Michael felt a heavy sensation come across his shoulders. He looked back at Peter to see what he was doing, but Peter was paddling away. Michael tried to shake it off, but the feeling remained. As the guide lead them to the sand shore inside the cave, Michael felt the strong urge to walk towards the back wall of the cave. His shoulders felt so heavy that he wanted to sit down and he began to worry if he had contracted some weird tropical disease. The rocks were sharp where he was standing, so he moved to an area where there was a flat rock to sit. He sat down with bent knees and placed his hand on the back of his neck. With his eyes shut, he took some deep breaths, before opening them. As he opened his eyes, Michael caught note of something silver and shiny amongst the rocks and sand. He picked it up and rubbed it clean to take a closer look. It was an Australian 50 cent piece.

Michael gasped. *Unbelievable! I wonder how this got here.*

It was as though someone had given Michael a shake; memories of him and his dad collecting 50 cent pieces returned to him. He hadn't thought about these specific memories for many years, but his dad had a jar that every time they got a 50 cent piece, they would put it in the jar on the kitchen bench.

His dad would always say, "Save your pennies and the pounds will look after themselves."

They used this saying all the time and, looking back, he realised that his dad was trying to teach him to save his money and show him that a little bit at a time will, eventually, become a lot. Michael smiled from ear to ear as he remember these moments and the heaviness from his shoulders lifted.

He spoke out loud to his dad, "Thanks for being with me here, Dad. I know you would be proud of me and, yes, I saved all my pennies for this trip and left your pounds safely in the bank for another day."

Michael was happy but, in a spilt second, he was grief-stricken. His heart ached and the reality of missing his dad hit him hard. He swallowed and tried to push his sadness away, but unfortunately there was no relief. He kept his head down and sobbed. He hadn't felt such sadness about his dad for many years. He had remained strong and focused on the love and happy memories they had shared instead.

Michael had become oblivious to his surroundings and hadn't realised that Peter was coming up close behind him.

"What ya doing?" Peter's voiced rang loud in Michaels ears.

Michael heaved in a big breath to try and contain himself, but it had no effect. Peter caught a glimpse of Michael's face and was surprised to see him in such a state. He wasn't sure if he should ask what was bothering him, or just sit down and be with his friend. Peter felt overwhelmed seeing his friend like this, it was a side of him that he had never seen. Michael had been a rock, but Peter knew firsthand that sadness could hit at any time and the smallest of things could trigger it. He sat down and put his arm around his mate to comfort him.

Peter felt the need to speak, "Your Dad would be so proud of you, man. You're such a good fella and a wise friend."

Michael heard the words and broke down again. He couldn't speak but knew his dad was there with him and it was an overwhelming realisation. He began to understand that his dad would always be with him, guiding him, and still loving him.

They sat in silence for a few minutes before Michael stood up and said, "Let's keep looking around."

He rubbed the 50 cent piece between his fingers and consciously put it in his pocket, never explaining anything to Peter. He was trying hard to hold on to the love and leave the sadness behind, but it was a struggle.

"GRIEF IS
UNPREDICTABLE."

44

JAKE & JOE – FINDING SOME PEACE

Jake found himself sitting at a coffee shop that he had never been in, but that Scott had convinced him would be good for him. He had agreed to meet a stranger that had, apparently, helped Scott get through things. Jake had managed to give up his drinking habit, but quitting had exacerbated his need to be a workaholic. Scott had recognised the change in Jake. He had been getting angry and frustrated with life when, before Justin's death, he was a placid man who lived to enjoy his family, he was funny and light-hearted. Scott felt the need to get Jake some help, so that his friend could grow instead of perishing.

Scott and Jake had been thrust together because of their wives; the women being sisters meant that it was expected the men would be friends. In the beginning, Scott was the one that made their friendship uncomfortable. He had never had a good male friend as he always kept everyone at a distance. Scott was scared of loving people and losing them, but Jake was just too friendly to resist. He kept including Scott in of all the family happenings and Scott knew that Jake had helped heal his heart a little. It was why he felt the need to reach out and help Jake. It was why they ended up sitting at a coffee shop waiting for Joe, the stranger, to talk to Jake.

Scott had warned Jake that Joe wouldn't be what he was expecting and that he should have an open mind. He had explained that he'd been chatting with Joe since the day of Justin's funeral. Scott couldn't put into words exactly what Joe had taught him, but he explained that he was better for having spent time with him. Frankly, Jake was sick of refusing Scott's invitations and felt he had nothing to lose.

Scott saw Joe walking up the street, smiling brightly and pushing his trolley straight towards the coffee shop as they had previously organised. Scott waved at him as Joe strolled over. Scott had already filled Joe in on what he knew of Jake's inner turmoil, but in reality, he knew nothing of his pain. Joe was open to talking with anyone, never showing any apprehension about a situation. Scott often wondered what had happened to Joe in his life for him to live the way he did, but anytime the conversation moved to him, Joe was great at turning the talking right back around to Scott.

Scott could see Jake assessing the situation; he had noticed Joe's shopping trolley. He said a little internal prayer, *Please, please, let this be a healing experience.*

Scott greeted Joe and introduced Jake as his brother-in-law and they all made small talk for a while.

Joe finally began the difficult conversation, "So, what brings you here today, Jake? Scott tells me you have had it pretty hard."

Jake nodded. He was a bit embarrassed, but also annoyed in the same second.

"If you call your kid dying 'pretty hard' then yeah, I suppose."

Jake wanted to embarrass Joe and make him feel

uncomfortable, but Joe simply nodded his head sympathetically. He was not deterred from the conversation.

"What are you struggling with the most?" Joe asked.

"What do you mean, the most?"

Scott could see that Jake was getting worked up and it was this behaviour that had made Scott grow concerned in the first place; Jake was quick to anger and then he would just shut down.

"What is troubling you the most about your son's death, Jake?"

"What the hell do you mean? Isn't it obvious? Mate, my kid is dead and I'm still alive and life is just all stuffed up."

"I know it doesn't seem fair when a child dies, it is hard to carry on." Joe wasn't giving up, he was trying to find a way in.

"Who are you, mate?" Jake squinted his eyes, "What the hell do you want from me?"

"I think you know. Scott wanted me to check in on you."

"Check in on me? What qualifies you as an expert, mate? You are pushing a trolley around town and I assume you're homeless. Pretty sure you don't know much." Jake shoved his chair back as he stood up, "I'm out of here!"

Jake took off with pace towards his car. Scott and Joe locked eyes and Scott shook his head, devastated at the outcome.

"I think I better go after him, Joe. I am sorry, I thought he would be more receptive."

"Sometimes you just must wait for someone to be ready to listen. No harm done. I'm sure I will see you soon."

Scott hesitated to leave.

"Go, go check on him," Joe insisted.

Scott caught up to Jake marching down the street, "Hey, Jake. Jake! Do you want some help or are you planning to live in this misery forever?"

Jake stopped and shook his head at Scott, his eyes seethed

with anger, "I am going home." He turned his back and headed for his car. Jake watched him walk away, more disappointed than he had been in his whole life.

Jake got to the car and slammed the door shut. He grabbed the steering wheel, acting as if he was going to rip it off, all the while yelling, "ARRGGHHHHH!!"

When he was finished letting off steam, he shook his head and his gaze fell to his lap. He was exhausted. Jake knew that he was not doing a very good job of life, but he didn't know what to do next. He sat in his car for a while, not knowing where to go or what to do. Scott had left in despair.

Jake didn't want to go home and he had had enough of work. If he visited anyone, they would ask the obligatory question, *How are you doing?*

Jake knew that it really meant, *How are you coping with life now your son is dead?*

After a while, he raised his eyes to the footpath, just as Joe was pushing his trolley past the car.

Far out, that guy. What a joke!

When Joe reached Jake's window, he turned his head and the men's eyes met. Jake was taken aback by the connection, but Joe was happy for it. He continued to walk on down the street towards Queens Park.

I suppose he's heading home, ready to set up camp for the night. Nastiness was dripping from every cell of Jake's body. He was trying hard to discredit Joe so that he felt ok about blowing the stranger off.

Jake was angry and bitter and he didn't know what to do with his emotions. He was talking things through in his head when he came to the conclusion that he hated God, he hated him for taking Justin away and letting him live. He hated the guilt he felt for living and he hated the pain and suffering that guilt caused. He hated God because now Jake hated life.

Jake was lost and had no idea what to do with himself. He began to think about what he had just done. Firstly, he thought about how he had probably embarrassed Scott. Secondly, he was feeling ashamed of how he had behaved. Finally, what did he have to lose speaking rationally to Joe, just to see what he had to say? Nothing in his life was getting any better, so why not?

Maybe I can find Joe in the park and have a civilised chat? It can't hurt, he rationalised.

Jake headed towards the park, before he could back out of his decision. As he approached the park, he didn't have to look far to find Joe. The man was sitting on a park bench, just inside the gate, and appeared to be chatting with a young man. Jake parked the car, ready to face Joe, but he was beginning to lose his nerve. He realised that he had been such an arrogant pig that he had probably blown his chance.

Jake's phone began to ring and the name 'Scott' appeared on the screen. He had no intention of answering it, so he just watched it ring out and go to message bank. The call made him question why Scott thought Joe could help him. Scott had been pushing Jake for months and months to talk with Joe, especially since he had stopped drinking.

Is there really any reason to push myself to go speak with Joe? Was I right before when I said I have nothing to lose? Jake's thoughts began to race.

Anxiety began to build within him, but Jake got out of the car and headed towards Joe anyway. As he approached, he could see that Joe was in deep conversation which slowed his momentum. He decided to sit on the park bench directly opposite Joe and patiently wait. After a few minutes, the young man speaking with Joe stood up and reached out to shake hands with him. Joe shook his hand and bowed his head. Jake continued to study Joe, intently. As the man walked off, Joe raised his line of sight to see Jake sitting directly in front of him.

"That didn't take too long," Joe whispered under his breath.

Jake peeled himself from the seat. His heart was racing and he still wasn't sure why he was talking to a homeless man, but continued his journey over to the opposite park bench to join Joe. Joe was welcoming and motioned for Jake to sit beside him.

Jake wasn't sure how to start the conversation but he needn't have worried because Joe spoke first, "You found me. What would you like to talk about, mate?"

Jake shrugged, "To tell you the truth, I'm not sure."

"Loss is tough and most people don't know how to start to heal. Actually, most people never heal."

Jake didn't react. It was taking everything within him to stay. He wasn't sure why he was so stressed, but it was continuing to build. The trees rustled in the breeze above their heads and Joe looked up, noticing the beautiful green of the branches and paying attention to how they were swaying. Jake remained sceptical about the homeless man sitting beside him.

"I think the best healing begins with the realisation that you are allowed to heal. You don't have to feel guilty about living because your loved one has passed away. Do you feel guilty, Jake?"

He hesitated before responding, "I don't know."

"Ok then, so do something for me... Imagine yourself doing something that you and your son did together... Did you ride bikes together or play football? Did you have a thing you did together that was uniquely yours?"

"We fished."

"Ok, can you imagine fishing now, without him?"

"No," Jake's voice remained quiet.

"Well, I want you to imagine fishing without him now. How would that feel?"

Silence fell over their conversation.

"I can't, it hurts too much," Jakes bottom lip quivered.

Joe wanted to reach out and comfort Jake but knew he didn't know the man well enough. Joe could feel Jake's pain, the air around them was palpable with it.

Joe let a minute pass before continuing, "That is guilt, Jake. Your son is gone but you need to know that you can still live. It is the first step to any sort of healing. I know it is hard to bear, but life does go on."

Joe knew firsthand that this step was hard, living while the person you loved is gone.

It was enough to break Jake, "Life goes on? Life goes on? You have no idea! If you knew anything about this then you would know better than to say anything even remotely like that!"

Joe nodded his head at Jake and very calmly said, "Jake, do you think that I would offer such advice if I didn't have any life experience in this area?"

Joe raised his eyebrows at Jake and he could see Jake's anger begin to melt.

"What do mean by experience, Joe? Have you had a kid die?"

"I have and all I wanted to do for a long time was to die myself." Joe looked down at his fingers in his lap, "It was a while ago now, but the first few years were rough. I just couldn't understand why I got to live. Guilt plagued me day and night. I found no joy in life. From the guilt within me grew anger, so much anger. I was so pissed off with the world and everyone in it. I did some pretty bad things, reckless and cruel. My attitude had changed. I wasn't the person I was before and I just didn't want to live. I started using drugs. I screwed my life up so much that I could never go back to how things were, nobody wanted me back. So, if you want to know if I understand where you are coming from, you now know."

Joe's words softened Jake. He had a thousand questions to ask Joe about his personal life, but his own reality set in. His own downward spiral; the alcohol, work, his inability to enjoy anything. The only thing that gave him a reason to live was his innocent little girl, Emma, but it had even been getting harder and harder to enjoy time with her.

"So, Jake, I had guilt." Joe emphasised the 'I'. "So much guilt about being alive. I know firsthand how to start to heal."

"How did you do it though? It's fine to say don't feel guilty, but how do you feel like that?"

Jake was now focused because he had asked this question of himself many times, *How do you come back from such a dark place?*

"I had to get out of my head and stop thinking so much. My thoughts were consuming my life. It would start with the smallest thing. Say it was raining and that would remind me of something with my family, the thought after that would build to a happy memory which would devastate me and I would want to die. It would go on, day and night, and I wouldn't sleep. Everything would be compounded. My guilt, my sadness, I couldn't get out of the loop. Then, one morning after a night of abusing myself, I found myself sitting on the steps of that church over there." Joe pointed across the park where you could just see the steeple of a church, "The sun was just rising and I remember thinking, 'Damn, morning has come around quickly.' A gentleman sat down beside me and asked me a simple but life changing question. I am not sure where he came from and I have never seen him since. I have looked many times. He gifted me a book about this thing called 'Mindfulness' and that was when my life started to feel a little better. Mind you, every day was a battle, but the feelings I began to have about living were a little more positive."

"I don't get it... You read a book, a guy asked you a question and your life was all better? It makes no sense. It's not that easy."

"I agree, Jake, it is not that easy."

———

JOE AND JAKE spent hours sitting on the bench, talking through the process of becoming mindful. How to catch thoughts built by the ego and how to use your breath to let them go. The conversation was the same one Joe had held with hundreds of people over the years. The same conversation that he had held with Scott and Jane. It focused on the use of breath to find peace, allowing thoughts to float through a person so they don't latch on and torment them. The more a person can allow their thoughts to build, the more powerful the emotions can become.

Joe spoke about allowing the good memories of the love Jake and Justin shared to lift Jake up, rather than let the sadness of losing him to drag him down.

Joe instructed Jake, just as he had with Jane.

"Close your eyes. Don't worry, I'll do it with you. Breathe deeply, concentrating on your breath. Breathe in through your nose and out through your mouth." Joe made exaggerated breathing sounds to guide Jake. "If a thought comes to your mind, thank it and ask it to move on or watch it drift off into the sky. Always bring your attention back to your breath. Imagine your chest light up with white light and your heart fill with love. Use a memory to find the love, a love-filled moment in your life. It could be a hug or a laugh with someone. Evoke the feeling using this memory and then hold it in your heart. Watch and feel the light spread across your body, then to your surroundings. Surrender to it, surrender to the love. Breathe in and breathe out…"

Both men sat there in silence with their eyes closed. Jake was bathing in the relief of his quiet mind and Joe was relishing in the love spinning within his own heart.

When they had finished with their mindfulness exercise, Joe looked directly at Jake.

"Now, this is what Justin would want you to feel, love and peace." Joe rubbed his heart centre, "Yes, he is gone, but keep the love you shared. Use it to fuel yourself and your happiness. It is better to have loved and lost, than to not have loved at all."

The sun was beginning to go down and a coolness spread over the park. Jake hadn't noticed the changes because he had been listening intently to Joe. A harsh breeze whizzed over them which brought Jake back to reality. He was surprised by the time of day.

"I suppose I should leave you be, Joe. It seems I have taken up too much of your time."

"Your choice, mate. It does seem to be getting cold. Will your family be wondering where you are?"

"Maybe."

Jake's energy seemed a little lighter, although his shoulders were still humped and the bags under his eye still exuded sadness.

"Can I just ask you one question? What did that man ask you on the church steps that made you see the light?"

Joe paused before he answered, he hadn't told anyone his story in a very long time.

"He asked, 'Do you want to live like this forever?'"

Joe hoped that Jake would ask himself that question, he hoped that he would make some changes, but he wasn't convinced.

A few minutes passed.

"Well, you know where to find me, Jake, if you ever want to chat again."

Jake stood up and turned to face Joe, "Are you going to be alright here, Joe? Why don't you come home with me? It seems as though it is going to be pretty cold here tonight."

Joe smiled brightly, "I'm ok, Jake, but thank you for the generous offer."

Jake grinned in response. He nodded his head, as if bowing to Joe, "Thanks for your patience with me today."

"Remember, Jake, the love you shared with Justin will never die. Use that love to energise yourself and everything you do. Go outside of yourself and help someone else with no reward required. You will forget your own pain."

RADIATE BOUNDLESS
LOVE TOWARD THE
ENTIRE WORLD."

-BUDDHA

45

JAKE & TINA - DO YOU WANT TO LIVE LIKE THIS FOREVER?

Jake sat in the car and he realised that life made a little more sense to him. He concurred with Joe that he did feel guilty for living while Justin was gone. Since when does a parent outlive their child? It was a monstrous feeling to have that whirling inside you.

"I am now letting that go," Jake spoke out loud as if he was making a promise to himself.

As he looked over at the front passenger seat, a memory of Justin sitting there in the front of the car with him made him smile; Justin just killing himself laughing after a fishing trip. They had been trying to get the boat on the trailer and Jake had been accidentally knocked off into the water. Jake had gotten really mad and yelled at Justin but Justin could only see the funny side to the incident. He had still been laughing at his father fifteen minutes later during their drive home. The memory made Jake smile a heartfelt smile and he even had a little giggle, *Man, that kid always had a happy outlook. He laughed so much.*

Jake took a few days to digest his time with Joe. Scott rang a couple of times a day which Jake assumed was to see if they were still talking, but he never answered. The question that was racing around in his head was the same question that was asked of Joe, *Do you want to live like this forever?*

Home was a sad place, except for little Emma's input, and he had realised that they probably had all made it that way out of the guilt of living. He realised that he must speak to Tina about what he was thinking, but the trouble was that they hadn't really talked for a long time. However, one day, he was determined to do something with his new information, he wanted to let it out and wanted to share it with his family. He burst through the back door, calling Tina's name.

"What, Jake? What are you yelling for?"

Anything that could remotely be an incident or accident, Tina got worked up about. Jake yelling her name had made her panic.

"I just want to talk to you, properly talk to you."

"What do you mean, properly talk to me?"

"I mean we need to talk about Justin. We need to talk about our future."

Tina looked annoyed. She had processed some of her grief, but life still hurt without Justin. The birth of her niece, Sophie, had helped teach her to love a little again and her relationship with Jane had grown which also helped.

"Really?"

"I just think we have been so sad that we have stopped being a couple and stopped being a family. We've stopped talking. Someone asked me recently if I want to live like this for the rest of my life and it has really made me think about things." He stopped talking, not knowing if Tina was processing anything he was saying. He was also out of breath trying to get everything out of his head out.

Just when Jake was about to speak again, Tina very deliberately said, "No."

Jake was taken aback. He clarified, "No, you don't want to live like this anymore?"

"No, I don't, but I don't know how to get rid of this pain, Jake. He was our boy."

"I know, Tina, it is just so painful."

They stood in the kitchen, face to face, heart to heart.

"I went to talk to someone a few days ago and I am feeling a bit better about life, better about our loss and better about living life."

"Wow. I couldn't image you going to see a counsellor, Jake. Who did you see?"

This is where Jake thought things would come unstuck. He didn't know what to say or how to explain his encounter so he chose to say that Scott had introduced them.

Without hesitation, Tina replied, "Oh, that must be the guy who Jane mentioned. She keeps bugging me to go and see him. She reckons he is not conventional but that he has been really helpful for her."

"Maybe," Scott was hoping not to be asked anymore questions.

"So, what was so profound about what he said, Jake?"

Jake walked to the fridge and grabbed a bottle of soft drink, "Do you want one?"

"Yeah, sure."

"Let's sit down."

Tina followed Jake into the lounge room, "I have to go and pick Emma up from dancing in ten minutes"

They both sat down. They hadn't spoken properly to each other for a long time, so they found it weird to be sitting together again. The girls always acted as a buffer between them.

"I don't know where to start really..."

"It's ok, Jane filled me in on some stuff. She has tried to explain things, but I just don't get it."

"To tell you the truth, I can't really put it into words. This guy helped me see that my guilt was torturing me and that I should still love Justin and enjoy other things in life."

"That is sort of what Jane tried to explain to me. It's hard to swallow." Jake spent the next ten minutes trying to get everything out of his head and pass it on to Tina. Tina sat and listened intently.

The evening passed by as it usually would, except Jake and Tina climbed into bed together, which was unusual because they had been avoiding times where they were alone together.

They lay there in the dark and Tina finally said, "Maybe I should talk to this guy, I don't want to live like this forever."

"Maybe you should," Jake replied in the darkness. He had hoped that Tina's answer to the question would be this.

"YOU HAVE TO BE
OPEN TO HEALING."

46

TINA & JOE – FORGIVENESS

Tina and Jake drove down the main street, heading directly for Queens Park.

"So, is he homeless, Jake?"

"He seems to be," Jake shrugged.

"And he makes sense, right?"

Tina was getting nervous. She didn't want to talk about her pain, she just wanted it gone. She could feel her insides quiver.

"So much sense. It's ok to be nervous, we might not even find him."

As they drove up to the car park in front of the gate, Jake quickly recognised Joe pushing his trolley through the park.

"There he is, Tina," Jake motioned to Tina.

"He looks so clean and well kept. He certainly doesn't look homeless, but the trolley gives it away."

"He is going to help you. I know you are nervous, I was a wreck, but I pushed myself to go and talk with him."

The car stopped and Jake took the key out of the ignition, "Are you ready?"

"I'm not so sure now."

Tina clenched her hands together. Jake turned to her and

grabbed her hands. They looked at each other and Jake whispered, "Trust me."

After a few seconds, Tina nodded her head in agreement.

Jake went back to the car after he made the introductions. Joe had been open and friendly, happy to see Jake. He had wrapped his arms around Jake and hugged him tightly. Jake felt like Joe was hugging some love straight into him. As Jake settled into his car seat, he could see the back of Tina and Joe sitting on the same park bench that they had been on a few weeks before. Jake had been able to share more of his experience with Tina, so he felt she was prepared. He had made sure she knew that Joe, too, had lost a child, hoping that it would soften her to everything Joe said. As he watched them talk, Jake realised that he could be waiting for a long while for Tina to return to the car.

One hour turned into two. Jake dozed off for a bit but, mostly, he recalled what Joe and he had spoken about the day they sat on that same bench. He remembered lots but he also feared that he had forgotten stuff. He realised that he had held onto all that he needed to know right now, but he knew, in the future, he would be talking to Joe again.

As he watched Tina and Joe, Jake noticed Tina lean against Joe's shoulder. Joe reached around her and gave her a sideways hug. Jake thought that this was a good thing; she was listening to his advice. They both stood up and Joe lent over his trolley, he appeared to be looking for something. He pulled out a book and handed it to Tina. They hugged again and Tina began to walk towards the gates of the park. Joe turned and saluted towards Jake, Jake sat up straight and saluted right back.

By the time Tina got to the car, she was crying hard, nearly hysterical. She opened the door and sat down. She wasn't hiding the tears from Jake, she couldn't contain herself.

"Tina, what's wrong?"

This was not what Jake expected. He began to feel very concerned if he had done the right thing.

"Joe said I must forgive the world or God or whatever I believe in, for taking Justin away. That is one tough call."

Tina was angry but appeared beaten. She was crying with exhaustion and despair.

"He said, if I forgive I will begin to heal."

Jake was looking through the centre console for some tissues. He found some and handed them to Tina.

"Forgiveness... That is big." Jake grabbed one of Tina's hands, "I didn't want Joe to upset you, I just thought it would help."

"He did help me. He made a lot of sense but, as I walked away from him, it just felt so hard to do what he asked of me. I have this hate, you know, inside of me, that gives me the right to be whoever I want to be. I hate the world and I hate the doctors that couldn't save my boy and I especially hate God for taking Justin from me." She paused, "If I let go, what do I have? If I forgive, who do I blame?"

Jake was struggling for words as Tina continued, "What if I found some peace and happiness? It wouldn't be fair on Justin."

At this, Jake interjected, "I don't know what to say, other than Justin wouldn't want us to be unhappy."

She looked at Jake. Their hands were still together and she squeezed his fingers in silent agreement, "That is what Joe said, forgiveness will set me free."

Jake and Tina drove home in silence. By the time they got home, they were both worn out. "We have to do this for the girls. We have to do life better, if only for them. We are damaging them."

"I just don't know how anymore, Jake. I can't remember how to be me."

"Don't worry. Follow Emma's lead, she will show us the way."

They found the girls sitting in front of the television, watching one of Emma's favourite movies. When Emma heard the door, she jump to her feet.

"Mum! Dad! I am starving! Can we please, please, please have pizza for dinner?"

Emma launched herself into her father's arms, she wrapped her legs around his waist and hugged him with all her might. Jake melted in the love. She jumped down and hugged her mother around the waist and motioned for her to bring her face close to hers.

"Mum", Emma whispered into her ear, "Let's have a Justin special... Three pizzas 'cause I am so hungry."

Tina stood up straight, laughed a little and agreed.

"I will order them," Sally had the phone up to her ear making the arrangements. Jake handed over his credit card for payment and he rubbed Sally's shoulder.

That evening, the four of them sat in front of the television, ate pizza and watched one of Emma's movies. They had a giggle and Emma spoke of Justin, which she did often. Jake and Tina didn't feel the usual pain, there was a tiny glint of happiness. This was new. This was progress. This was healing in action.

———

As they were getting ready for bed, Tina said, "I have to do it, Jake, I have to. Those girls lost their brother and have been emotionally alone since Justin died. I have to forgive. I am only poisoning all our lives. If I keep going, I am going to end up unhappy until the end of my time on this planet. You know you asked me that question 'Do I want to live like this forever?'

I certainly do not." She paused to turn around and face Jake, "I am going to start practising right now."

"How do you practise it, Tina?"

"I forgive, I forgive, I forgive," Tina repeated. She closed her eyes, focused her attention on her heart and breathed deeply. Just as Joe had told her to. Jake could hear her whispering until he drifted off to sleep, "I forgive, I forgive, I forgive."

The next morning, Jake was thinking about forgiveness and he began to get frustrated with himself. If Tina could forgive the situation, why couldn't he? He just could not let it go that Justin was taken away. He kept thinking, *How can I say it is alright that Justin died?*

He was all worked up when she entered the kitchen, "Look, I am happy for you that you can forgive God or whatever for Justin, but I just cannot say that it is alright that he is gone."

"You're up early."

"I just couldn't sleep. Why is it so important that I forgive? It is just an impossibility for me."

Tina was trying to work out how she could articulate what Joe had told her, but she was having trouble finding the words and Jake was being impatient.

"Look, I will do my best at trying to explain." She paused, "It is not actually about forgiving the act of the death, but about forgiving the situation. Joe explained that if you cannot forgive, it creates hatred and anger within you. That is where we are, now, feeling hate and anger. Part of changing things is changing how you feel and forgiveness is key in this process."

Jake tried to digest what Tina was saying but he was so worked up he couldn't take anything in, "Do you really think you can forgive?"

"I have to, Jake."

"I just don't get it."

"Look, Jake, if Joe can forgive for his situation, then we certainly can give it a go."

Jake looked puzzled. Joe hadn't told him much about his own loss, so Jake had just assumed that he had also lost a child.

"What is Joe's situation? He never told me anything really."

"He didn't tell you?"

"Truthfully, I was pretty hostile during our talk."

"Joe lost his three children, his wife and his mother in an accident."

"What? Thee children?" Jake was totally blown away by this information, "And his wife and his mother?" He began to feel behind him for one of the stools to sit on. "Oh my God, are you for real?" Jake couldn't comprehend this information.

"So, can you see, Jake?" Tears welled in Tina's eyes, "We can do this. We still have two children, our families and each other."

"How did they die, Tina?"

"A fatigued truck driver drove straight over the top of their car. They were all killed instantly."

"No wonder he turned to drugs..."

"Drugs? What are you talking about?"

"Joe told me he hated the world and used drugs to cope."

They both digested all this information in silence.

Tina broke the silence, "Imagine, Jake. Losing everyone, imagine the pain..."

"I don't want to think about that, Tina. That really is too much."

"So, you see, Jake, I am sure we can forgive our situation. I'm not saying that Justin dying is ok, I'm just going to forgive the fact that it happened."

"There is no difference in what you just said. It is not ok any way that you look at it."

"There has to be, Jake, that is the only way we can move through this."

Jake stormed off with his keys, he had every intention of going to find Joe. Tina felt comfortable with Jake leaving because she knew exactly where he was going.

"FORGIVENESS IS AN ACT
OF SELF LOVE."

- DR. WAYNE DYER

47

JOE & JAKE – THE HOMELESS MAN

Jake found himself in the car park of Queens Park, but Joe was nowhere to be seen. The peace he had cultivated over the past few weeks was now gone and he could only focus on his anger. He sat and recalled his conversation with Joe and instantly realised that he was doing exactly what they had discussed; allowing his ego to take him over. His thoughts were causing pain and torture. Flashes of Justin's face on his death bed, his funeral, the coffin being lowered... the torture flowed freely. Jake shook his head. It began to feel like his head was going to explode, his heart ached, his throat was all choked up.

How can I possibly be ok with this, with him not being here?

Jake remembered the night before, their family time with the girls happy, and the guilt took another blow at his heart. He was resting his head in his hands on the steering wheel when there was a quiet tap on his window. Jake slowly turned his head to see Joe.

They found themselves on the same park bench.

"What has been happening, mate?" Joe broke the ice.

"I don't know, I just can't let the pain go this morning. What do I do?"

"You know, Jake, I spent a lot of years looking for something

I should 'do' so I would feel better. Something I could achieve that would put me in a place of eternal peace. The truth of it all is that there is nothing of the sort, you have to work at it every day. There is no magic pill or one spiritual lesson you have to concur that frees you. You have got to work at it, you have got to be present."

"I am struggling, Joe. I couldn't possibly forgive the fact that Justin is dead, no matter what anyone says. Tina said that I should be able to forgive and that is just never going to happen."

"Forgiveness is not what you think it is, Jake. You are not forgiving the cause, you are just forgiving the circumstance."

"What the hell does that mean? Forgiveness is forgiveness. I can't understand how you forgave that truck driver that killed your family." It came out of Jake's mouth before he thought too much about it and he regretted it instantly.

"Forgiveness isn't about saying what another person has done is ok, forgiveness is about forgiving the situation so you can let it go. It's so the poison and the darkness don't eat you up."

Jake shook his head in disbelief.

"You see, Jake, I had to forgive a person, but my forgiveness doesn't mean I condone their actions. I am forgiving the situation, forgiving that my family is gone, letting go of the hatred for that driver. This really helped me because now I have no need to judge which means I am free to find peace. If I had held on to all of my pain and torture, it would have only damaged me and stopped me from living and enjoying life. Can you see that this forgiveness connects with releasing the guilt that we spoke about and your ability to be mindful and find some peace?"

Jake was calming down, but he was still finding it hard to understand what Joe was saying.

"Let's walk, Jake. I have got something to give you."

They walked through the park and Joe pointed out some beautiful views on the way. He asked Jake to be present and just enjoy the natural beauty. Joe hoped that Jake would leave his mind chatter behind. Jake did his best to empty his head, he hadn't had such a sad and angry day in while. They walked in silence for most of the way.

Jake remembered that days like this, with all his mind torture, were prior to meeting Joe for the first time. He realised that the other stuff Joe had shared with him had been working, so there was no reason why what he was saying wasn't truth now.

Finally, Jake spoke, "Joe, I think that I was triggered back into my bad habits of thinking too much and I just couldn't get out of the loop. It is hard to think about being ok with the fact that Justin is gone. It makes me so uncomfortable."

"I have been there, Jake, but you have to realise that it is a necessary step in having the ability to love again and to live life with love. Do you want life to be like this forever?" Joe asked the question again, the same question he asked himself regularly.

"You are right, Joe. I know you are."

"This stuff takes practice. It takes dedication, patience and love."

Jake nodded. Before he realised, they were standing on a street curb about to cross the street. They were walking towards a row of terraced houses and were making a direct line to one with a red door. Jake followed Joe, not knowing what they were doing. Joe reached into his pocket, pulled out a key, unlocked the door and gestured for Jake to go inside. Jake was gobsmacked, he had no idea what was happening.

"Let's have a coffee. You want a flat white?"

Jake realised that they were in Joe's house. It was clean and tidy, well-furnished but nothing extravagant.

"Take a seat and clear your mind while I make us coffee."

Jake looked around Joe's little house. He assumed that Joe lived alone. There was a massive floor-to-ceiling bookshelf, at least eight metres wide, filled with books.

"Wow, you have read a lot, Joe," Jake shouted out to Joe as Joe prepared the coffee.

"I have, but there is still lots more for me to read."

Joe placed the coffee in front of Jake.

"Can you see how you can distract your busy mind with a mindful walk. Jake? You did eventually realise that it was your own mind torturing you. Your own mind," Joe highlighted the last three words, slowly.

Jake nodded and sipped his coffee.

The two men chatted for a while and when the conversation came to its natural end, Jake stood up to excuse himself.

"Oh, hang on a minute. Come with me," Joe beckoned.

They walked towards the front door and Joe opened a large cupboard, "I want to give you something, Jake. Something you can refer back to, to ensure you realise you have the power and knowledge with you, always." Joe unzipped one of the bags from his trolley and pulled out a book, "I want you to have this book. If you don't like to read, download the audible copy and listen to it regularly. It is about how to silence your mind and allow happiness."

"Thank you, Joe, that is very kind. Thank you for your precious time, you don't know how much this means to me."

Joe smiled, "Oh, Jake, but I think I do."

Joe bowed his head, placed his hands together in prayer position over his heart and said, "Shanti, shanti, shanti. Go with peace in your heart."

Jake reached out and embraced Joe, "Thank you."

"You know where I live now, so call in any time."

Jake smiled turned around and headed back to the park, feeling so much better than he had that morning. Jake had wanted to ask Joe a lot of questions about his situation, the trolley, his house and all his belongings, but he felt that Joe wanted to keep his life private.

Jake got into the park and felt the need to sit down and gather himself. Thoughts of Joe were circling in his head.

So, he is not homeless. He is well read. His trolley, which I thought held all his worldly possessions, is actually a trolley of books. He doesn't sleep rough and he has a place to call home. I am puzzled. His family is dead, it seems like he lives alone and counsels strangers on the art of finding peace. People wouldn't believe me if I told them this story.

Jake looked down at the book Joe had given him and read the title out loud, "Find Peace in Your Inner World. Written by Joe Finch."

He paused and a puzzled look appeared on his face. *He is an author!*

Jake kept looking back at the red door he could see in the distance, *What a surprising fella!*

He took out his phone and typed 'Joe Finch' into the search engine. He scrolled through the searches and opened a few articles which helped fill him in on Joe's life. A couple of academic papers showed up, photos in academic attire and the front cover of his book. Then, he came across a surprising newspaper article which read, 'Man's Whole Family Killed in Horrific Accident.'

Joe's name appeared in the story which outlined the details of accident. It also included a picture of a younger Joe with his family. The impact of what Jake read moved him. He sat for a while and shook his head in disbelief, wondering how on earth this man had recovered from such devastation. A tear welled in Jake's eye, recalling how the impact of Justin's death had changed and challenged him in ways that were unimaginable. He recalled how he relied on alcohol to remove himself from reality. Jake totally sympathised with Joe losing his whole family. He looked up again at the red door across the park and he could feel his admiration for Joe growing fast. Over the past few weeks, he had doubted some of what Joe had said. Maybe it was just that healing was hard sometimes, but now without a doubt, he knew everything Joe said was truth. It was the way forward and it was the way to finding peace.

As Jake continued to scroll through his phone, he found another newspaper article that read, 'Finch Awarded $24 Million Dollars in Compensation After Losing His family in a Devastating Accident.' Jake couldn't believe the words on the page. It was dated over ten years ago.

Gosh, you should not judge a book by the cover. Twenty-four million dollars. Twenty-four million dollars!

Jake's thoughts raced about how lucky Joe was to have all that money and that he was free to do anything, but then a realisation came to him; he was positive that Joe would give it all back if he could have his family back, the love in his life back, his normal back.

He sure doesn't live like a millionaire; he doesn't live like he has money. Maybe he gave it away or maybe he wasted it on drugs years ago.

Jake recalled Joe's clothes and the house he had just visited. The only extravagance Joe had was his books. Jake decided that that was not a sign of a millionaire. The guilt of his family dying and then being given all that money must have been overwhelming.

Maybe he gave it all away? I wouldn't want money that I

gained from the death of my family. Man, he has reconciled some stuff.

Jake sat on the bench as his admiration grew for Joe. He knew, for sure, that he would learn more from Joe in time and he began to feel it was a great privilege that this stranger had come into his life.

Jake took some deep breaths and picked up the book that was sitting beside him on the bench. He opened the cover and began to read.

"YOU NEVER KNOW SOMEONE ELSE'S STORY. JUDGE LESS AND BE KINDER."

48

SALLY - NEVER HEALING

It had been years since Justin's death and Sally's take on life had not changed. She was still angry, bitter and distant from the world around her. Secretly, she still grieved about what she perceived as her loss, the abandonment that Justin had inflicted on her. Her friends from school fell away and any new friends she made in life were always kept at an emotional distance. Although she did keep people around her to disguise her pain, she did not allow them to get close. She did, however, allow a man to get close, but she still wasn't completely open with him. She always held a little bit of herself back as she feared the pain of what she perceived as abandonment.

Sally and Ben had been together for eight years and lived together, when Sally fell pregnant. As the days got closer to the birth of their child, anxiety began to rise within Sally. Different scenarios of her child dying consumed her thoughts. Every situation she was in, she thought of a way that her child could die or be killed and she began to feel very unsafe. She did not share her agony with anyone.

The day of the birth, Ben had gone out to work; he worked odd hours as a paramedic but had promised to keep his phone on and close by in the event Sally went into labour. Ben was a nice guy, but he was emotionally numb which is what had attracted Sally to him, just the same as she had become. They didn't have a big circle of friends.

As Sally heard the garage door close, she began to clean up the sink and stacked the dishes in the dish washer. She was big, tired and uncomfortable from her pregnancy and was wishing the baby would be born soon. She already loved her unborn child and had made a vow to herself that she would do her best to always keep him, or her, safe. To some extent, she blamed her parents for Justin's death. She decided that they had given him too much freedom and, if they had kept tighter rules, he would still be alive.

While Sally was wishing that her child would be born soon, her thoughts began a downward spiral into birthing scenarios that ended in her child's death. Then, they took an even darker turn and she thought how she would prefer to die and allow her child to live. Her breathing began to quicken and tension tightened in her throat. She pictured the birthing suite, with a dead lifeless baby laying on her chest. She was scared, as frustration began to grip her body. Her version of the events of Justin's death soaked her thoughts and provoked even more frustration and despair. Sally was convinced that her parents didn't do enough to save Justin. She rubbed her forehead hard as the frustration leaked out of every pore of her body. The concept of keeping her baby safe had become something she felt she had to prove to her parents. Sally felt the urge to walk to the mirror in the hallway and take a look at herself as her face became red. She rubbed her belly, and her forehead as if she was comforting both herself and her unborn child.

As she stood there, she was startled by the interruption of the doorbell chiming. Her eyes widened as she looked in the mirror to check her reflection because she didn't want anyone to know what troubled her; she wanted to ensure everyone thought she was capable and together.

As she reached the door, Sally remembered that Emma was due to come over to hang out with her for the day while Ben was a work, since it was so close to her due date. Emma and Sally had stayed close over the years. Emma knew that she could never allow Sally to get too far from her, emotionally, as she was so closed off to the rest of the world. Emma had been very surprised by the development of Sally and Ben's relationship, but she was overjoyed that Sally had connected with another person in this way.

Over the years, Emma had found her thoughts to be consumed by Sally; how to help her and pull her back into the person she was before Justin's death. Emma was only young when it happened, but she vividly remembered what her sister was like before she shut the world out. Emma had been Sally's consistent person over the years, always there and always the same. Tina and Jake had had their up's and down's, emotionally. They were never the same after Justin's death. They worked hard at trying to hold themselves together, but Sally could feel the disconnection between them. Emma was the guiding light for the entire family, including her Aunt Jane and Uncle Scott, always drawing them back to reality and truth.

Emma had processed her loss following Justin's death, but she had realised that it had stolen her childhood. She had to grow up very fast, emotionally, and she had seen the ugliness of grief firsthand. Emma had studied social work and spent her summers travelling and chasing spiritual insight into inner peace, in the hope of bringing some insight to her family. She had always wanted to help them move past their pain. She had recently found a job with an adoption agency that worked to adopt children from India into Australian families. Many of

Emma's travels had taken her to India and she had seen the number of homeless children and wanted to devote her life to helping this process.

Sally opened the door.

"What up, Sis? You had a baby yet?"

Sally pointed to her belly to indicate the obvious. As Emma took a closer look at Sally, she realised her sister's face was flushed. She reached out and grabbed Sally's hand, "Are you ok?"

"Yeah, yeah, I'm fine, just want this baby out of me."

Emma wrapped her arms around her sister and rubbed her back, "You sure that is all it is?"

"Yeah, I am fine."

Emma squeezed her sister a little harder and she began to do something that an Indian friend taught her on her travels; she allowed the love that she felt for Sally to expand and imagined a warm white light surrounding them both.

"Ok, that is enough of that Emma."

Sally turned and walked back to the kitchen as the feelings of frustration and fear bounced straight back. With her back turned to Emma, she continued to stack the dishwasher with dishes and listened to Emma natter away about the movies they should watch today and how they should go down to their favourite café. Sally was half listening, but she was also working on gaining control of herself. Flashes of a dead baby kept speeding through her mind.

"Hey, Sal, are you listening to me?"

Emma noticed Sally raise her hand to her face and she was rubbing her forehead. She was concerned by what she saw. She raced around the kitchen bench and pulled her sister by the shoulders so that they were face to face.

"You are not alright. What is troubling you? A worry shared, is a worry halved."

"No, no, it's nothing. I'm just anxious to have the baby."

"Rubbish, Sally. Tell me the truth."

There was a long pause with Sally looking at the ground and shaking her head, "No, nothing, just stupid thoughts."

"Thoughts about what?"

"I just keep seeing a dead baby..."

"It is natural to worry about the baby."

Sally, finally, broke down and let out what had been worrying her for months, "How am I going to keep this baby safe, this child safe, this teenager safe? It is a lot. I didn't think this all through, not properly."

Emma wasn't sure what to say or where this was coming from. She had spent a lot of time with Sally during her pregnancy and there had been no signs of Sally's stress or strain.

"You just go one day at a time, one minute at a time and make the best decisions you can."

Emma hadn't seen her sister emotional for many years and it made her panic. She had been trying to break through that hard exterior for a long time and she knew that she was the only one on the planet who Sally was real with, but she felt helpless now that her sister was actually upset.

Sally was silent and Emma wasn't sure what to do. "Look, let's sit and have a cuppa tea," she walked Sally over to the lounge and sat her down. "Do you want a green tea or regular?"

Sally shrugged her shoulders. Emma decided to make them both a green tea and she returned to sit next to Sally on the lounge chair.

"I just have this deep unrest within me, Em. This feeling that life is out of control."

"In what way are things out of control?"

"I can't control this birth thing... What if something happens to the baby during the birth?"

With those words, the baby gave Sally a kick and she raised her hand to her belly with a surprised look on her face.

"What's the matter?" Emma could see something had just happened with the baby.

"It's ok, the baby just gave me a whopping kick."

Emma reached out and placed her hand on Sally's, over the bump, "We, of all people, know that life is out of our control, that there is a plan for us and we have to trust and roll with it." A few seconds went by in silence, "There has been no reason to think that anything will go wrong with your birth. You are healthy and the baby is healthy."

"That means absolute shit to me, Emma. Anything can happen, the world is out of our control."

"I hear what you are saying but projecting stories of what may or may not happen in the future is fruitless. Thinking about the possibilities only torments you and no one else."

Emma had been learning about mindfulness and happiness and how they relate to each other. What she had learnt and integrated into her way of being had changed her sense of wholeness and peace. She had tried to share it with Sally previously, but it had all fallen on deaf ears. She realised that this was her chance to really reach out and help her sister feel some happiness again.

Sally began to become more agitated, "You don't understand! It has happened before; people being ripped away without any warning. It could happen again. Do you know that I already love my child? I love them not knowing who they are. What if it happens again? Emma, what if it happens again?"

"If it happens, then you deal with it then, but what if I said it doesn't happen? How would you feel then? What if you get to know and love your child until the day you die when you are an old lady?"

"But how do you know it isn't going to happen? How can you be that calm?"

"I am calm because right now, in this very second, I know everything is ok, everything is working and things are good. I am sitting with my sister and we are both safe."

"But that could change at any time, you don't know..."

Emma interrupted Sally and spoke slowly and with perfect focus, "I don't know anything about the future, I only know about this moment in time, the present moment, and I know that I am living this moment and no other. I am not living in the times when Justin died and we were all broken and so sad. I am not living in the future, freaking out that I will never find a partner and have a family. I know that in the present, right now, all is well. You are good. Look at you, healthy and pregnant! We are in your house, we are warm and there is food in the cupboard and, all in all, we are both happy." Emma smiled at her sister, "Do you get it? If you are always in the past or the future, you are never living your life in the present, right now and enjoying it."

Their eyes were locked and Emma continued, "Justin didn't leave us as punishment or abandon us to be cruel. It was just what happened. It is just life... You desperately need to come to terms with that. Going through such a life changing, sad and hurtful experience is there to teach us and push us to grow in compassion and love. No matter how much you think about Justin's death and what happened to our family after it, you will never be able to rationalise it, you will never understand it. You know, it is about growing as a soul and a spirit to develop your ability to love and be compassionate and kind. You see, you can become bitter and stay bitter and never enjoy life again, or you can grow and love Justin forever. As a little girl, I saw the love and friendship you and Justin had, the connection and unspoken understanding you had. I saw how he loved Mum and Dad, and I felt how he loved me." Tears welled in Emma's eyes, she still loved Justin with all her heart.

"You see, it is up to you. You can remain scared to love, and worry how that love could be taken away, or you could realise that the love you have for Justin can carry you through the rest of your life. You can spread it to everyone you meet, especially your own child. Justin's soul is with us, always. His energy can never die. You just have to be open to feel it and allow it to fill every cell in your body. He lives forever in every person he met and every person he touched."

By now, Sally was bitting her bottom lip, her face was red and she felt as if her head was going to blow. She could hear the words and she was fighting the truth of them. She knew everything Emma was saying was true, but her anger over losing Justin from her life drove her to hate the situation without him.

"Do you see, my darling sister? We have to keep our hearts open and love, no matter what happens. You are only tormenting and torturing yourself by keeping your heart closed."

Sally gasped for air. She was holding so much in and she didn't want to let her guard down. It had been up for so long, she didn't know any different.

Emma shook Sally's hands as if to wake her out of her thoughts, "Do you see what I am saying?"

Sally threw Emma's hands away, got up off the chair and began to yell at Emma, "You just don't understand the pain and hurt! He was my best friend and my brother!"

Emma didn't want Sally to get caught up in herself, so she stood up and also raised her voice, "What do you mean I don't know? When Justin died, I lost everything I knew: my mother, my father, my brother and my sister. I lost every single thing that I knew. I was a little girl, unprotected and vulnerable. I was abandoned and left to fend for myself."

"I was there, what are you talking about?" Sally shot back.

"What? Were you the same loving, kind and gentle person that took me to the park and laughed with me, who loved me? You weren't! You were only a shell, the same as Mum and Dad."

Sally sobbed "I don't know, I don't know! We were all so messed up, Em. Why are you not so messed up, like me?"

Sally sobbed. She did want a way out, but she was so confronted by the possibility of hurt again.

"I am not so messed up because, like I said, I still love Justin with all my heart and I thank God every day that he was in my life. I am who I am because I love him. I am who I am because I still love him. I feel him with me and I know with all the truth within me that I will be with him again. I just continue to love."

"You make it sound so easy, baby sister," Sally rubbed her belly and closed her eyes, "I do want to be a better person for my baby. I want my baby to be happy and feel loved."

Emma walked towards Sally and wrapped her arms around her. Sally rested her head on Emma's shoulder and returned the embrace with all the love she could muster. In that moment, the sisters felt the love they had for each other. They both relished in every single second of it. They both felt lighter and it tingled as they held each other tight. They felt safe, peaceful and like they were in the hands of something special. It was unconditional love!

"WHEN YOU RECOGNISE THAT YOU WILL THRIVE NOT IN SPITE OF YOUR LOSSES AND SORROWS BUT BECAUSE OF THEM, THE WORD FOR THAT IS HEALING."

- CHERYL STRAYED

49

SALLY – THE BIRTH

As the girls talked through Sally's pain and Emma continued the explanation of being present and not projecting, Emma felt Sally's energy changing. The house was becoming calm and peaceful as her voice, her demeanour and posture all softened.

"Explain what you mean by projection again, Emma."

Emma was so grateful to hear Sally speak of such things. She was uplifted by Sally being interested in healing and growing from the person she had warped into. She knew the loving, kind and cheeky person her sister had been before Justin passed and she saw glimpses of her that day.

"Projection is when you are thinking and living in the future or the past. Assuming what others are thinking and feeling. Making stories of pain and hurt and avoiding the present moment. This is the torture you essentially make up. Think of the moment you are in, better yet be, live and experience the moment you are in."

Sally nodded. She looked exhausted from the emotional few hours they had had. Emma could see that it was enough discussion for the time being and encouraged Sally to have a rest on the lounge and watch a movie that was playing on the television. Sally laid her head in Emma's nap and, after only 15 minutes, she was asleep. Emma stroked her hair as Sally lay there and continued to feel the love they shared. Eventually, Emma also rested back on the chair and fell asleep.

————

THE SISTERS FOUND themselves in the delivery suite with the midwife telling Sally there was only one more push. Sally looked at Emma as she squeezed her hand, "Ben is going to miss it."

"I think so. He is still ten minutes away."

The midwife encouraged, "You are one good patient, Sally, only one more push."

"But Ben is not here, we have to wait!"

"My sweet girl, babies don't wait! We just have to do this." The midwife rubbed Sally's leg and said, "Ok, you're contracting now, push!"

Before anyone knew it, a tiny little baby was placed on Sally's chest, quiet as a mouse. Sally wrapped her arms around him and his little face was turned towards Emma.

"It's a little boy, Sal, a little boy."

"Oh my gosh, he is so beautiful!"

Sally was looking at every feature of his tiny little face when he began to blink his eyes so very gently. As they opened, both the girls gasped at what they saw. They looked at each other and grinned.

"Justin," they both said in unison.

Emma leaned over to hug her sister, "I am so happy you're my big sister. I love you."

The doors burst open and Ben raced in, "Oh, Sal, I am so sorry. What is happening?"

Ben's words trailed off as he comprehended what he saw. His eyes widened and his heart quickened.

"It is ok, sweetheart, we are both ok. You have a little boy, we have a son."

Emma stepped out of the way and allowed Ben to get closer to Sally and their son. She stood back and watched them all together, tears of joy running down her face. The midwife came from nowhere to stand beside Emma, putting one arm around her and giving her a squeeze.

"Quite the show, hey?"

Emma breathed out a sigh, a sigh of relief that the baby was born and he was safe. The baby had Justin's big round blue eyes. He would be the family's reminder to hold on to the love they all had for Justin. He would help with healing her family. Emma left the room so they could all be together.

As Emma walked out of the delivery room, she could see her Mum and Dad racing down the hallway.

"Are they ok? Is everything ok? Emma, where are they?"

"It's ok, Mum, everything is perfect. Sally was amazing and the baby was born about five minutes ago. He is perfect."

Emma smiled as both her Mum and Dad smiled with genuine happiness.

Tina, Jake and Emma all walked into the delivery room together. Sally was sitting up in the bed with Ben tucked in beside her. They were both smitten with the baby, watching his every move.

"Oh well done, Sal," Tina congratulated her daughter as she got close to the bed. Jake walked over to shake Ben's hand but Ben stood up and hugged Jake.

"Congratulations, Ben! Looks like you are going to have your hands full with this little fella."

Ben nodded, he was lost for words.

"Mum... Dad... I hope you will be ok with it, but Ben and I have decided to name our son Justin."

Jake nodded while Tina reached to pick the baby up out of Sally's arms. Sally handed him to her with tears of love and joy. Tina turned around and, with her back to the family, took a look at the little baby who was to be her grandson. The baby blinked a little and opened his eyes to look directly up at his grandmother. Tina gasped; she recognised those eyes. She assessed his features and couldn't believe how much he looked like her Justin. Her heart skipped a beat. She hadn't felt such love for many years.

Tina lifted little Justin close and kissed his forehead. She whispered, "Welcome, Little Man. l love you already."

She felt a little part of her heal, a little part of her soften, a little part of her come back to reality. Tears of joy fell from her eyes and she walked over to Jake so that he could see baby Justin's little face.

"Hello, Baby Justin." It hurt Jake a little to say Justin's name out loud but, when he leant down and kissed his forehead, he felt a flood of peace come over him. Jake wondered how he felt so good, he didn't realise it was love.

Little Baby Justin would distract them all from their past and encourage them to live in the present.

"GRIEF IS A MATTER OF THE HEART AND SOUL. GRIEVE YOUR LOSS, ALLOW IT IN AND SPEND TIME WITH IT. SUFFERING IS THE OPTIONAL PART. LOVE NEVER DIES AND SPIRIT KNOWS NO LOSS. KEEP IN MIND THAT A BROKEN HEART IS AN OPEN HEART."

- LOUISE HAY & DAVID KESSLER

50

KATE & SALLY – FORGIVENESS

Kate had always been wise beyond her years. When Justin died, she had persevered with Sally for many years trying to sustain their friendship. As adults, she still sent the obligatory Christmas and birthday cards, with little to no response from Sally. She thought about Justin often and her memories mainly focused on the love that they shared and the fun their families had experienced together. Kate couldn't deny that she was hurt by Sally's rejection, she still missed their friendship. However, she worked through it the same way as she worked through Justin's death, holding on to the love and the good memories.

Kate heard that Sally had given birth to a healthy baby boy and had named him Justin. Her mother, Natalie, had told her the day of the birth. Kate was overjoyed and secretly hoped that Sally having a baby would help her heal and learn to love freely again.

Kate had been married for a few years and had two children of her own who Sally had never met. Emma, Tina and Jake were all still part of Kate's life and knew her children well.

Not long after baby Justin's birth, Kate's little dog, Charlie, followed her to the letterbox to collect the mail. As Kate pulled the letters from the box, she noticed an envelope addressed to her that was handwritten. She pulled it from the bunch of bills and was intrigued to find out what the contents were. As she opened the envelope, Kate realised it was an announcement card of the birth of Sally's baby. She was surprised and didn't know what to think about this out of the blue contact. It had been many years since they had seen or spoken to each other. As she opened the card, a folded piece of paper fell onto the ground. She reached down to pick it up and she smiled as she noticed the photo of little Justin printed on the front of the card.

Kate unfolded the piece of paper and saw Sally's handwriting on the page. She looked around and found a spot to sit alongside the letterbox, feeling an urgency to read Sally's words. Charlie lay down on the grass beside her.

To my Dearest Kate,

I hope this letter finds you. I have a lot I need to say, but I am finding it hard to find a place to start.

I suppose I should start with an apology, an apology that I have owed you since Justin's death. I am sorry that I pushed you away and that I was so cruel after Justin's death. I am sorry that I inhibited our friendship and that I just removed myself from our lives together.

I know it has been a long time, but I would love to see you. I do understand if you don't want a part of any of this because I must have hurt you very badly and I know it has been a long time.

Since I have had baby Justin, I have had some tough realisations and feel I need to right some wrongs that I have created in my life. I know now that I have missed you, every day. In my mind, you are still my best friend, my confidant and a kindred spirit, even though we haven't spoken for more years than I care to say.

I am so, so sorry and I really would love to see you some time.

I don't know what else to say other than sorry because our relationship only ended because of me. I have added my contact details if you can find it in your heart to forgive me.

Love and friendship,

Sally

X

Kate was in shock over the contents of the letter. She had resigned herself to the fact that her friendship with Sally was over, although she wished it not to be true. She reached down to pat Charlie and then took herself back into the house.

Kate's children, Billy and Paige, were both sitting on the floor playing with their toys. Paige raced over to her and wrapped her arms around her waist.

"Hello, Sweet Pea."

"What are you doing, Mummy? What is this?" Paige asked as she took the card and letter from Kate's hand.

"It's a letter, Sweetheart."

"What does it say?" Paige was four years old and was full of conversation. She was articulate and inquisitive so Kate was forever talking things through with her. Kate sat down on the couch and Paige followed.

"So, Mummy, tell me what it says. Oh, that baby has big eyes!" Paige exclaimed as she examined the card.

Kate took the card and had a close look at baby Justin.

"Why, yes, he does, Paige. Actually, he looks like someone I used to know." Kate was taken aback as she saw the reflection of Justin in baby Justin's eyes.

"Who did you used to know?"

"A boy who was Uncle Peter's best friend from when we were children, like you."

"Oh, what was his name Mummy?"

"His name was Justin."

"What is this baby's name?"

"Actually, he is also called Justin."

"Well, that is funny that they have the same names," Paige giggled.

"Read me this letter," Paige pushed the letter towards her mother.

Kate took the letter and sighed.

"What's the matter?" Paige could see that her mother wasn't too enthusiastic to read it to her.

Kate looked up at her daughter and swept the hair from her eyes. She thought about how much she loved her and what a sweet little creature she was.

"Mummy, can't you tell me? Is it privacy?" Paige had recently learnt the meaning of the word private, but she often got the pronunciation wrong.

Kate took the letter and began to read it to Paige. Part way through the letter, Paige interrupted her mother, "Did Justin die? How did he die Mummy?"

Kate had always been truthful with her children. Billy was only two so didn't ask too many questions, but Paige was full of them.

"Justin died when he was about 16 years old. He hit his head really hard and his brain got broken."

Paige's eyes widened. "That is really sad, Mummy."

"Yes, it was. I suppose it still is."

"Well, finish the letter, Mummy."

Kate finished reading the letter and tried to distract Paige from its contents by showing her the announcement card with the photo of baby Justin on it again.

"So, Mummy what do you think? Do you think you can forgive this letter?"

"You mean forgive Sally who wrote the letter."

"Yes, Silly, that is what I meant!"

Kate studied Paige's little eyes and said, "Actually, there is nothing to forgive. I let it all go a very long time ago."

Paige turned her head, "Oh, that Sally is pretty silly then, hey. She should come and visit us and me and Billy can play with her."

"That is very kind of you, Paige, but Sally is big like Mummy."

"Well, she could come over and play with you then."

With that, Paige returned to the floor and continued to play. Kate stayed on the couch and read the letter again. She knew that she had been hurt when Sally rejected her but, over the years, she realised that she should forgive Sally and continue to love her.

Kate walked over to her phone picked it up to dialled the phone number that was noted on the letter.

"Hello?" Sally's voiced beamed from the other end of the phone.

"Hello, Sally," Kate returned.

Sally immediately recognised Kate's voice, "Hi Kate."

"REMEMBERING A WRONG IS
LIKE CARRYING A BURDEN ON
THE MIND."

- BUDDHA

51
LUCAS JOHNS - YOU
NEVER KNOW

Lucas stood on the podium and accepted the trophy that was thrust at him. In adulthood, Lucas remained humble, quiet and focused. This was his fifth season playing football professionally and his second 'Best Player of the Season' accepting the Summons Cup.

"Congratulations, Lucas!" Peter Scott, the President of the league, announced to a cheering crowd of thousands, "May I just say to you all, this award does not come as a surprise to any of us. Lucas is a strong and talented player but what makes him the best, is his ability to rally his team, his ability to bring the best out in everyone he plays with. We saw it last season with the Rebels and again this year with the Foxes." He paused and looked over at Lucas, who was staring at the ground, "I have never seen such a humble, yet valuable, player. Congratulations, mate! No one could deserve this more than you."

Peter stepped away from the microphone, "Are you going to say something this year, Lucas?"

Lucas made eye contact with Peter and nodded.

Lucas walked over to the microphone and the crowd went wild with excitement. He was a quiet and humble man who always took the time to get to know the people he had to spend time with in the game. Lucas kept his eyes glued to the ground. He cleared his throat and began to speak. The crowd took a few moments to quieten down.

"I would just like to thank the league for this honour, I do truly appreciate it, so thank you. I want to dedicate this award to a person that was only in my life for a short while, but who has had the most significant impact on my game and on my ability to dig deep and be the best player I can be. When I was a young, I always felt like I held back a little. Maybe I was scared of the attention or maybe I was just not confident with my skills. A fella that coached me made me be my best, he made me do my best and he connected with me. He saw something in me and gave me the confidence to use it. I attribute my whole professional career to this guy because, without him encouraging me when I played under 14's, I don't think I would have been given the opportunities I have had so far. So, I dedicate this award to Justin Point, who was taken away from us all before his time but he sure left his mark on me, on my success and on my desire to connect with others. I hope Justin's parents are watching tonight so they realise that Justin's legend lives on in me. Thank you, Justin, and I will never forget what you did for me."

As Jake watched the television, he felt the lump in his throat tighten. He watched Lucas walk down the stairs and hold the trophy in the air. He couldn't recall Lucas in Justin's life and he didn't know that Justin had had anything to do with him. Jake was a big football fan and knew that Lucas attended the same school his own children had been to, but didn't realise there was any connection between Lucas and his son. Tears ran from his eyes, just as they had the day Justin passed away in their living room. Ten years had passed but, to Jake, it was always so close.

Recently, Jake had been having reoccurring thoughts, questioning if Justin's life mattered to anyone but the people that were closest to him. Jake had worked hard to be mindful over the years but, at times, he slipped. This time he was caught off guard by the dedication to Justin, which triggered him feeling such pain. Joe and he did keep in contact and their friendship developed over the years. Jake felt safe knowing that Joe was there for support but, more than that, he felt they were friends. Jake had learnt a lot about Joe's life, which always inspired him to work to live a loving happy life. Jake knew deep in his soul that Joe had saved him from a life time of misery.

As the words that Lucas had just spoken settled into Jake's mind, his pain shifted to love. The lump of pain in his throat began to dissipate when his mobile phone rang. Peter's name flashed on his phone screen. Peter and Jake had kept in touch. Jake and his family had moved to try and lose the painful memories of Justin's death, but Peter always kept in touch.

Jake picked up the phone and put on a brave voice, "Hey, Pete."

"Hey, Mr P, are you watching the footy?"

"You know I wouldn't miss it, mate."

"Did you see Lucas? Did you hear Lucas?"

"I did mate, I did."

"I just wanted to make sure you heard it and I want you to know that not a day goes by when I don't think about him, how much I love him and how good he was for me too."

Silence fell as they let the words and feelings sink in.

"You know, I went through a stage of wishing Justin and I hadn't been best friends, wishing that I didn't know him and experience life with him. I thought I would have been better without him in my life at all but, without him, I wouldn't be me."

Jake was lost for words.

"His life was so worth it for me. I still love him and his death has pushed me to be what I am today. To love life and appreciate everything I have."

More silence, Jake was speechless.

"Justin shaped Lucas but he also shaped me too, Mr P. I just wanted to let you know."

Peter had been wanting to tell Jake how he felt for some time but had never found the right moment. He had been so moved by Lucas's dedication that he felt he had to speak up.

A minute passed in silence.

"Hey, we are having birthday drinks for Abigail at ours Saturday at 4pm if you feel like coming round?"

Abigail was Peter's girlfriend. She was a lovely girl and they were both very family orientated, always having their best and closest to their place for a catch up. Jake often went.

"Yeah sure, mate, I'll see you then."

"Right, Mr P, see you then!"

Jake caught Peter just before he could hang up, "Thanks for saying that, Pete. The world goes on and that's hard because I don't want him to be forgotten," he paused. "I often feel heartbroken and feel like everyone has moved on and forgotten him. Tonight has shown me that he did more for people than I will ever know."

Peter could hear the desperation in Jake's voice. He took a breath and tried to explain something that had taken him a lot of years to discover, "It used to make me so angry when I looked around and saw people getting on with their lives. I would question God and ask, why isn't everyone as sad as me? It took me a lot of years and a lot of hatred to see that people mostly grieve on the inside, in private. The sadness doesn't go away, it is just hidden deep. If you are one of the lucky ones, you can use that sadness to grow, instead of allowing your soul to shrivel and your ego to rise. I don't think people forget; people just learn to manage it. Personalities change, attitudes change, your ability to love changes. For me, Michael helped me to grow from my relationship with Justin and cope with the loss of Justin. I hope I have become a better person, a kind person, a person with peace in my heart. Some days, I feel that Justin just lived for me because he has taught me so much."

Peter took a breath. He hadn't said those things out loud before, he had only reconciled these things inwardly. As the silence grew, Peter's gut began to ache with worry. He was always wary around Justin's dad, he never knew how Jake was really coping, even after ten years.

Then Jake spoke, "You know, Pete, that is a very healthy way of thinking of things. You are wise beyond your years."

Peter didn't respond.

"You have given me a lot to think about."

The conversation came to a natural end with Jake promising to attend the birthday party at Peter's on the weekend.

"YOU DON'T KNOW WHO YOU INFLUENCE, WHO YOU INSPIRE AND WHO YOUR LOVE TOUCHES."

52

TINA - THE PAIN CONTINUES

TINA ADORED HER GRANDCHILDREN, ESPECIALLY JUSTIN. She tried her best to reach for happiness in each moment, but there was an element of resentment and her health was deteriorating. As the years passed, Tina's health began to become a concern. She developed severe asthma and had to take medication that depleted her immune system which, in turn, caused many other issues. Her illness helped distract her from her loss which she just couldn't let go of. Tina was a great actress and, to the outside world, she appeared mostly adjusted. Although, on the inside, a deep sadness remained.

Tina and Joe sat side by side on the same park bench where they had met years before. Despite her hidden inner pain, Tina always seemed to find time to catch up with Joe. Joe was still doing the same thing, walking and talking to anyone that needed a shoulder to cry on and offering his wisdom on inner peace. Joe could see the superficial happiness Tina was projecting to the world.

"How's your chest going. Tina? You seem pretty wheezy today."

"Not too good. I'm doing all I can to manage it."

"Would you say we are friends, Tina?"

"Yes, sure, Joe."

"I want to speak truthfully to you..." He paused, "Are you willing to listen?"

Tina was surprised by the question and she had no idea where Joe was going with it.

"Look, your health has bothered me the last few times we have seen each other, along with your deeply hidden unhappiness."

Tina was silent and she slumped a little in the chair as she realised she had been found out.

Joe continued, "I have noticed and can feel that your grief and sadness is still plaguing you. I know it has been a long time, but I realise you have still not moved on."

Tina sighed. She knew Joe was right, but he hadn't realised that her sadness had grown in the past few years.

"Your chest illness is a big give away. Grief causes ill lung health."

Tina had nothing to say. She knew Joe was correct and she had no fight in her to dispute it. Joe reached into a bag in his trolley and pulled out a book, the same book he gave to Tina years before.

"Do you remember this book, Tina?"

"Yes, of course I do."

"I want you to have this copy. I can say the same thing I have been for years, but I know you have heard it all before. You must find that little part of you that is holding you back from healing and release it. Give yourself permission to let the sadness go. Justin would want you to find some peace. It has been a long time."

Silence fell over them. Joe was determined to allow the silence. He wanted Tina to respond to what he said, he wanted her to be confronted.

After a few minutes, Tina answered Joe, "I don't know

what happens to me, Joe. I just get lost in sadness." She looked down and fiddled with her fingers, "Don't worry, I'll do better."

"You know you will become sicker if you don't let this stuff go."

"I know Joe, I know."

Joe handed Tina the book and the two of them sat on the park bench in silence.

It was the last time Joe ever saw Tina. Over the next ten years, she became sicker and enjoyed the suffering. She hoped to die. She liked the pain, it made her feel like she was still connected with Justin. It was as though she was proving to him that she loved him with all her heart. All the while, Tina hid her pain from her family as best she could. A senseless waste of life.

"PAIN IS INEVITABLE,
SUFFERING IS OPTIONAL."

- BUDDHA

"Even though our rational mind has been trained to believe that when a person dies his spirit is gone, the truth is that the spirit does not die, it simply changes form. Your spirit can't die because it has no boundaries, no beginnings and no end."

- Dr. Wayne Dyer

HOW TO NURTURE YOUR SPIRIT THROUGH GRIEF

Finding space within to nurture yourself can be a challenge, but during grief it can be exceptionally challenging. What you can see in this story is that when people lose themselves in their thoughts, they then get lost in their suffering. Mindfulness is the key to getting through the grieving process, controlling the computer brain that torments us all.

In a nutshell, mindfulness is about becoming aware of what you think. Now, I know that this sounds like a concept that makes no sense. Of course, you are aware of what you think because you are thinking the thoughts, but what if your thoughts can drive you if you let them? What if your computer brain can do the thinking for you, without your conscious control?

You could be thinking of any infinite number of things that your mind/brain can get lost in. In general, we are thinking of scenarios of the past or the future. A lot of the time we are making up situations and emotions, having thoughts filled with possibilities rather than reality. These thoughts evoke emotions and these emotions can cause us to suffer, unless we take control.

CHALLENGE

Spend a few days, or even a few hours, monitoring your thoughts. What do you spend time thinking about? You can go through an entire day, or even your entire life, lost in your thoughts. Set an alarm to remind you to take note of what you are thinking about. Write down what you have been thinking about and then mark the thoughts that are about the future or the past; the what if's, the pain and the stories.

This can be a very confronting process, realising how much your mind torments you and how you have allowed it to happen. Your mind also relives pain. At times, you can become addicted to the pain which would, in turn, allow your mind to replay your torture. If you are honest, you will realise how much time you spend living in the past or the future, torturing yourself. Releasing your thoughts will allow you to concentrate on the present moment.

With a provoking life event, such as death and loss, we can easily be led with our sadness and pain down the path of eternal inner torture. Being able to catch our thoughts and change them, gives us the power to change our energy and, therefore, our lives.

It is all well and good to stop the incessant thinking, but what does your mind/brain do if it is not tormenting you? This is why it is important to replace your thoughts with wanted ones such as thoughts of love. Remember, grief is love with no place to go, continue to love.

When working through grief or the loss of a loved one, sadness and painful thoughts easily prevail. What if we could think about death differently? What if we could find peace in death? What if we could focus on continuing the love we shared with the person we lost?

Across a lot of cultures, death is seen as the end. However, in cultures and religions that see death as a blessing and a happy time, they leave inner torture behind.

Spiritual guru, Dr. Wayne Dyer, says:

> *"Even though our rational mind has been trained to believe that when a person dies his spirit is gone, the truth is that the spirit does not die, it simply changes form. Your spirit can't die because it has no boundaries, no beginning and no end."*

So, do we ever end? Do we live on? If we live on then we are only sad for ourselves that we have lost the person we mourn. Working as a nurse, I have seen life and many deaths and know, for sure, that the energy that powers us, the energy that makes the sun rise, makes the trees grow and the animals run, leaves our earthly body and moves on. If this is the case, then we only have ourselves to save from our own grief, how we think and feel about it. We can use mindfulness to remedy our pain.

Can we replace our pain with love? Can we continue to love someone after they have left our physical side? This is a question you have to answer for yourself. If you change your way of thinking, you can relieve your pain and suffering. Culturally, we see death as a bad thing. What if we all started delighting in having experienced life with the person that has left our physical plane? It is all about what we choose to think. You become what you think. Movement to a place of being grateful, to have known and loved the ones you have lost, is a very powerful movement of energy. Gratitude.

Grief is only love with nowhere to go.

So, if we can catch ourselves suffering and replace that suffering with the love and gratitude you felt for the one you have lost, we can find peace. Focus on the love. Love is the key to peace and joy in your life.

It is hard to change your programming, but your mind is a computer. Whatever you put into your mind grows, so why not stop the sadness and pain and replace it with gratitude and love?

Why can't the end of suffering be simple? Yes, loss is sad, but it doesn't have to cause endless suffering. It is a choice we can make, what we choose to think about.

———

In this story, you saw some of the characters use breathing as a technique to quieten their mind, a form of meditation. Don't be put off by the term or idea of meditation. Meditation is not complex. It is about finding some quiet in your mind and the breath work is an easy way to find that. When you find yourself lost in grief and sadness with your mind running wild with scenarios and pain, just listen to your breathing.

Consciously counting your breath in for any count you choose. I believe eight is a good count because it will give you enough time and space to let the tormenting thoughts go.

Closing your eyes and sitting in a comfortable upright position with your hands in your lap are both simple ways to support the process of quietening the mind as you consciously breathe. Start with a few minutes. Work up to sitting with any empty mind, without the prompting of your breath, for 20 minutes twice a day. You will find that profound peace develops within.

It sounds easy but believe that the mind is an incessant machine that will keep trying to sabotage your peace. So, it may not be as easily as it sounds but, like everything with discipline and practice, your skills will improve.

Another powerful way of finding your peace is heart focused meditation. In the story, you saw the power of focusing on your heart. Your heart is everything; it is the mind of your soul. Read about the significance of your heart, spiritually, and you will be amazed. First, use the breathing meditation technique to quieten your mind. Then, take your awareness to your chest, where you feel your heart resides and watch it expand and become bright and feel light. Evoke the feeling of love and allow it to resonate in your chest. If you have trouble feeling love, remember a time in your life you felt love and use that memory to evoke it within you. Feel the love and light expand within you and allow it to expand beyond yourself, out into the world around you. Remember everything is energy. You can do this for any length of time. Even a few minutes is going to improve the quality of your life.

A vital part of progressing in a happy life and feeling peace and love is meditation and taking note of your thoughts, regularly. Also, think about waking a little earlier and beginning your day with a meditation. Feel and write down what you are grateful for. You can also end the day in the same way. Review your day and see if you got lost in your thoughts and suffering. Begin to watch your thinking and see if you can catch yourself and replace your suffering with gratitude and love. What triggered you into suffering? How can you, or did you, end it? Find yourself a notebook and document your progress.

They say changing a routine takes time. Be strong and make a promise to yourself that you will get into the habit of practising mindfulness, gratitude and love. End your suffering.

"Pain is inevitable, suffering is optional."

A NOTE FROM THE AUTHOR

For me, grief has been a rough road. Everyone on this planet has their own story about grief and loss. If it isn't the loss of a person, it could be loss of a job, lifestyle, material possession, a friendship; everyone has felt it. A great loss in my family's life triggered a lot of pain and, for a few years, a lot of suffering.

I was inspired to write this book by a power bigger than myself. The story kept coming to me and it includes everything that I have learnt, spiritually, through a very tough personal journey. Elements of my own experience are written in these pages for you to connect with.

The hardest lesson I have learnt through the grieving process, is that you can't fix things for anyone else. You can't take their pain away. Standing by a grieving person's side, being unable to do anything to help, is gut wrenchingly painful. It took me years of private agony to learn this lesson and to begin my own healing process. I learnt that, if I can heal, this energy also has the ability to help the people around me. I also realised that just because those around me are suffering, doesn't mean I have to suffer as well. It is not about walking away from your loved ones who are suffering, it is all about your own healing.

I have read other people's stories of finding faith and spiritual understandings of life through the grieving process. For me, I had faith in Universal Source; God or whatever you would like to label it. I am not an active member of any religion, but I am an independent spiritual seeker. Loss strengthened and tested this faith. It forced me to live my spiritual truth. Part of that truth was to write this story to connect with others, to commence or strengthen their journey of faith and spiritual understanding of life, to assist with spreading love and peace across the planet.

The words in these pages do not hold new information. They are words that have been spoken of by every spiritual writer, teacher and preacher. My hope is that, by reading this book, you will be motivated and inspired to seek out the truth of life, learn to love and find peace within.

Find someone that inspires you and who you feel speaks the truth. You will find that the spiritual messages are the same, but written or explained in a slightly different way. Some of my most powerful spiritual teachers have been:

A Course in Miracles
Alan Cohen
Deepak Chopra
Dr Brian Weiss
Eckhart Tolle
James Redfield
Louise Hay
Marianne Williamson
Michael Beckwith
Michael Singer
Neale Donald Walsh
Paulo Coelho
Ram Dass
And my ultimate guru, Dr. Wayne Dyer

I have found that every one of these authors resonates with the others, speaking of common themes and understandings.

I am always reading, learning and (I hope) growing from the assimilation of information, or what I would call truth, into my life. There are always ups and downs, highs and lows, but I have come to realise that my faith always centres me and helps me find peace, joy and love.

My hope is that, by reading this book, you can see the massive significance of finding the peace that lies within you, and that you continue to love, for grief is love with nowhere to go.

Much love, light and laughter,
   Lisa xx

"May I be a lamp for those in darkness,

a home for the homeless,

and a servant to the world."

- **Shantideva (8th Century)**

Also by Lisa Rogers

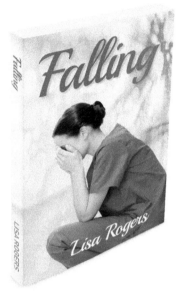

AVAILABLE ON

amazon

Connect with Lisa

WWW.LISAROGERSAUTHOR.COM

LISAROGERSAUTHOR@GMAIL.COM

FACEBOOK: LISA ROGERS AUTHOR

ACKNOWLEDGMENTS

I want to acknowledge a man I never met or had any personal contact with but has had a profound effect on my spirit, Dr Wayne Dyer. The assimilation of Wayne's work into my life has changed me and is still changing my understanding of existence and love daily. The way Wayne interprets sages and guru's teaching into useable understandings of life in modern day words is magical. I acknowledge the impact Wayne has had on my soul and my writing.

Thank you, Wayne, for your dedication to changing humanities understanding of life.

I also want to acknowledge life's devastations as my greatest teacher. My grief forced me to seek a true relationship with my soul and to truly live with connection to a force greater than myself.

Lastly, I want to acknowledge my biggest fan, my daughter Abbie for all her encouragement and creative input. You are a beautiful soul and my love for you is endless.

Milton Keynes UK
Ingram Content Group UK Ltd.
UKHW020708290424
441924UK00017B/1070

9 781914 447822